HOUGHTON MIFFLIN SOCIAL STUDIES

From Sea to Shining Sea

*O*beautiful for spacious skies,

For amber waves of grain,

For purple mountain majesties

Above the fruited plain.

America! America! God shed His grace on thee,

And crown thy good with brotherhood

From sea to shining sea.

Katharine Lee Bates

Beverly J. Armento
J. Jorge Klor de Alva
Gary B. Nash
Christopher L. Salter
Louis E. Wilson
Karen K. Wixson

From Sea to Shining Sea

Houghton Mifflin Company • Boston

Atlanta • Dallas • Geneva, Illinois • Princeton, New Jersey • Palo Alto • Toronto

Consultants

Program Consultants

Edith M. Guyton
Associate Professor of Early
  Childhood Education
Georgia State University
Atlanta, Georgia

Gail Hobbs
Associate Professor of Geography
Pierce College
Woodland Hills, California

Charles Peters
Reading Consultant
Oakland Schools
Pontiac, Michigan

Cathy Riggs-Salter
Social Studies Consultant
Hartsburg, Missouri

Alfredo Schifini
Limited English Proficiency Consultant
Los Angeles, California

George Paul Schneider
Associate Director
  of General Programs
Department of Museum Education
Art Institute of Chicago
Chicago, Illinois

Twyla Stewart
Center for Academic Interinstitutional
  Programs
University of California—Los Angeles
Los Angeles, California

Scott Waugh
Associate Professor of History
University of California—Los Angeles
Los Angeles, California

Teacher Reviewers

David E. Beer (Grade 5)
Weisser Park Elementary
Fort Wayne, Indiana

Jan Coleman (Grades 6–7)
Thornton Junior High
Fremont, California

Shawn Edwards
  (Grades 1–3)
Jackson Park Elementary
University City, Missouri

Barbara J. Fech (Grade 6)
Martha Ruggles School
Chicago, Illinois

Deborah M. Finkel
  (Grade 4)
Los Angeles Unified
  School District,
  Region G
South Pasadena,
  California

Jim Fletcher (Grades 5, 8)
La Loma Junior High
Modesto, California

Susan M. Gilliam
  (Grade 1)
Roscoe Elementary
Los Angeles, California

Vicki Stroud Gonterman
  (Grade 2)
Gibbs International
  Studies Magnet School
Little Rock, Arkansas

Lorraine Hood (Grade 2)
Fresno Unified School
  District
Fresno, California

Jean Jamgochian
  (Grade 5)
Haycock Gifted and
  Talented Center
Fairfax County, Virginia

Susan Kirk-Davalt
  (Grade 5)
Crowfoot Elementary
Lebanon, Oregon

Mary Molyneaux-Leahy
  (Grade 3)
Bridgeport Elementary
Bridgeport, Pennsylvania

Sharon Oviatt
  (Grades 1–3)
Keysor Elementary
Kirkwood, Missouri

Jayne B. Perala (Grade 1)
Cave Spring Elementary
Roanoke, Virginia

Carol Siefkin (K)
Garfield Elementary
Sacramento, California

Norman N. Tanaka
  (Grade 3)
Martin Luther King Jr.
  Elementary
Sacramento, California

John Tyler (Grades 5, 8)
Groton School
Groton, Massachusetts

Portia W. Vaughn
  (Grades 1–3)
School District 11
Colorado Springs,
  Colorado

ISBN: 0-395-54890-X
  56789–VH–96 95

Development by Ligature, Inc.

Acknowledgments

    Grateful acknowledgment is made
for the use of the material listed below.
10–17 *Where the River Begins* by Thomas
Locker. Copyright © 1984 by Thomas
Locker. Reprinted by permission of
the publisher, Dial Books for Young
Readers.

–*Continued on page 286.*

From Your Authors

B lack Kettle licked buffalo grease from his lips and sighed happily. He looked at the other Cheyenne sitting around the campfire and knew they felt the same way. Their stomachs had not been full for a long time.

So begins the story of Black Kettle, a Cheyenne Indian boy about your age. In Chapter 5 of this book, you will have the chance to read more about Black Kettle and about those Indians who followed the buffalo.

Many of the people you will meet in this book lived long ago in places that may seem far away from your home. But they all had feelings just like yours. They had many of the same needs that you have today.

As you read about these people, places, and events, we hope you will ask many questions. Some questions may be about what things were like long ago. Other questions may be about the land. "What was it like in that place?" or "Why did those people choose to live there?" Still other questions may be about how they lived. "How did they get their food? or "What kind of houses did they live in?"

Most of all, we hope you continue to ask questions like these. We hope you enjoy asking questions and finding out answers, now and in the years to come.

Beverly J. Armento
Professor of Social Studies
Director, Center for Business and
Economic Education
Georgia State University

Christopher L. Salter
Professor and Chair
Department of Geography
University of Missouri

Louis E. Wilson
Associate Professor
Department of Afro-American Studies
Smith College

J. Jorge Klor de Alva
Professor of Anthropology
Princeton University

Gary B. Nash
Professor of History
University of California—Los Angeles

Karen K. Wixson
Associate Professor of Education
University of Michigan

Contents

Understanding Skills

Each "Understanding Skills" feature gives you the chance to learn and practice a skill.

Understanding Concepts

Each "Understanding Concepts" feature gives you information about an idea that is important to the lesson you have just read.

Making Decisions

Much of history is made up of people's decisions. Here you see how people make decisions. Then you practice how to make good decisions for yourself.

Explore

The story of the past is hidden in the world around you. "Explore" pages tell you the secrets of how to find it.

Literature

Reading these stories will help you experience what life was like at other times and places.

Primary Sources

Reading the exact words of people who lived long ago is a good way to learn about that time.

A Closer Look

Take a closer look at the objects and pictures on these pages. With the clues you see, you'll become a detective.

A Moment in Time

You can pretend to be there, at a moment in time. You'll get to know someone or something by the words and pictures on these pages.

Charts, Diagrams, and Timelines

These pictures help give you a clearer idea of the people, places, and events you are studying.

Maps

Often the land shapes the way things happen. Each map in this book tells a story about things that have happened and the places where they happened.

Starting Out

What makes this textbook so much more interesting than others you've used? Take some time, and look at each part of your book.

When and what? This number tells you which lesson you are reading. The title tells you what the lesson is about.

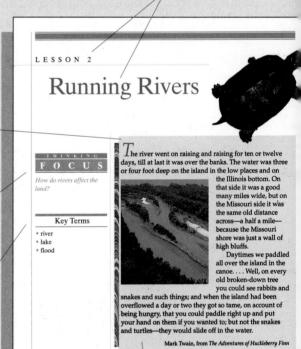

From unit to chapter to lesson— the art and photos show you where events happened.

Right from the beginning the lesson opener pulls you into the sights, the sounds, the smells of life at another time, in another place.

Like a road sign, the question that always appears here tells you what to think about while you read the lesson.

Look for these key terms. They are listed here so that you can watch for them. The first time they appear in the lesson they are shown in heavy black print and defined. Key terms are also defined in the Glossary.

Every age has its great storytellers. Each chapter includes short examples of fine writing from or about the period.

Take a closer look, in this case at the Grand Canyon. Look at the layers and layers of rock cut out by the river. Trace the route of the river on its way to Mexico.

A CLOSER LOOK
The Grand Canyon

The power of a river can change the earth. The Colorado River has formed a huge canyon by working its way through layers of rock. Every year, for millions of years, the canyon has become deeper and wider.

Millions of years ago, sand, gravel, and boulders were swept along by the river. These materials scraped away layers and layers of rock.

What was once a river bed is now the Grand Canyon. The Colorado River started out on flat land. Today it is a mile deep and almost 20 miles wide in some places.

John Wesley Powell, standing on the right, explored the Grand Canyon by boat, in 1869. Few people knew about the canyon's beauty until Powell shared information he learned on his journey.

The Route of the Colorado River

Utah

Nevada

Colorado River

Colorado

California

Grand Canyon National Park

Arizona

New Mexico

MEXICO

Trace the route of the Colorado River. It starts in Colorado and flows almost 1500 miles to Mexico. The gold area on this map shows Grand Canyon National Park. Each year, millions of people visit this park.

Fossils may be found where the Colorado River has cut down through layers of rock. Fossils are the remains or traces of past plants or animals. This fossil shows a fern that once grew in the canyon.

21

A **lake** is a pool of water on land. Like rivers, most lakes have fresh water. One difference between rivers and lakes is that rivers flow from place to place.

Constant Motion

Rivers start in different ways. Some rivers begin in lakes. Look at the map. Where does the Hudson River begin? Other rivers start from underground streams. Heavy rains or melting snow can also cause rivers. Rivers carry extra water that the land can't soak up.

The Hudson River

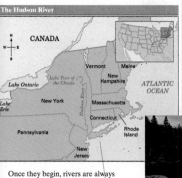

CANADA

Vermont Maine

Lake Tear of the Clouds

New Hampshire

Lake Ontario

ATLANTIC OCEAN

New York

Massachusetts

Lake Erie

Connecticut

Rhode Island

Pennsylvania

New Jersey

Once they begin, rivers are always moving. Most rivers run into another body of water. Some rivers flow into other rivers. Some rivers end in lakes or oceans. Others may just disappear underground.

Rivers may be wide or narrow. They may be deep or shallow. But all river water moves because it flows downhill. If the land is flat, water runs slowly. If the land is steep, water runs quickly. The Colorado River often flows fast because it runs downhill through very steep land. ■

▲ The Hudson River starts in Lake Tear-of-the-Clouds, which holds water from Mt. Marcy. Where does the river end?

■ How do rivers begin and end?

19

Pictured at a moment in time is this cactus in an Arizona desert. Look at its blossoms and the birds and rabbit that come to visit it. You will learn what happens to the cactus after a spring rain.

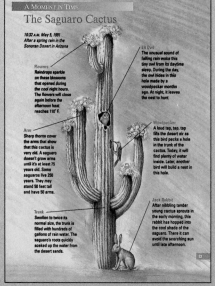

A MOMENT IN TIME
The Saguaro Cactus

10:32 A.M. May 5, 1991
After a spring rain in the Sonoran Desert in Arizona

Flowers
Raindrops sparkle on these blossoms that opened during the cool night hours. The flowers will close again before the afternoon heat reaches 110° F.

Elf Owl
The unusual sound of falling rain woke this tiny owl from its daytime sleep. During the day, the owl hides in this hole made by a woodpecker months ago. At night, it leaves the nest to hunt.

Arm
Sharp thorns cover the arms that show that this cactus is very old. A saguaro doesn't grow arms until it's at least 75 years old. Some saguaros live 250 years. They may stand 50 feet tall and have 50 arms.

Woodpecker
A loud tap, tap, tap fills the desert air as this bird pecks a hole in the trunk of the cactus. Today, it will find plenty of water inside. Later, another bird will build a nest in this hole.

Jack Rabbit
After nibbling tender young cactus sprouts in the early morning, this rabbit has hopped into the cool shade of the saguaro. There it can avoid the scorching sun until late afternoon.

Trunk
Swollen to twice its normal size, the trunk is filled with hundreds of gallons of rain water. The saguaro's roots quickly soaked up the water from the desert sands.

Every map tells a story. The map on this page tells the story of where the Hudson River in New York State runs and what the land is like there.

Continuing On

As you read about your world and the people in it, you'll want ways of understanding and remembering them better. This book gives you some tools to use in learning about people and places and remembering what you've learned.

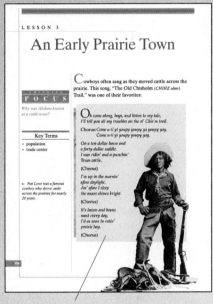

The people of the past speak directly to you in special parts of the text.

The titles give the main points of the lesson. On this page the red title tells you how rivers shape the land. On the next page the red title tells how rivers flood the land.

You're in charge of your reading. See the red square at the end of the text? Now find the red square over in the margin. If you can answer the question there, then you probably understood what you just read. If you can't, perhaps you'd better go back and read that part of the lesson again.

Diagrams make clear things that are hard to understand. Here the diagrams show the loops a river makes as it flows toward the sea.

Some tools you'll always use. The Understanding pages help you learn skills that you will use again and again. On this page you learn how to make a summary by listing the main ideas of what you've read.

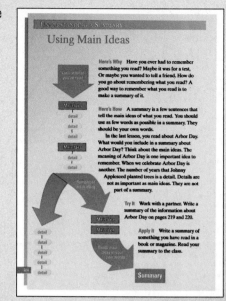

You get the inside story when you read two special paragraphs. One, called How Do We Know?, tells you where information about the past comes from. Another, Across Time & Space, connects what you're reading to things that happpened long ago or far away. (See page 81 for an example.)

A picture is worth a thousand words. But just a few words in a caption can help you understand a picture, a map, or a photograph.

A special kind of Understanding page looks at the big ideas that help put all the pieces together. This section helps you understand ideas like how we use our natural resources—our water, land, and trees.

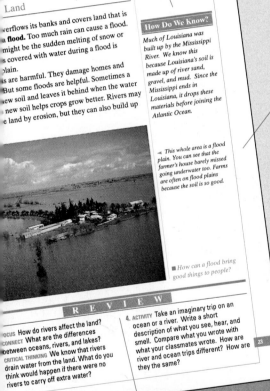

Land

...verflows its banks and covers land that is ...a **flood.** Too much rain can cause a flood. ...might be the sudden melting of snow or ...s covered with water during a flood is ...plain.

...s are harmful. They damage homes and ...But some floods are helpful. Sometimes a ...new soil and leaves it behind when the water ...new soil helps crops grow better. Rivers may ...e land by erosion, but they can also build up

How Do We Know?

Much of Louisiana was built up by the Mississippi River. We know this because Louisiana's soil is made up of river sand, gravel, and mud. Since the Mississippi ends in Louisiana, it drops these materials before joining the Atlantic Ocean.

◄ *This whole area is a flood plain. You can see that the farmer's house barely missed going underwater too. Farms are often on flood plains because the soil is so good.*

■ *How can a flood bring good things to people?*

R E V I E W

...OCUS How do rivers affect the land?
...CONNECT What are the differences ...etween oceans, rivers, and lakes?
...CRITICAL THINKING We know that rivers ...drain water from the land. What do you think would happen if there were no rivers to carry off extra water?

4. ACTIVITY Take an imaginary trip on an ocean or a river. Write a short description of what you see, hear, and smell. Compare what you wrote with what your classmates wrote. How are river and ocean trips different? How are they the same?

23

After you read the lesson, stop and review what you've read. The questions and an activity help you think about the lesson. Chapter Review questions help you tie the lessons together. (See pages 24 and 25 for an example.)

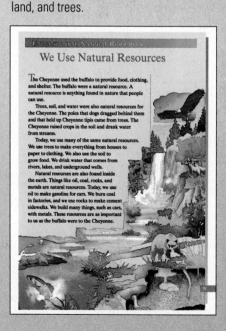

Also Featuring

Some special pages show up only once in every unit, not in every lesson in the book. These features continue the story by letting you explore an idea or activity, or read a story about another time and place. The Time/Space Databank in the back of the book brings together helpful pages you will use again and again.

What would you do? The Making Decisions pages show you an important decision. Then you practice the steps that will help you to make a good choice.

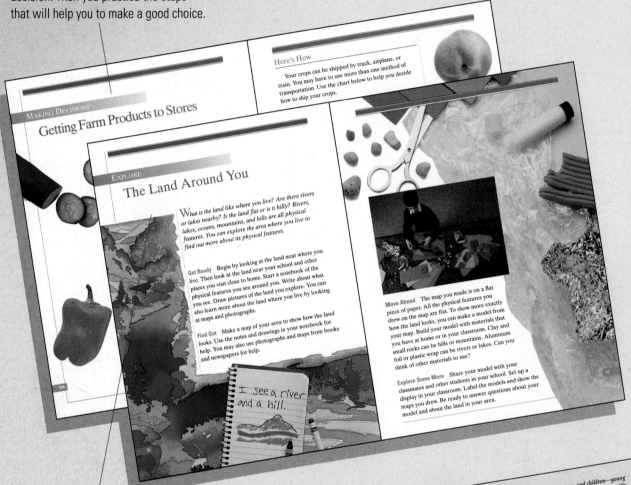

School isn't the only place where you can learn social studies. This feature gives you a chance to explore people and places outside the classroom—at home or in your own neighborhood.

Stories have always been important parts of people's lives. Each unit in the book has at least one story about the time and place you're studying. In this case, it's a story about a pioneer family in Kansas.

Many years ago, men, women, and children—young and old alike—went west to find a new land to settle. Travel was not easy. Houses and food were hard to find. But, always, other people helped. Read this excerpt from a story about a pioneer family in Kansas.

LITERATURE

WAGON WHEELS

Written by Barbara Brenner
Illustrated by Don Bolognese

Chapter 1—THE DUGOUT

"There it is, boys," Daddy said. "Across this river is Nicodemus, Kansas. That is where we are going to build our house. There is free land for everyone here in the West. All we have to do is go and get it."

The Time/Space Databank is like a reference section of a library at your fingertips. It's the place to go for more information about the places, people, and key terms you meet in this book.

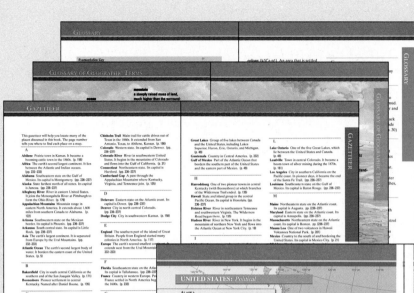

GLOSSARY

Preinstiction Key

colony (kŏl'ə-nē). An area that is settled

GLOSSARY OF GEOGRAPHIC TERMS

mountain
a steeply raised mass of land,
much higher than the surround-

ocean

GAZETTEER

This gazetteer will help you locate many of the places discussed in this book. The page number tells you where to find each place on a map.

A

Abilene Prairie town in Kansas. It became a booming cattle town in the 1860s. (p. 198)
Africa The earth's second largest continent. It lies between the Atlantic and Indian oceans. (pp. 232–233)
Alabama Southeastern state on the Gulf of Mexico. Its capital is Montgomery. (pp. 236–237)
Alaska State farthest north of all states. Its capital is Juneau. (pp. 236–237)
Allegheny River River in eastern United States. It joins the Monongahela River at Pittsburgh to form the Ohio River. (p. 179)
Appalachian Mountains Mountain range in eastern North America. It extends about 1,600 miles from southern Canada to Alabama. (p. 122)
Arizona Southwestern state on the Mexican border. Its capital is Phoenix. (pp. 236–237)
Arkansas South central state. Its capital is Little Rock. (pp. 236–237)
Asia The earth's largest continent. It is separated from Europe by the Ural Mountains. (pp. 232–233)
Atlantic Ocean The earth's second largest body of water. It borders the eastern coast of the United States. (p. 5)

B

Bakersfield City in south central California at the southern end of the San Joaquin Valley. (p. 171)
Boonesboro Pioneer settlement in central Kentucky. Named after Daniel Boone. (p. 135)

C

California Western state on the Pacific coast. Its capital is Sacramento. (pp. 236–237)
California Trail Southern branch of the Oregon Trail. It was used by pioneers traveling to California. (p. 149)
Canada Country to the north of the United States. Its capital is Ottawa. (pp. 232–233)
Chicago City in northeastern Illinois on the shore of Lake Michigan. (p. 198)

Chisholm Trail Main trail for cattle drives out of Texas in the 1860s. It extended from San Antonio, Texas, to Abilene, Kansas. (p. 198)
Colorado Western state. Its capital is Denver. (pp. 236–237)
Colorado River River in southwestern United States. It begins in the mountains of Colorado and flows into the Gulf of California. (p. 21)
Connecticut Northeastern state. Its capital is Hartford. (pp. 236–237)
Cumberland Gap A pass through the Appalachian Mountains where Kentucky, Virginia, and Tennessee join. (p. 135)

D

Delaware Eastern state on the Atlantic coast. Its capital is Dover. (pp. 236–237)
Denver City in north central Colorado. (pp. 236–237)
Dodge City City in southwestern Kansas. (p. 198)

E

England The southern part of the island of Great Britain. People from England started many colonies in North America. (p. 117)
Europe The earth's second smallest continent. It extends west from the Ural Mountains. (pp. 232–233)

F

Florida Southeastern state on the Atlantic coast. Its capital is Tallahassee. (pp. 236–237)
France Country in western Europe. People from France settled in North America beginning in the 1600s. (p. 233)

G

Georgia Southeastern state on the Atlantic coast. Its capital is Atlanta. (pp. 236–237)
Germany Former country in Europe, now split into two countries. German people came to settle eastern North America in the 1700s. (p. 233)
Grand Canyon Canyon of the Colorado River in northwestern Arizona. It is 217 miles long and 4 to 18 miles wide. (p. 20)

Great Lakes Group of five lakes between Canada and the United States, including Lakes Superior, Huron, Erie, Ontario, and Michigan. (p. 49)
Guatemala Country in Central America. (p. 233)
Gulf of Mexico Part of the Atlantic Ocean that borders the southern part of the United States and the eastern part of Mexico. (p. 49)

H

Harrodsburg One of two pioneer towns in central Kentucky (with Boonesboro) at which branches of the Wilderness Trail ended. (p. 135)
Hawaii State and island group in the central Pacific Ocean. Its capital is Honolulu. (pp. 236–237)
Holston River River in northeastern Tennessee and southwestern Virginia. The Wilderness Road began there. (p. 135)
Hudson River River in New York. It begins in the mountains of northern New York and flows into the Atlantic Ocean at New York City. (p. 19)

I

L

Lake Ontario One of the five Great Lakes, which lie between the United States and Canada. (p. 49)
Leadville Town in central Colorado. It became a boom town of silver mining during the 1870s. (p. 161)
Los Angeles City in southern California on the Pacific coast. In pioneer days, it became the end of the Santa Fe Trail. (pp. 236–237)
Louisiana Southeastern state on the Gulf of Mexico. Its capital is Baton Rouge. (pp. 236–237)

M

Maine Northeastern state on the Atlantic coast. Its capital is Augusta. (pp. 236–237)
Maryland Eastern state on the Atlantic coast. Its capital is Annapolis. (pp. 236–237)
Massachusetts Northeastern state on the Atlantic coast. Its capital is Boston. (pp. 236–237)
Mauna Loa One of two volcanoes in Hawaii Volcanoes National Park. (p. 201)
Mexico Country to the south of and bordering the United States. Its capital is Mexico City. (p. 21)

UNITED STATES: *Political*

The Atlas maps out the world. Large maps show you the parts of your world and your country. One large map shows you the physical regions of the United States.

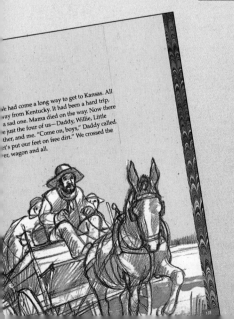

We had come a long way to get to Kansas. All way from Kentucky. It had been a hard trip, a sad one. Mama died on the way. Now there just the four of us—Daddy, Willie, Little ther, and me. "Come on, boys," Daddy called. 't put our feet on free dirt." We crossed the er, wagon and all.

Map and Globe Handbook

*Y*ou're about to start an exciting journey around the world. You'll make this journey across maps and globes. The journey will first take you across the United States. You'll make some stops—New Mexico, Michigan, Mississippi. Then you'll travel on, over distant lands and great oceans. You're sure to see mountains and deserts. You'll even see the earth from space.

Your journey will show you how to use globes and maps. You'll learn of places all over the world. Move on to page G1 to begin your adventure.

Contents

Mapping Our World

    A map is a special kind of drawing. It shows the whole world or just a part of the world. The map below shows a very small part of the world. It shows a little bit of one town. A mapmaker looked closely at the photo to draw this map. Both the map and the photo show the town as you would see it from an airplane.

From above, in an airplane, you see the top of a building. What part of the building would you see if you were standing next to it?

From the airplane, you can look down at cars on the street.

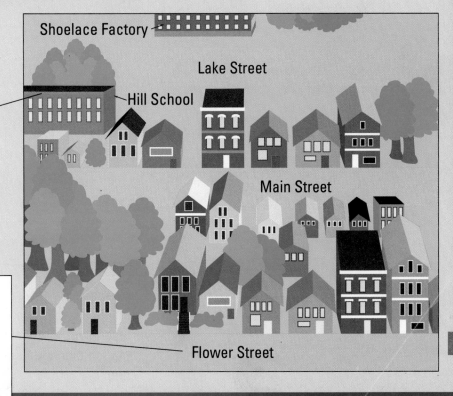

Buildings on this map have the same shape as the buildings in the photo. The map also tells you the names of some buildings.

Shoelace Factory

Lake Street

Hill School

Main Street

The map does not show cars. Instead, it shows the names of the streets.

Flower Street

Understanding a Map

Look through this Map and Globe Handbook. You'll see that each map has a different size and shape. Each also shows a different place. For example, the map on page G9 shows a farm community. The map on page G12 shows the kinds of trees in the United States.

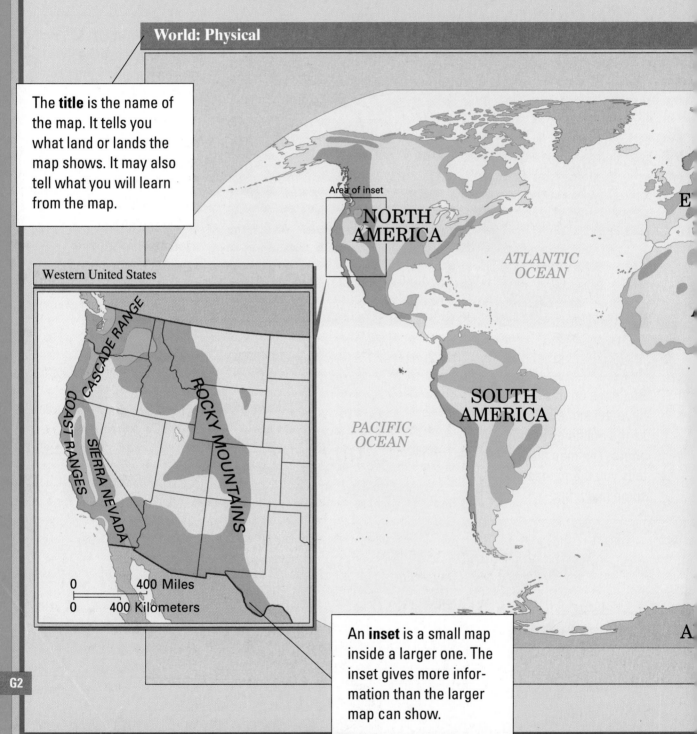

World: Physical

The **title** is the name of the map. It tells you what land or lands the map shows. It may also tell what you will learn from the map.

Area of inset

NORTH AMERICA

ATLANTIC OCEAN

E

Western United States

CASCADE RANGE

COAST RANGES

SIERRA NEVADA

ROCKY MOUNTAINS

PACIFIC OCEAN

SOUTH AMERICA

0   400 Miles
0   400 Kilometers

An **inset** is a small map inside a larger one. The inset gives more information than the larger map can show.

A

Now, go through the handbook more carefully. Look at the parts of each map. While maps may differ, they all have many of the same parts. Every part of a map tells you something important. What parts can you find on almost every map? The map below shows some useful parts of a map. You'll be able to read a map more easily once you know how to use its main parts.

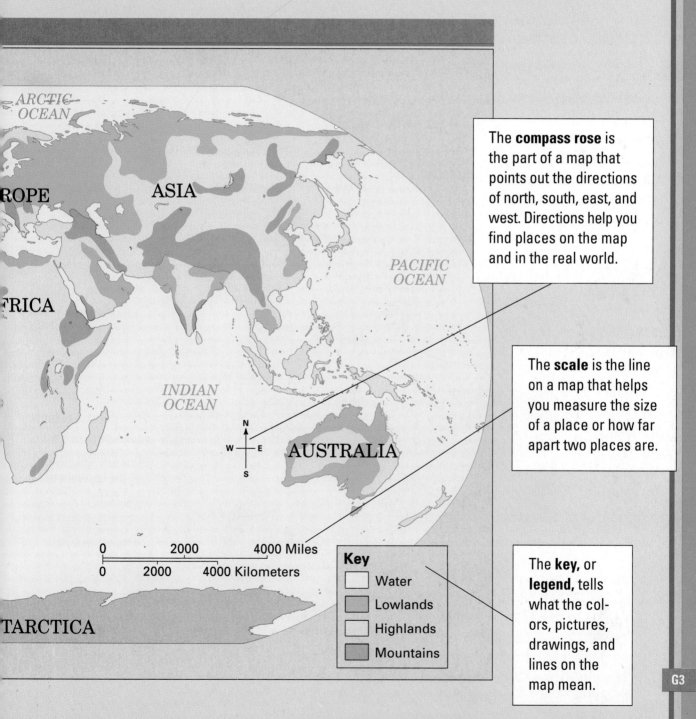

The **compass rose** is the part of a map that points out the directions of north, south, east, and west. Directions help you find places on the map and in the real world.

The **scale** is the line on a map that helps you measure the size of a place or how far apart two places are.

The **key,** or **legend,** tells what the colors, pictures, drawings, and lines on the map mean.

Key
Water
Lowlands
Highlands
Mountains

0   2000   4000 Miles
0   2000   4000 Kilometers

ARCTIC OCEAN
ROPE
ASIA
PACIFIC OCEAN
RICA
INDIAN OCEAN
AUSTRALIA
TARCTICA

Using a Compass Rose

Suppose you're in an amusement park called Circus World. You want to find the roller coaster. You have a map. You can use its compass rose to figure out which way to walk. A compass rose is the drawing on a map that shows directions. You can use the compass rose to find your favorite rides and places at Circus World.

▲ *A direction sign is like a compass rose. Both help you decide which way to go.*

As you enter Circus World, you face north. The Big Top Circus Tent is straight ahead. The Carousel lies west, to your left.

A compass rose shows the main directions. **N** stands for north. **S** stands for south. **E** stands for east. **W** stands for west.

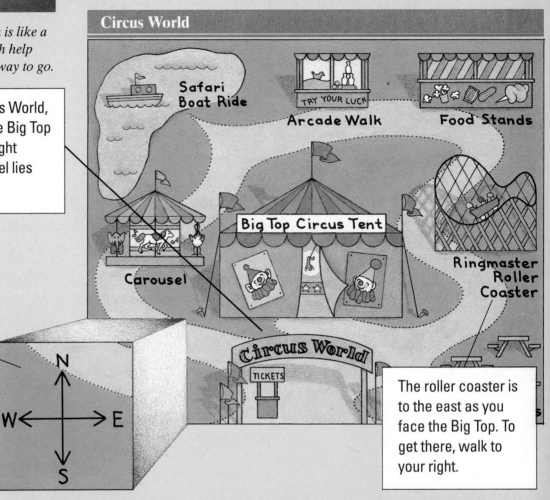

Circus World

Safari Boat Ride

TRY YOUR LUCK

Arcade Walk

Food Stands

Big Top Circus Tent

Carousel

Ringmaster Roller Coaster

Circus World

TICKETS

The roller coaster is to the east as you face the Big Top. To get there, walk to your right.

MAP SKILLS

1. **REVIEW** Which direction on the compass rose is to the left of north (N)?

2. **THINK ABOUT IT** Look at the treasure map on page 9. What other letters are on that compass rose? What directions do you think those letters stand for?

3. **TRY IT** Draw a map of your classroom. Show each desk in its place, and other important things. Ask your teacher which way is north. Draw a compass rose on your map.

Using a Map Scale

You can use a map scale to find out how far one place is from another. The scale tells you how much smaller the map is than the area it shows. One inch on this map equals 500 feet in Parkview. On a world map, one inch might equal 2,000 miles.

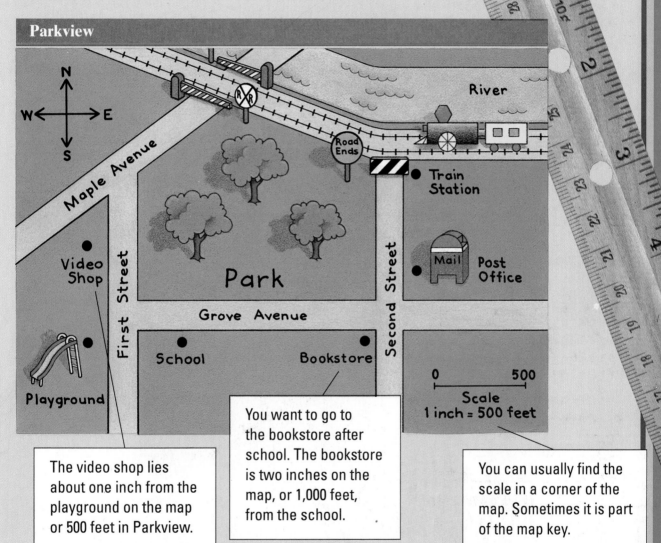

Parkview

River

Maple Avenue

Road Ends

Train Station

Video Shop

First Street

Park

Second Street

Mail

Post Office

Grove Avenue

School

Bookstore

Playground

0   500
Scale
1 inch = 500 feet

The video shop lies about one inch from the playground on the map or 500 feet in Parkview.

You want to go to the bookstore after school. The bookstore is two inches on the map, or 1,000 feet, from the school.

You can usually find the scale in a corner of the map. Sometimes it is part of the map key.

MAP SKILLS

1. REVIEW Two inches on the map stand for what distance in Parkview?

2. THINK ABOUT IT Look at the map on page 109. It shows the area around Bright Star's village. Is the scale on the map of the village the same as the scale on this map? Why would the scales be different?

3. TRY IT Draw a map of a part of your town. Create a scale for the map. Decide what distance will equal one inch.

Using a Map Key

What do stars mean on a map? Maps use stars and other symbols to tell you where places and things are. A symbol is a drawing, shape, or line on the map that shows where something is located. On some maps, the color of an area tells you something about that area. The key, or legend, tells you what the map's symbols and colors mean.

A Key with Symbols

All kinds of symbols can appear on a map. Symbols on the map below show capital cities and borders. A border is a line that separates two places, such as states.

A map usually uses a star to show a capital city. This star shows Jackson, the capital of Mississippi.

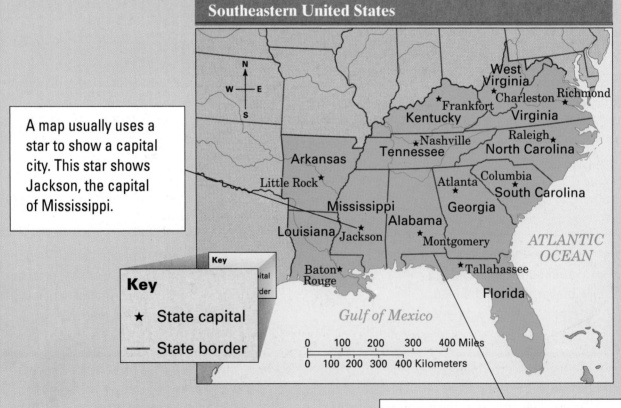

Southeastern United States

Key

Key

★ State capital

— State border

The thick lines show state borders. This line lies between Florida and Alabama. Such lines often show the borders of states and countries.

A Key with Colors

On many maps, colors have special meanings. A key tells you what the colors mean. On this map of Kansas, colors show three climate areas. Climate is the kind of weather an area has over a long time. Look at the map and pictures. Imagine what it might be like to live in each of the climate areas of Kansas.

▲ *Do you enjoy cold weather? If so, you'd like to be in Wichita during the winter.*

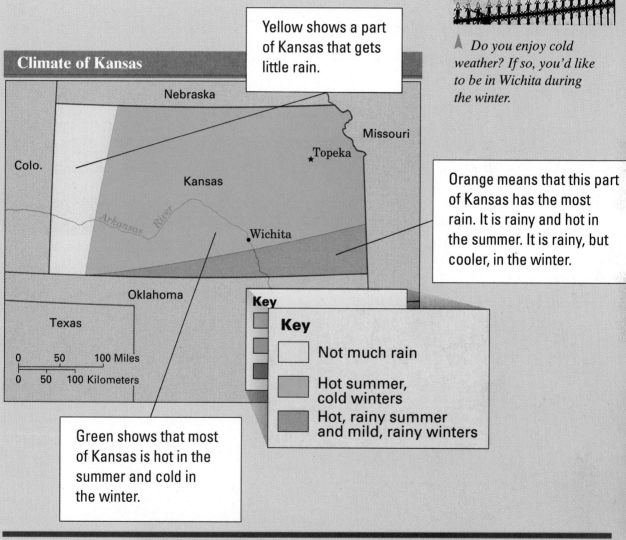

Climate of Kansas

Yellow shows a part of Kansas that gets little rain.

Orange means that this part of Kansas has the most rain. It is rainy and hot in the summer. It is rainy, but cooler, in the winter.

Green shows that most of Kansas is hot in the summer and cold in the winter.

Nebraska

Missouri

Colo.

Topeka

Kansas

Arkansas River

Wichita

Oklahoma

Texas

0   50   100 Miles

0   50   100 Kilometers

Key

Key

☐ Not much rain

☐ Hot summer, cold winters

☐ Hot, rainy summer and mild, rainy winters

MAP SKILLS

1. **REVIEW** Look at the map on page G6. Name one state and one state capital shown on the map.

2. **THINK ABOUT IT** What is the map color of the part of Kansas where you're most likely to need a raincoat? Explain how the map key helps you to answer this question.

3. **TRY IT** Find your state and its capital city on the map on page G6. If they are not on that map, use the map on pages 268 and 269.

Using an Inset Map

Sometimes one map isn't enough. The map below shows Mississippi and its neighbors. But it doesn't show where Mississippi is in the United States. The inset tells you that. An inset is a small map inside a larger one. The inset gives different information than the larger map does.

▲ *Part of the Mississippi River carves out the western border of the state of Mississippi.*

This inset shows where Mississippi is in the United States. This kind of inset map is called a locator. It helps you find, or locate, a place.

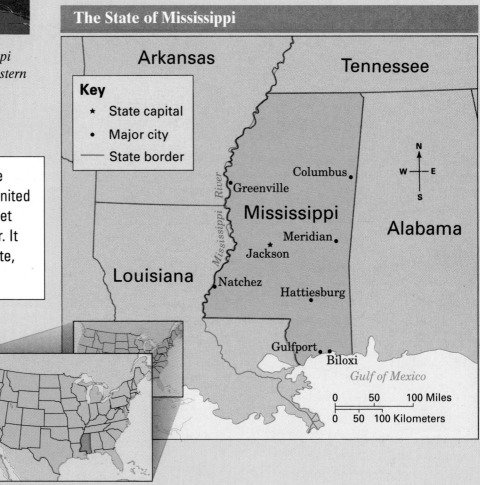

The State of Mississippi

Arkansas

Tennessee

Key
★ State capital
• Major city
— State border

Mississippi River

Columbus

Greenville

Mississippi

Alabama

Meridian

Jackson

Louisiana

Natchez

Hattiesburg

Gulfport

Biloxi

Gulf of Mexico

N
W — E
S

0   50   100 Miles
0 50 100 Kilometers

MAP SKILLS

1. **REVIEW** Is the state of Mississippi in the northern or southern United States? Is it in the eastern or western part?

2. **THINK ABOUT IT** Think of a title for the inset on this page. Then tell why your title fits this inset map.

3. **TRY IT** Trace a map of your state. Then make a locator inset to show where your state is in the United States. Trace a map of the United States. Then look at the map on pages 266–267 to find your state. Color your state on the inset.

Using a Map Grid

You want to swim and pick apples at the Bailey farm. The map grid will help you find the places to go. A grid is a set of lines on a map that cross and form squares. On this map, numbers run across the top of the grid. Letters run along the side. A square on the grid is named by its letter and number.

This list gives you the names of squares where you'll find different places on the map.

A Farm Community

Key
Apple Orchard, D5
Barn, C3
Corn Field, B2
Cow Pasture, D4
Foley School, A3
Hay Field, C4
Moon's Diner, A4
Farm House, C1
Old Well, D1
Pond, D2
Water Tower, A1

This square lies across from **D** and below **3**. That's why it is called square **D3**.

The cow pasture lies in square **D4**. That is the square across from **D** and below **4**.

MAP SKILLS

1. REVIEW Look at the map above. In which square is the old well? In which squares can you find the pond?

2. THINK ABOUT IT What kind of places does the map grid on page 158 help you find?

3. TRY IT Make a map of your schoolyard or of a nearby park. Draw a grid on the map. Put in numbers and letters. Then, make a list of five objects on the map. Name the grid square of each object.

Using a Globe

Look to the left at the picture of the earth. The earth is shaped like a ball. Then look at the globe below. The globe is also shaped like a ball. A globe is a small model of the earth. It shows all the land and water on the earth. Like most maps, a globe also has grid lines to help you find places.

The North Pole is the farthest point north on earth.

A grid line called the equator circles the globe halfway between the North Pole and the South Pole.

When you look at a globe, you can see only half the world at one time.

NORTH POLE

PRIME MERIDIAN

EQUATOR

Another grid line on the globe is the prime meridian. It runs from the North Pole to the South Pole.

SOUTH POLE

The South Pole is the farthest point south.

GLOBE SKILLS

1. **REVIEW** Take turns finding the United States on a globe. Is the United States north or south of the equator?

2. **THINK ABOUT IT** On the globe, put your finger on the equator. Turn the globe until your finger touches the prime meridian. Where do the two lines cross?

3. **TRY IT** Write a plan telling how you would make a globe. Would you use a balloon? Would you use clay?

Reading Different Kinds of Maps

Maps answer many questions. How do people use the land? What kind of trees grow in nearby forests? Where did your neighbors stop on their trip? What resources does your state have? Look at the next four maps. Think about what you can learn from each.

A Land Use Map

One kind of map shows how people use the land to produce food and other things. For example, people use the wood from forests to make houses and skateboards. Here, the color of an area shows the main way people use the land. The key tells what each color means.

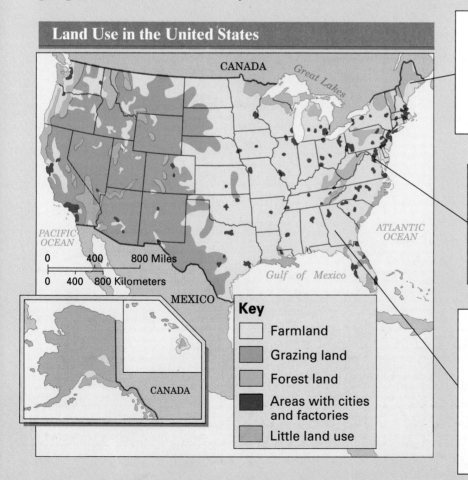

Land Use in the United States

CANADA
Great Lakes
PACIFIC OCEAN
ATLANTIC OCEAN
Gulf of Mexico
MEXICO

0 400 800 Miles
0 400 800 Kilometers

ALASKA
CANADA

Key
- Farmland
- Grazing land
- Forest land
- Areas with cities and factories
- Little land use

Large parts of the United States were once forest. If you visit the state of Maine today, you still see thick, green forests.

These purple areas stand for cities and large towns where many people live and goods are made.

Farmland takes up large parts of the United States. The yellow parts of the map are farming areas. These areas also have small towns.

A Vegetation Map

What would the land in your area look like if people had never settled there? A vegetation map can tell you. It shows the trees, grasses, and other plants that would grow if there were no cities, towns, or farms. You can also use such a map to learn what plant life grows in forests and parks near your home. The map below shows forests, one kind of vegetation.

These forests in Alaska have trees that do not lose their leaves in winter. They are called evergreen trees.

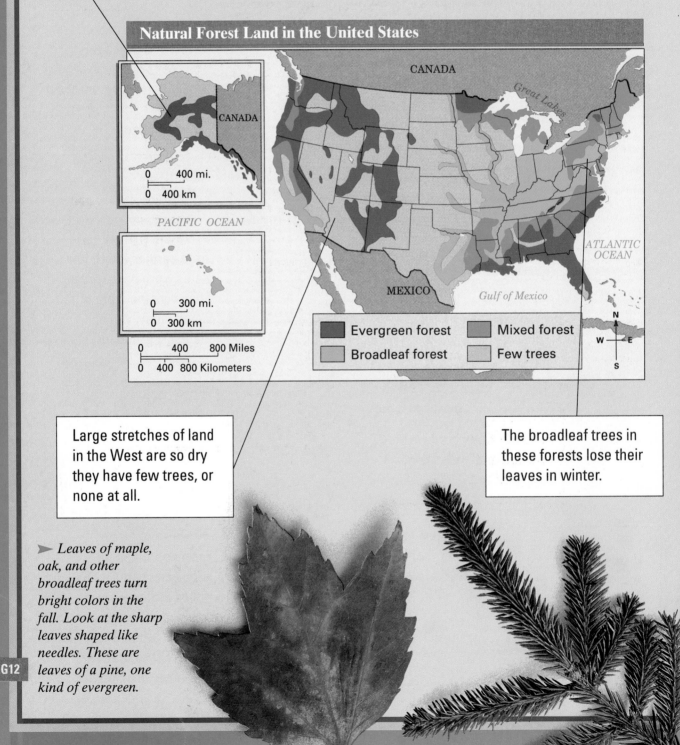

Natural Forest Land in the United States

CANADA

Great Lakes

CANADA

PACIFIC OCEAN

ATLANTIC OCEAN

MEXICO   Gulf of Mexico

| | Evergreen forest | | Mixed forest |
| | Broadleaf forest | | Few trees |

N
W — E
S

0   400 mi.
0   400 km

0   300 mi.
0   300 km

0   400   800 Miles
0   400   800 Kilometers

Large stretches of land in the West are so dry they have few trees, or none at all.

The broadleaf trees in these forests lose their leaves in winter.

➤ Leaves of maple, oak, and other broadleaf trees turn bright colors in the fall. Look at the sharp leaves shaped like needles. These are leaves of a pine, one kind of evergreen.

A Route Map

A route map shows the movement of people or goods from place to place. On this map, a line with arrows shows the route the Martinez family took on their trip. They went from Milwaukee to the lands of the Menominee, Native Americans in Wisconsin. The Martinez family also visited the city of Green Bay.

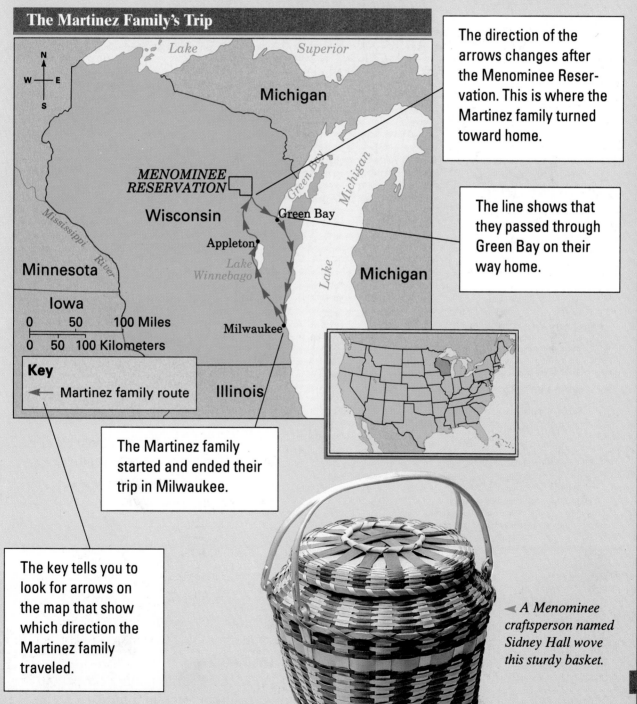

The Martinez Family's Trip

The direction of the arrows changes after the Menominee Reservation. This is where the Martinez family turned toward home.

The line shows that they passed through Green Bay on their way home.

The Martinez family started and ended their trip in Milwaukee.

The key tells you to look for arrows on the map that show which direction the Martinez family traveled.

Key
← Martinez family route

◄ *A Menominee craftsperson named Sidney Hall wove this sturdy basket.*

A Resource Map

A natural resource is something found in nature that people can use. The oil that workers find in the ground is one resource. It provides fuel to run cars. The natural gas that workers find in the ground is also a resource. Gas heats water. Gas also makes homes warm in winter. This map shows where oil and natural gas are found in the state of Michigan.

Oil and Natural Gas in Michigan

On this map, the flame is a symbol for natural gas.

The symbol for oil looks like an oil well. Workers use such wells to pump oil from the ground.

Key
- ⚒ Oil
- ♦ Natural gas
- • Major city
- ★ State capital

```
0        100        200 Miles
0    100   200 Kilometers
```

Minnesota · Lake Superior · CANADA · Wisconsin · Lake Michigan · Michigan · Lake Huron · Grand Rapids · Lansing · Detroit · Lake Erie · Indiana · Ohio

You can see that oil and natural gas are usually found side by side.

MAP SKILLS

1. **REVIEW** What kind of map shows where forests grow in the South?
2. **REVIEW** What natural resources does the map on page 161 show? What kind of resource was found closest to Leadville?
3. **THINK ABOUT IT** Look at the route map on page 156. How would you change this map to show the route from eastern cities to Abilene?
4. **TRY IT** Make a route map to show how to get to school from your house.

Using Geographic References

What does a mountain look like? Where do New York and New Jersey meet? Where can you find a map that shows Ohio? The Time/Space Databank on pages 263 to 281 can help answer such questions.

The Atlas on pages 264 to 271 has a map of the world and maps of the United States. This part of the United States political map on pages 268 and 269 shows the border between New York and New Jersey.

O

Ohio North central state. Its capital is Columbus. (pp. 268–269)

Ohio River River formed in Pennsylvania where the Allegheny and the Monongahela rivers join. It flows into the Mississippi River at the southern tip of Illinois. (p. 179)

Oklahoma Southwestern state. Its capital is Oklahoma City. (pp. 268–269)

Oregon Northwestern state on the Pacific coast. Its capital is Salem. (pp. 268–269)

The Gazetteer on pages 272 to 275 is a list of places. If you look up "Ohio" under "O," you'll find this entry. It tells Ohio's location and capital. It also gives the page number of a map showing Ohio.

The Glossary of Geographic Terms on pages 276 and 277 tells you about land and water features of the earth. This part gives the meaning of "mountain." The picture helps you see what a mountain is.

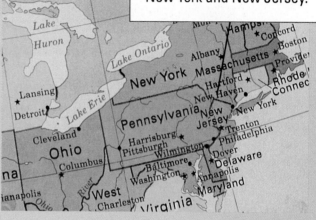

mountain
a steeply raised mass of land, much higher than the surrounding country

tree line
on a mountain, the area above which no trees grow

REFERENCE SKILLS

1. **REVIEW** Use the Time/Space Databank to make a list of states that touch Texas. Did you use the Atlas, the Gazetteer, or the Glossary of Geographic Terms?

2. **THINK ABOUT IT** What is a harbor? What does it look like? Look at the Atlas map of the United States on pages 268 and 269. Find and name some cities you think might have harbors. Why?

3. **TRY IT** Look up your state in the Gazetteer. Find a map of your state. Name the states that lie next to yours.

Unit 1

Listen to the Land

Before people came to the land, only the sounds of nature could be heard. Water from melting snow rushed noisily down mountain peaks, and moose called in thick green forests. Today, roaring cars and planes can make them hard to hear, but—if you listen—you can still hear the beautiful sounds of the land.

David Muench. Beaver Lodge. Grand Teton National Park, Wyoming.

Chapter 1

Mighty Waters

The story of this land begins with a look at its mighty waters. The United States is touched by two great oceans and crossed by many rivers and streams. Pounding ocean waves eat away at the shores and make sandy beaches. Powerful rivers and streams carry soil from one place to another. The United States is a land shaped by water.

Oceans are filled with beautiful sea creatures. This animal is called a starfish, or a sea star. Starfish live in every ocean of the world.

Powerful waves have formed these cliffs along the Pacific Ocean.

The waters of the Atlantic Ocean broke up rocks and shells to form the sand on this beach.

The Earth is mostly covered with water. The United States lies between the Atlantic and Pacific oceans.

The Mississippi River, which winds through the middle of the United States, is the longest river in North America.

Sand and Salt

How do oceans change the land?

Key Terms

- ocean
- coast
- erosion

The sun was hot, but Matt didn't notice. He piled cool, damp sand onto his sand castle. The crashing waves of the ocean were so loud that he could barely hear the sea gulls calling. Matt picked up more sand and noticed something white, round, and flat. He carefully brushed off the sand. It was the first sand dollar Matt had ever found. He gently placed it next to the shells he had gathered.

Matt looked at the waves rolling toward him. He licked his lips, which tasted salty. Soon the waves would wash away his sand castle, but Matt didn't mind. He'd always have the sand dollar to remind him of the sea.

Pacific and Atlantic

The waves that rolled toward Matt came from the Pacific Ocean. An **ocean** is a large body of salt water. Oceans cover more than half the earth's surface. The Pacific Ocean is the largest ocean. It borders the United States on the west. Hawaii is surrounded by the Pacific Ocean.

If Matt could see 3,000 miles across the United States, he would see another ocean! That one is the Atlantic Ocean, the second largest ocean in the world. Find the Pacific and Atlantic oceans on the picture of the globe. ■

Coastal Land

Oceans constantly change the land. The land along the edge of an ocean is called the **coast.** Ocean waters act like a scraper on coastal land. Crashing waves slowly grind up the soil and rock and carry it away. This wearing away of land is called **erosion.**

Across Time & Space

Many scientists believe that the earth was once one giant piece of land and one giant ocean. Look at the world map on pages 264–265. Imagine that Africa and South America are pieces of a puzzle. Fit them together.

■ *What oceans border the United States?*

◄ *Large ocean waves like these can change the shape of a coast.*

Ocean waves are very powerful. Over hundreds of years, they can wear away even the hardest kinds of rock. In some places, crashing waves turn land along the coast into steep, rocky cliffs.

How Sea Cliffs Are Formed

1. A sea cliff starts out as a hill. Over many years, waves weaken the lower part of the hill.

2. Bit by bit, the earth and rock there begin to break into chunks and slide into the ocean.

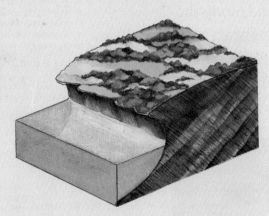

3. Now the upper part of the hill hangs out over the water. When it becomes too heavy, that part begins to crumble and fall.

4. Finally, the side of the hill has become a steep cliff.

Ocean waves do not just cause erosion. They can also add to the land. When waves wash up on a shore, they may leave sand and mud behind. After years of sand and mud piling up this way, new beaches are formed.

Where does sand come from? You may be surprised to learn that it was once rocks and shells. Rocks and shells are pounded by waves against other rocks and shells. This constant pounding breaks them down into small bits. Then the waves wash the small bits onto the shore.

Not all beaches are alike. In some places, rocks and shells are broken into tiny bits and become sand. In other places, rocks do not break into such small pieces. That is why some beaches are sandy and others are rocky. ■

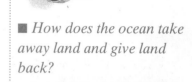

■ *How does the ocean take away land and give land back?*

◄ *In some places, waves break rocks into very tiny pieces, and sandy beaches form. In other places, rocks are left in bigger pieces as on the rocky beach above.*

R E V I E W

1. **FOCUS** How do oceans change the land?
2. **CONNECT** Do you live closer to the Atlantic Ocean or the Pacific Ocean?
3. **CRITICAL THINKING** Is a sea cliff a safe place to build a house? Why?
4. **ACTIVITY** Draw a line down the middle of a piece of paper. On one side, draw a picture of things to do on a sandy beach. On the other side, draw a picture of things to do on a rocky beach.

Using a Compass Rose

Here's Why You know that the Pacific Ocean borders the United States on the west. The Atlantic Ocean is on the east. Canada is to the north. Mexico is to the south. North, south, east, and west are the main, or cardinal, directions.

Suppose you want to find a place between north and east, or between east and south. Then you need in-between directions. In-between directions are called intermediate directions. Knowing how to use intermediate directions will make it easier to locate places on a map.

Here's How You will find a compass rose on many maps. A compass rose shows directions. Find the compass rose on the treasure map on the next page. North is at the top. South is at the bottom. East is to the right. Where is west?

Now find the direction halfway between north and east on the compass rose. Northeast is the intermediate direction between north and east. What two letters are used for this direction? Find the direction halfway between south and east on the compass rose. That direction is labeled SE. What does SE stand for? What is the intermediate direction halfway between south and west? What is the intermediate direction halfway between north and west?

Try It Look at the treasure map again. Imagine that you are looking for hidden treasure. You walk north

along the path and then turn east. You come to the hut, but the treasure isn't there. You decide to look under the table. In which direction is the table from the hut? Maybe the treasure is under the bridge. In which direction is the bridge from the table?

Apply It Now work with a partner. Plan your own treasure hunt. Use the map to decide where to hide your treasure. Give your partner a starting point and directions to find it. When your partner has found the treasure, it's your turn to search. Follow your partner's directions until you find the treasure.

9

*Two boys watched the river and
wondered where it began. They asked
their grandfather, who had lived near
the river all his life. Together, they set
out to find the beginning of the river.
Read about their trip.*

LITERATURE

WHERE THE RIVER BEGINS

**Written and Illustrated by
Thomas Locker**

Once there were two boys
named Josh and Aaron who lived
with their family in a big yellow
house. Nearby was a river that
flowed gently into the sea. On
summer evenings the boys liked
to sit on their porch watching the
river and making up stories about
it. Where, they wondered, did the
river begin.

Their grandfather loved the river and had lived near it all his life. Perhaps he would know. One day Josh and Aaron asked their grandfather to take them on a camping trip to find the beginning of the river. When he agreed, they made plans and began to pack.

They started out early the next morning. For a time they walked along a familiar road past fields of golden wheat and sheep grazing in the sun. Nearby flowed the river—gentle, wide, and deep.

At last they reached the foothills of the mountains. The road had ended and now the river would be their only guide. It raced over rocks and boulders and had become so narrow that the boys and their grandfather could jump across.

In the late afternoon, while the sun was still hot, the river led them into a dark forest. They found a campsite and set up their tent. Then the boys went wading in the cold river water.

The first long day away from home was over. That night, around the flickering campfire, their grandfather told Josh and Aaron stories. Drifting off to sleep, they listened to the forest noises and were soothed by the sound of the river.

Dawn seemed to come quickly and the sun glowed through a thick mist. The boys were eager to be off, but their grandfather was stiff from sleeping on the ground and was slower getting started.

The path they chose led them high above the river. On a grassy knoll they stopped to gaze around. The morning mist had risen and formed white clouds in the sky. In the distance the river meandered lazily. It was so narrow that it seemed almost to disappear. They all felt a great excitement, for they knew they were nearing the end of their journey.

Without a word the boys began to run. They followed the river for an hour or more until it trickled into a still pond, high in an upland meadow. In this small, peaceful place the river began. Finally their search was over.

As they started back, the sky suddenly darkened. Thunder crashed around them and lightning lit the sky. They pitched their tent and crawled inside just before the storm broke. Rain pounded on the roof of their small tent all night long, but they were warm and dry inside.

In the morning long before dawn they were awakened by a roaring, rushing sound. The river had swelled with the storm and was flooding its banks. They tried to take a shortcut across a field but were soon ankle deep in water. Grandfather explained that the river drew its waters from the rains high up in the mountains.

They came down out of the foothills in the soft light of late afternoon. The boys recognized the cliffs along the river and knew they were close to home. Their weariness lifted and they began to move more quickly down the road.

At last they reached their house on the hill. The boys raced ahead to tell their mother and father about the place where the river began. But their grandfather paused for a moment and in the fading light he watched the river, which continued on as it always had, flowing gently into the sea.

Running Rivers

THINKING FOCUS

How do rivers affect the land?

Key Terms

- river
- lake
- flood

*T*he river went on raising and raising for ten or twelve days, till at last it was over the banks. The water was three or four foot deep on the island in the low places and on the Illinois bottom. On that side it was a good many miles wide, but on the Missouri side it was the same old distance across—a half a mile—because the Missouri shore was just a wall of high bluffs.

Daytimes we paddled all over the island in the canoe. . . . Well, on every old broken-down tree you could see rabbits and snakes and such things; and when the island had been overflowed a day or two they got so tame, on account of being hungry, that you could paddle right up and put your hand on them if you wanted to; but not the snakes and turtles—they would slide off in the water.

Mark Twain, from *The Adventures of Huckleberry Finn*

The author who wrote these words lived along a river bank and often saw the water rise after a big rain. A **river** is a stream of water that flows across land. Rivers are different from oceans in two ways. First, oceans are much bigger than rivers are. Oceans cover most of the earth. Second, oceans are salty. Rivers are not. Water that comes from rivers is called fresh water.

A **lake** is a pool of water on land. Like rivers, most lakes have fresh water. One difference between rivers and lakes is that rivers flow from place to place.

Constant Motion

Rivers start in different ways. Some rivers begin in lakes. Look at the map. Where does the Hudson River begin? Other rivers start from underground streams. Heavy rains or melting snow can also cause rivers. Rivers carry extra water that the land can't soak up.

The Hudson River

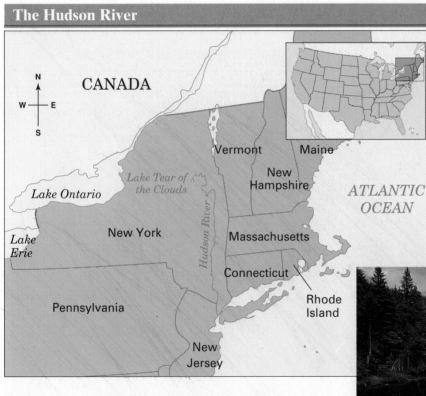

◄ *The large map shows where the Hudson River flows. To learn how to use the inset map, see page G8 of the* Map and Globe Handbook.

Once they begin, rivers are always moving. Most rivers run into another body of water. Some rivers flow into other rivers. Some rivers end in lakes or oceans. Others may just disappear underground.

Rivers may be wide or narrow. They may be deep or shallow. But all river water moves because it flows downhill. If the land is flat, water runs slowly. If the land is steep, water runs quickly. The Colorado River often flows fast because it runs downhill through very steep land. ■

▲ *The Hudson River starts in Lake Tear of the Clouds, which holds water from Mt. Marcy. Where does the river end?*

■ *How do rivers begin and end?*

19

The Grand Canyon

The power of a river can change the earth. The Colorado River has formed a huge canyon by working its way through layers of rock. Every year, for millions of years, the canyon has become deeper and wider.

Millions of years ago, sand, gravel, and boulders were swept along by the river. These materials scraped away layers and layers of rock.

What was once a river bed is now the Grand Canyon. The Colorado River started out on flat land. Today the canyon is a mile deep and almost 18 miles wide in some places.

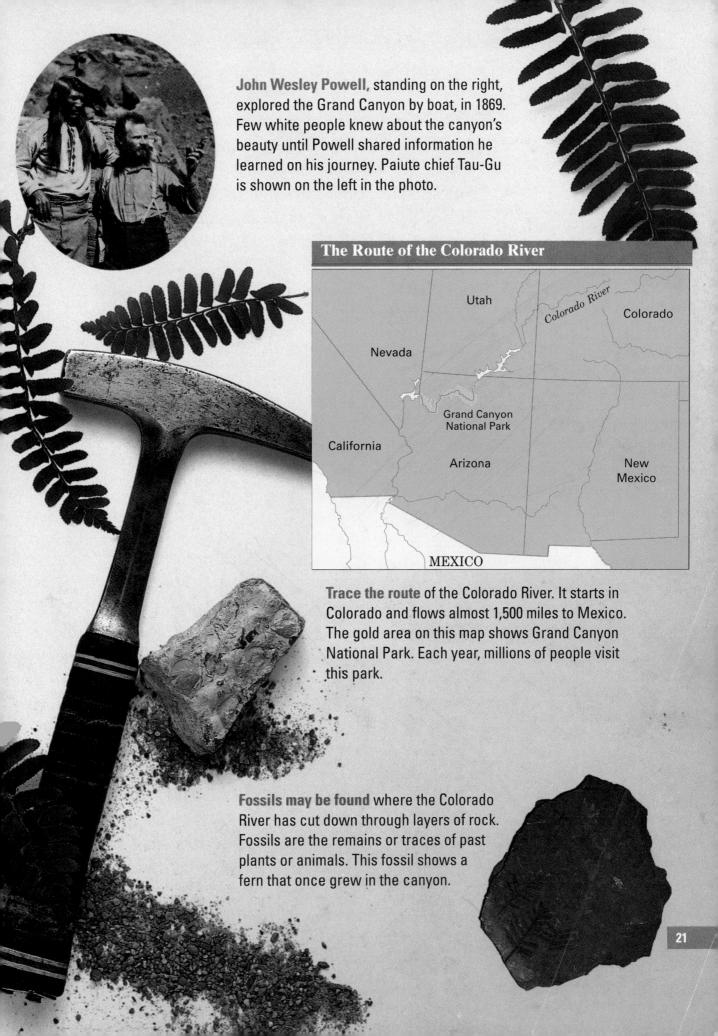

John Wesley Powell, standing on the right, explored the Grand Canyon by boat, in 1869. Few white people knew about the canyon's beauty until Powell shared information he learned on his journey. Paiute chief Tau-Gu is shown on the left in the photo.

The Route of the Colorado River

Utah

Colorado River

Colorado

Nevada

Grand Canyon National Park

California

Arizona

New Mexico

MEXICO

Trace the route of the Colorado River. It starts in Colorado and flows almost 1,500 miles to Mexico. The gold area on this map shows Grand Canyon National Park. Each year, millions of people visit this park.

Fossils may be found where the Colorado River has cut down through layers of rock. Fossils are the remains or traces of past plants or animals. This fossil shows a fern that once grew in the canyon.

Shaping the Land

You saw how the mighty Colorado River carved a deep canyon into the surface of the earth. Other rivers cut valleys into the land, too. At first a river valley is narrow with steep sides, like the letter V. Over many years, the flow of water wears away the soil and rock of the banks and of the river bottom. In time, the V becomes deeper and wider.

Often the valley becomes very wide. The river may wander in winding loops from side to side. A river may change directions. This makes the valley even wider. If a river changes directions many times, it starts to look like many winding loops. Sometimes a river cuts off one of these loops, forming a C-shaped lake. ■

▼ *Look at the winding loops of this big, old river.*

■ *How do rivers change the shape of a valley?*

The Changing River

A loop in a river is called a meander.

In time, the river may flow out of its banks, straight ahead. The loop it leaves behind is called an ox-bow lake.

Flooding the Land

Water that overflows its banks and covers land that is normally dry is a **flood.** Too much rain can cause a flood. Another cause might be the sudden melting of snow or ice. Land that is covered with water during a flood is called a flood plain.

Most floods are harmful. They damage homes and carry off soil. But some floods are helpful. Sometimes a flood brings new soil and leaves it behind when the water dries up. The new soil helps crops grow better. Rivers may take away the land by erosion, but they can also build up the land. ■

◄ *This whole area is a flood plain. You can see that the farmer's house barely missed going underwater too. Farms are often on flood plains because the soil is so good.*

■ *How can a flood bring good things to people?*

R E V I E W

1. **FOCUS** How do rivers affect the land?
2. **CONNECT** What are the differences between oceans, rivers, and lakes?
3. **CRITICAL THINKING** We know that rivers drain water from the land. What do you think would happen if there were no rivers to carry off extra water?
4. **ACTIVITY** Take an imaginary trip on an ocean or a river. Write a short description of what you see, hear, and smell. Compare what you wrote with what your classmates wrote. How are river and ocean trips different? How are they the same?

Chapter Review

Reviewing Key Terms

coast (p. 5)　　lake (p. 19)
erosion (p. 5)　ocean (p. 5)
flood (p. 23)　　river (p. 18)

A. Write the key term for each meaning.

1. a pool of water on land
2. the wearing away of land
3. a large body of salt water
4. the land that is along the edge of an ocean

B. Write the correct key term for each numbered blank.

On his vacation, Jack saw big waves of salt water in the __1__. His mother told him that the waves caused __2__ of the land. Amy went to a __3__, which is a large pool of fresh water. From it, a __4__ began and flowed downhill between its banks. One day, too much rain caused a __5__.

Exploring Concepts

A. Copy the chart below. Fill in the missing information in the two empty spaces. In the second column, fill in the kind of water that rivers have. In the last column, fill in the size of oceans. Your chart will show two ways in which rivers and oceans are different.

B. Write one or two sentences to answer each question.

1. How are floods helpful and how are they harmful?
2. How are some new beaches formed?
3. Explain why some river water runs slowly and some runs quickly.

Bodies of water	Kinds of water	Size
Rivers		Smaller than oceans
Oceans	Salty	

Reviewing Skills

1. Find Denver, Colorado, on the map on pages 268–269. Travel northwest from Denver to Canada. When you get near Canada, in what state will you be?
2. In what intermediate direction would you travel to go from Atlanta, Georgia, to the coast of Maine?
3. What state is next to and east of Mississippi? What two states are next to Mississippi on the west?

Using Critical Thinking

1. You know that rivers change the land. How do you think the Colorado River will continue to change the Grand Canyon?
2. Suppose you take a boat trip down a long river. You go all the way to the end of the river. What might you see there?

Preparing for Citizenship

1. **ART ACTIVITY** Look at the river pictures on the right. Then read Mark Twain's description of the river on page 18 again. Draw a picture that shows the scene described by Mark Twain. Color your picture if you want to.

2. **COLLABORATIVE LEARNING** Work with a partner. Have one person be a newspaper reporter who asks the other person questions about the effects of a flood on the land. Then switch roles so that the reporter becomes the person who answers questions. Finally, work together to write a newspaper story about the effects of the flood. Be sure to include some of the interview answers. If you can, read your story to your class.

Chapter 2

Rustling Leaves and Grasses

Our mighty rivers flow across a huge land. Not all of this land looks the same. The rivers flow through great tree-covered lands called forests. They also cross huge grasslands called prairies. Forests and prairies are very different from each other, but they are both home to many kinds of animals.

A sage grouse can hide from its enemies in the tall grasses of a prairie.

This is turkeyfoot prairie grass. The tops of the grass separate into many parts and look like turkeys' feet.

Forests grow in much of the eastern half of the country. Forests also grow in many mountains and along the coasts in the West. Prairies cover much of the middle part of our land.

The color of this gray fox's fur makes it hard to see against the greens and browns of the forest. This helps it sneak up on the animals that are its food.

Many of the trees in this forest are oaks and maples. Sugar maple trees grow from seeds like the ones at the top of this page.

Wonderful Woodlands

THINKING
FOCUS

Why are forests important?

Key Terms

- forest
- humus

Imagine being able to swing, hop, or fly from tree to tree all the way from the Atlantic Ocean to the Mississippi River without ever touching the ground! Long ago, the trees were so thick that a squirrel could have done just that. Most of the eastern half of our country was one big **forest,** a large area of land thickly covered with trees.

United States Forests

Today, trees no longer cover so much area. About 100 years ago, most of those forests were gone. As our country grew, people cut down trees to make room for farmland and cities. Today, people plant new forests to help replace some of those that once covered much of America.

Three types of forests grow in the United States. One kind has trees that lose their leaves in the fall. Another type of forest has trees that stay green all year. The third kind is a mixed forest. It includes trees that stay green and trees that lose their leaves. What kinds of trees grow where you live? ■

■ *What types of forests grow in the United States?*

Types of United States Forests

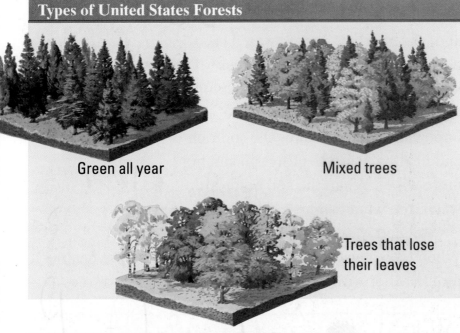

Green all year

Mixed trees

Trees that lose their leaves

◄ *Here are three types of forests in the fall. The trees that always stay green are called evergreens. The forest on the right is a mixed forest. Trees that lose their leaves have bare branches in the winter.*

How Do We Know?

Some trees can grow to be thousands of years old. Look at a round tree stump sometime. You can tell how old the tree was by counting the number of rings on the trunk. Each ring stands for one year.

Trees and Soil Help Each Other

Trees are important because they help stop erosion. You have already seen how water in oceans and rivers wear away the land. Wind can cause erosion, too.

Trees help stop erosion in two ways. First, their roots hold the soil in place. The roots act like tiny fingers. When the wind blows, the "fingers" grab on to the soil and keep the wind from taking it away. Trees also stop erosion by "feeding" the land. When a tree dies, its branches, roots,

The green moss on this dead log makes a good place for mushrooms and insects to live.

▲ *Mushrooms get their food from dead plants. Mushrooms help break down dead trees into humus for rich new soil.*

■ *How do trees help the land?*

and leaves decay, or rot away. This decayed material is called **humus** (*HYOO muhs*). The dark brown color of soil comes from humus. More important, humus makes the soil rich and healthy. Rich, healthy soil can hold more water. When the soil holds more water, the wind cannot easily blow it away.

Soil and water feed trees and other plants. When the soil is well-fed, trees and plants can be healthy, too. In other words, trees help soil and soil helps trees. ■

Trees and Animals Need Each Other

Soil and trees are not the only things that depend on each other. Forest plants and animals need each other, too. The forest gives food and shelter to many animals. Squirrels and birds make their homes in tree branches. Raccoons live in holes in tree trunks. Insects live in tree bark. Many animals eat the seeds and nuts that grow on trees. Deer eat bark. Insects eat leaves, wood, and roots.

In return, the animals help more trees and plants

Birds and squirrels help forests grow. By eating berries, this thrush scatters seeds on the ground from which new plants sprout. By burying an acorn, and then forgetting to dig it up later for lunch, this squirrel helps plant new oak trees.

to grow. How? Trees and plants grow from seeds and nuts. Birds scatter seeds that allow new plants to grow. Have you ever seen a squirrel bury an acorn? Squirrels bury more nuts than they can eat. Each nut they bury has a chance to become a new tree.

Animals help the trees in another way. When they die, their bodies decay on the ground. The decaying bodies add to the humus in the soil that feeds the trees. The forest feeds its creatures, and the animals die and become food for the trees. In this way, forest life can go on and on.

So forest animals and plants depend on each other in many ways. If one living thing is damaged or destroyed, another may suffer, too. If whole forests are cut down, animals may lose their homes and die. Soil washes away and new plants cannot grow. If we learn how living things depend on each other, we can help forest life continue. ■

■ *How do trees and animals help each other?*

R E V I E W

1. **FOCUS** Why are forests important?
2. **CONNECT** Would you rather visit a river or a forest? Why?
3. **CRITICAL THINKING** How might a forest be different if no animals lived in it?

4. **ACTIVITY** Draw a picture of a forest. In your picture, show how trees give shelter and food to animals.

Finding Supporting Details

Here's Why Writers often write about one main idea in each paragraph. Other sentences give details that support, or explain, the main idea. Knowing how to find main ideas and their supporting details will help you understand what you read.

Here's How Think of a chart such as the one below when you read a paragraph. The large box at the top has the main idea. The smaller boxes have the details. Read this paragraph:

> The forest is home to many animals. Birds make their nests in tree branches. Hollowed-out tree stumps are homes for raccoons and other animals. Deer sleep and hide among the trees in forests.

The main idea of the paragraph is: *The forest is home to many animals.* The other sentences tell how the forest is home to the animals. They give the details that support the main idea.

Main Idea: **The forest is home to many animals.**

Detail: Birds make their nests in tree branches.	Detail: Hollowed-out tree stumps are homes for raccoons and other animals.	Detail: Deer sleep and hide among the trees in forests.

Try It Read the second paragraph on page 29 again. The main idea is stated in the first sentence. What details support the main idea?

Apply It Work with a partner. Write a paragraph about forests or forest animals. Make a chart of your main idea and supporting details.

A Sea of Grass

Picture yourself standing in a field of grass. The grass is moving in the wind, like waves on the ocean. The land stretches out as far as you can see. Suddenly, the ground begins to shake. The land ahead looks dark and smoky. You begin to think the whole earth might be on fire! A rumbling sound grows louder and louder. Now you know that you are not looking at the smoke of a raging fire. What you see is the darkness of thousands of pawing and charging buffaloes coming toward you. A great cloud of dust blackens the sky for miles around.

THINKING FOCUS

How are prairies different from forests?

Key Terms

- prairie
- predator

◄ A Herd of Buffaloes on the Bed of the River Missouri *was painted by William Jacob Hays in 1860.*

What Is a Prairie?

Across Time & Space

Two hundred years ago, millions of buffaloes roamed the U.S. prairies. Later, after the arrival of white people, hunters killed all but about 500. Now buffaloes live in areas that are protected from hunters.

■ *What would you see if you were standing on a prairie?*

▼ *This prairie in Nebraska grows short grass about two feet tall.*

People traveling across the United States long ago would often write about seeing these giant animals. During the fall, small groups, or herds, of buffaloes joined together to form larger herds. In the winter, these huge herds would move across the prairie to warmer areas. There they searched for food. A **prairie** is an area of flat or hilly land covered by grasses.

If you stood in the middle of a great prairie, you would see nothing but grass and sky. In the distance, you might notice a low hill. You would not see many trees.

The amount of rain that falls on prairies affects the height of the grass that can grow there. Eastern prairies get more rain than western prairies. Because of this, grass in the east can grow as tall as a person!

Prairie soil is very rich. Grasses and farm crops, such as wheat and oats, grow well in such soil. Because of this, much of the prairie land shown on the map on page 35 is now used for raising animals and crops. ■

CANADA

Montana

North Dakota

Minnesota

South Dakota

Wisconsin

Wyoming

Michigan

Nebraska

Iowa

Indiana

Colorado

Illinois

Kansas

Missouri

Oklahoma

UNITED STATES

New Mexico

Texas

PACIFIC OCEAN

ATLANTIC OCEAN

MEXICO

Key
☐ Shortgrass Prairie
▨ Mixed Prairie
▩ Tallgrass Prairie

Prairie Life

Prairies are home to many creatures. The animals that live on prairies have special ways to protect themselves from predators. A **predator** is an animal that hunts other animals for food. Forest animals use the trees to hide from their enemies. Since few trees grow on prairies, the animals there have other ways to escape predators.

Some prairie animals, such as badgers and prairie dogs, dig underground tunnels, or burrows, to protect themselves from predators. If an enemy is near and there is no burrow around, a badger will quickly dig a new one to hide in. Prairie dogs nibble down the grass around their burrows. Doing so makes it easier for prairie dogs to see predators coming.

▲ *For help in reading a vegetation map, see page G12 in the Map and Globe Handbook.*

◄ *Badgers have large front paws with sharp claws. How does this help them in their prairie life?*

35

A Prairie Dog Town

If you were to visit a prairie, what animals do you think you'd see? Prairie dogs live on prairies in large groups called towns. A town may have 50 to 100 burrows.

Prairie grass for lunch? Sounds delicious! Prairie dogs eat mostly grasses and grain. They also eat small insects.

Home means being together! Many prairie dogs live in one burrow. The entrance is called a mound.

Let's take a tour of a prairie dog burrow:
a. *emergency exit*—used to escape predators
b. *nursery or bedroom*—used to sleep or give birth
c. *bathroom*—used only during bad weather
d. *listening room*—used to listen for predators
e. *dry room*—used during floods

◄ The pronghorn's long legs help make it one of the fastest animals in the world.

▼ The coyote can leap 14 feet. How does this help make it a good predator?

Pronghorns protect themselves from predators by living in herds. When a predator is near, the animals warn each other. The animals in a herd also stay together. It is much harder for an enemy to attack a whole herd than to attack a single animal. If an animal gets separated from the herd, its best chance to escape is to outrun its enemy. Being able to run fast helps many animals stay alive on the prairie.

Who are these enemies? Coyotes *(ky OH teez)* are among the most feared predators. Coyotes hunt everything from the smallest prairie dog to the largest pronghorn. They are also very fast. Coyotes can outrun many small animals and are very good hunters. They have to be. After all, coyotes must stay alive in the sea of grass, too. ■

■ How do prairie animals protect themselves from predators?

R E V I E W

1. **FOCUS** How are prairies different from forests?
2. **CONNECT** Compare the way forest and prairie animals escape from predators.
3. **CRITICAL THINKING** Tell how living in a burrow in a prairie dog town is like living in an apartment in a big apartment building. How is it different?
4. **ACTIVITY** Imagine you are a traveler long ago, seeing a prairie and its animals for the first time. Write a paragraph in your journal telling what you see.

37

Line Graphs and Circle Graphs

Here's Why Have you ever heard the expression "a picture is worth a thousand words"? Line graphs are like pictures of number facts. Knowing how to read line graphs will help you see changes over a period of time.

Circle graphs compare the amount of things. Knowing how to read circle graphs will help you understand differences in amounts.

Here's How As you know, line graphs deal with numbers. The dots on a line graph represent numbers. We use line graphs to see how something changes. Look at the line graph below. It shows the amount of rain that fell on a prairie for six months during one year.

The numbers down the left side of the line graph are inches of rain. For April, the dot is at three inches of rainfall. The dot for May is at a larger number. The June

Prairie Rainfall for Six Months

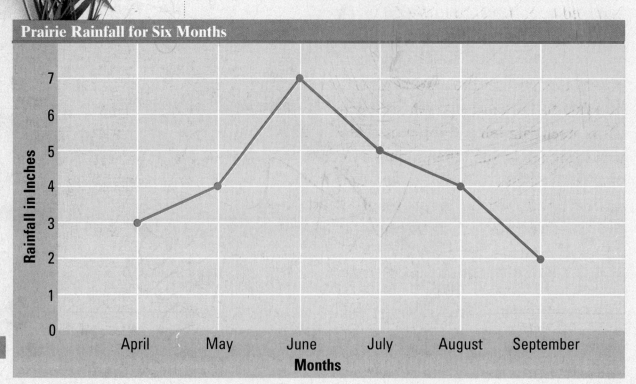

dot is at a still larger number. The dots are connected by lines to show the amount of change in rainfall during the six months. Which month had the most rainfall? Which had the least?

Circle graphs show parts of a whole. You have learned that different kinds of forests grow in the Northeast. The circle graph on this page shows how much of the Northeast is covered by each kind of forest. The key above the graph shows what the colors in the graph stand for. What color stands for mixed trees? You can see that most of the forest area is mixed trees, because that is the largest part of the circle.

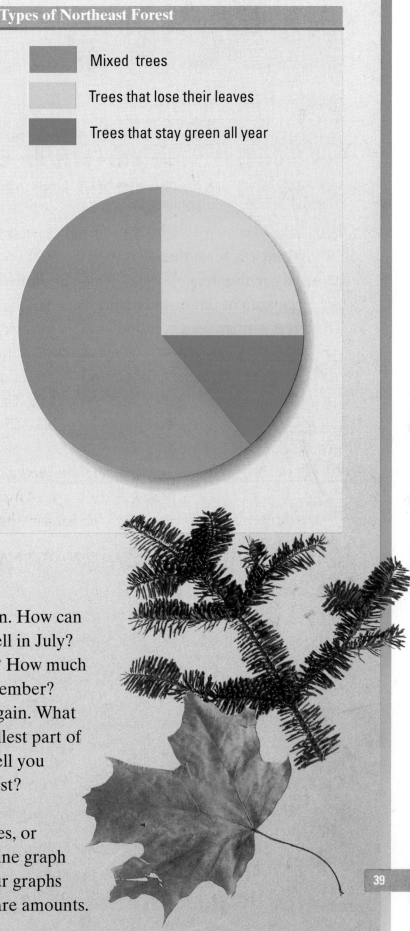

Types of Northeast Forest

Mixed trees

Trees that lose their leaves

Trees that stay green all year

Try It   Look at the line graph again. How can you find the amount of rain that fell in July? How much rain fell in September? How much more rain fell in June than in September?

Now look at the circle graph again. What type of forest is shown by the smallest part of the graph? What does the graph tell you about the trees in that type of forest?

Apply It   Look in books, magazines, or newspapers for graphs. Find one line graph and one circle graph. Tell how your graphs show change in amounts or compare amounts.

Chapter Review

Reviewing Key Terms

forest (p. 28)   prairie (p. 34)
humus (p. 30)   predator (p. 35)

A. Write the key term that best completes each sentence.
1. A large area of flat or hilly land covered with grasses is called a _____.
2. Decayed tree branches, roots, and leaves help make _____.
3. A _____ is an animal that hunts other animals for food.
4. A large area of land covered with trees is called a _____.

B. Write *true* or *false* for each sentence below. If a sentence is false, rewrite it to make it true.
1. All trees lose their leaves in the fall.
2. Prairies in the United States are mainly near the west coast.
3. Farm crops grow well in prairie soil.
4. There are more trees in forests now than there were many years ago.

Exploring Concepts

A. The chart below shows three animals that live in the forest or the prairie. Copy the chart on a piece of paper. Fill in the second column to show where each animal lives. Fill in the third column to show what each animal eats.

B. Write one or two sentences to tell why each sentence below is true.
1. Forest animals help trees and other plants.
2. Prairie animals escape from predators in different ways.

Animal	Where it lives	What it eats
Squirrel		
Prairie dog		
Coyote		

Reviewing Skills

1. Write three supporting details for this main idea: *Many animals find food on the prairie.*

2. The line graph shows the number of people who visited Grand Teton National Park in seven months. Which month had the fewest visitors? Which month had the most visitors?

3. Look again at the circle graph on page 39. How many kinds of forests are shown on the graph?

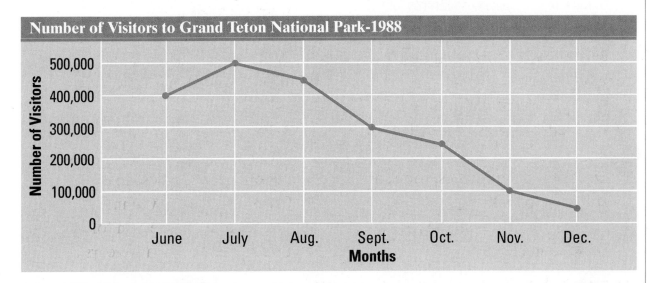

Number of Visitors to Grand Teton National Park-1988

Number of Visitors: 500,000 / 400,000 / 300,000 / 200,000 / 100,000 / 0

Months: June, July, Aug., Sept., Oct., Nov., Dec.

Using Critical Thinking

1. If much of the eastern forest had not been cut down many years ago, how would our country be different today?

2. What happens to forest animals when trees are cut down or burned?

Preparing for Citizenship

1. **ART ACTIVITY** Many grain crops, such as corn and wheat, are grown on the prairie. Find out what kinds of foods are made from wheat. Breakfast cereals and breads are two examples. Then cut out pictures from a magazine. Use your pictures to make a poster showing how wheat is used for foods.

2. **COLLABORATIVE LEARNING** Make a class book about what animals do in winter. Work in small groups. Each group should choose one kind of animal, such as birds, bears, deer, foxes, or rabbits. Make drawings and write a paragraph that tells what the animal does in winter. Put the work from all the groups into a class book.

Chapter 3

Majestic Peaks and Deserts

Much of the land in the western United States is made up of towering mountains or dry deserts. Mountaintops can be very cold, and deserts are often very hot. The animals and plants that live on these kinds of land must have special ways of staying alive.

Cactus plants have spines that protect them from animals that live in the desert. Without their spines, these plants would be eaten for the water inside.

This brightly colored lizard is a Gila *(HEE luh)* Monster. It is right at home in the blazing summer heat of an Arizona desert.

Bighorn sheep move easily over jagged rocks in high mountains.

This is one of the Sawtooth Mountains in Idaho. Few plants grow at the top of this high peak, but below you can see evergreen forests.

LESSON 1

Touching the Clouds

How do mountains affect the land around them?

Key Terms

- mountain
- physical feature
- temperature
- timberline

➤ *These are the beautiful Teton (TEE tahn) Mountains in northwestern Wyoming. Find the highest peak. It is called Grand Teton.*

Ann stood on the edge of a cliff and caught her breath. She had been mountain climbing for years, but this sport was new to her. She was almost ready to go. She thought about her teacher's directions.

One end of her rope was firmly attached to the mountain. Ann had hooked the rope to her body, and now she gripped it with both hands. She backed slowly over the edge of the cliff and pushed off into space!

Down, down, down she went. The wind whistled past her ears. Her hands fed out more and more rope. Her feet touched the cliff face again and again. Ann was rappelling *(ra PEHL ihng)* down a mountain for the first time, and she loved it!

44

Height Makes a Difference

Mountain climbing, like rappelling, has many exciting moments. Climbing to the peak of a mountain is also hard work. And it's no wonder. A **mountain** is a piece of land that is higher than a hill and stands much higher than the land around it. This **physical feature,** or natural part of the earth's surface, is easy to see. A mountain has steep sides and a pointed or rounded top.

Air is cooler in high places than it is in low places. At the top of tall mountains, the temperature is very cold. The **temperature** of air is how hot or cold it is.

What does this colder air mean to plant life on mountains? Few plants are able to grow in the highest parts of tall mountains. The plants that do live there must be strong, indeed. They must be able to grow in very cold air and wind.

Different kinds of plants grow well at different heights. Oak and aspen trees grow well on the lower parts of a mountain. Only the very toughest trees, such as bristlecone pines, can grow at higher levels. No trees are able to grow at the highest levels. The height where trees can no longer grow is called the **timberline.** A few small plants can live above the timberline. Columbines and moss campions are wildflowers that can grow in this bitter cold.

The chart below shows two kinds of small flowers and two kinds of large trees that can grow at different heights on a mountain. When a person is standing far from a mountain, the wildflowers are too small to be seen.

Plant Life on a Mountain

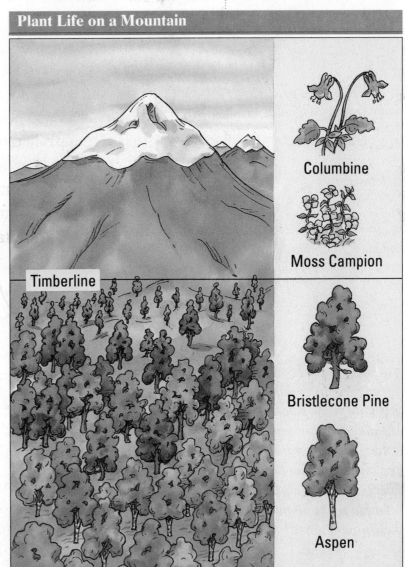

Columbine

Moss Campion

Timberline

Bristlecone Pine

Aspen

Because of the low temperatures, very few animals live above the timberline. Some animals, such as bighorn sheep, live there during late spring and summer. When fall comes, these wild sheep go down the mountain to avoid deep snow that will cover the grasses they feed on.

Bighorns have very little trouble traveling up and down the mountains. They are able to jump and climb quickly, even in very steep places. For this reason, bighorns can easily escape predators on rocky mountainsides. ■

➤ *"Bighorn" is a good name for these animals. Some bighorns have horns that are over four feet long.*

■ *How does height affect the plant and animal life on a mountain?*

Across Time & Space

Standing in the Rocky Mountains today, you'd never guess that this land was once under an ocean. Fossils of sea creatures are found in rocks all over these mountains.

46

A Powerful Force

Mountains affect more than just the plants and animals that live on them. Mountains are a powerful force that can change the weather a long distance away.

In the United States, clouds usually move from west to east. They must rise to pass over mountains. Remember that air gets colder at higher levels. Cold air cannot hold as much water as warm air can. As clouds begin to rise, the damp air grows cooler, so the clouds cannot hold as much water. The water falls in the form of rain or snow.

How Mountains Affect the Weather

West

East

◀ *How do you think the different amounts of rainfall on the east and west sides of a mountain affect the plant life on each side?*

As the clouds drift over mountains, they may drop more water. By the time the clouds have moved farther east, most of their water is gone. This means more rain falls on land west of mountains and less rain falls on land east of them.

In the same way, mountains usually protect land to the east of them from high winds and snowstorms. These storms move from west to east, just as rain clouds do. The west sides of mountains get most of the storms, while the land east of the mountains is protected. ■

■ *How does a mountain affect the weather in the area around it?*

R E V I E W

1. **FOCUS** How do mountains affect the land around them?
2. **CONNECT** How does melting mountain snow affect some rivers?
3. **CRITICAL THINKING** How is plant and animal life on the highest parts of mountains different in the summer than it is in the winter?
4. **WRITING ACTIVITY** Decide whether you would rather live on the east side or the west side of a mountain. Write a paragraph telling why.

Reading a Physical Map

Here's Why   You know that mountains are one of the physical features of the earth's surface. Mountains and other physical features of an area can be shown on a physical map. There are many kinds of physical maps. One kind shows lowlands, highlands, and mountains. Lowlands are large areas of land that are at about the same level as the sea, or ocean. Highlands are high above sea level. Physical maps also show water features, such as oceans, lakes, and rivers.

Land Above Sea Level

Highlands

Lowlands

Sea Level

Here's How   Most physical maps use different colors to stand for different things. Blue usually stands for water. Green usually stands for lowlands. Every map has a map key that shows what the colors on the map stand for.

Look at the map key for the physical map on page 49. Notice the colors and what they stand for. What does orange stand for? What does brown stand for?

Now look at the map itself. Find Lake Ontario. How does the map show that Lake Ontario is a body of water? Two rivers are also shown on the map. Trace the route of the Mississippi River with your finger. It begins in a northern state and ends at the Gulf of Mexico.

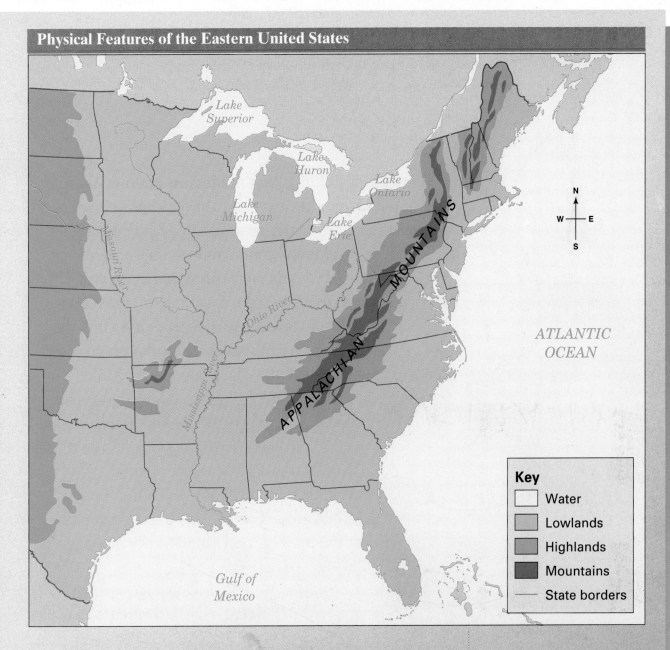

The map shows a long range of mountains through the eastern states of our country. Can you name any of these mountain states?

Try It Work with a partner. Ask each other questions about the physical map on this page. For example, what is the largest lake shown on the map?

Apply It Look at the physical map of the United States in the Atlas on pages 270–271. How are mountains shown on the map? Name two rivers that flow into the Mississippi River. What physical features are in or near the state of Alaska?

Physical Features and People

You have learned that physical features are the natural parts of the surface of the earth. A physical feature may be part of the earth's land or water. For example, a mountain is a land feature and an ocean is a water feature. A town is not a physical feature because it is not a natural part of the earth. A town is made by people. A drawing of many physical features is shown on pages 276–277 of the Time/Space Databank.

The earth's physical features have a lot to do with where people live and how people live. Many cities, for example, grew next to a river. Rivers have always provided transportation for people and the things people grow or make. Find some river cities on the map of the United States on pages 268–269 of the Atlas.

St. Louis, Missouri

Cities have also grown on ocean coasts. These cities often started near a harbor, which is an area of the ocean that is partly surrounded by land. The harbor provides a safe place for ships. Find some ocean cities on the map of the United States on pages 268–269.

There are many ways that physical features affect our lives. We do different things on a mountain than we do in a lowland. We may even eat different foods. As you study about our country, you will learn more about the effects of physical features on the lives of people.

Boston, Massachusetts

A Dry Place

Katie pressed her nose against the glass. Inside the clear case, the creature stared back. Its body was covered with tiny scales and it had a long, thin tail.

"Wow!" said Katie. "Look at that funny-looking animal. Maybe it's from another planet."

"Now, Katie," Mrs. King said, smiling. "That's not from another planet. It's an animal called an iguana (*ih GWAH nuh*)."

"Why are its toes so long?" Tony wanted to know.

"To help it walk," Mrs. King said. "It comes from a very dry and sandy place. When an iguana walks, it spreads its long toes. Doing this helps it stay on top of the sand instead of sinking into it."

"Are you sure it's an iguana?" Katie asked. "It sure looks like something from another planet to me!"

THINKING FOCUS

How do plants and animals adjust to living in the desert?

Key Terms

- desert
- climate

The Desert Land

A **desert** is an area where little rain falls and few kinds of plants grow. Katie's iguana, like the one shown here, can be found in the deserts of the southwestern United States. This area includes the states of Arizona, Texas, New Mexico, California, Nevada, Utah, and Colorado. Look for this area on the map on page 52.

N
W ← → E
S

CANADA

UNITED STATES

Oregon
Idaho
Wyoming
Nevada
Utah
Colorado
California
Arizona
New Mexico
Texas

PACIFIC OCEAN

ATLANTIC OCEAN

MEXICO

Key
Desert

Most deserts are very hot, but not all deserts are the same. Some deserts are hot during the day but cool at night. Many deserts are hot in summer and cold in winter. Hot temperatures and changes from very hot to very cold make it hard for plants to live in deserts.

Temperatures are not the only problem for desert plant life. Little rain falls in deserts, so the soil is very dry. Desert soil is also rocky or sandy. Many plants do not grow well in such soil. Because there are not many plants in the desert, there are few decaying plants to form humus. Humus helps soil hold water. The sandy desert soil dries out quickly even after a hard rain.

Even though a desert is hot and dry and the soil is poor, some plants grow well there. You will see on the next page that the saguaro (*suh GWAHR oh*) cactus has special ways to live in the desert. ■

▲ *How does this desert look different from prairies?*

■ *Why don't many plants grow well in the desert?*

The Saguaro Cactus

10:32 A.M. May 5, 1991
After a spring rain in the
Sonoran Desert in Arizona

Flowers

Raindrops sparkle
on these blossoms
that opened during
the cool night hours.
The flowers will close
again before the
afternoon heat
reaches 110° F.

Arm

Sharp thorns cover
the arms that show
that this cactus is
very old. A saguaro
doesn't grow arms
until it's at least 75
years old. Some
saguaros live 250
years. They may
stand 50 feet tall
and have 50 arms.

Trunk

Swollen to twice its
normal size, the trunk is
filled with hundreds of
gallons of rain water. The
saguaro's roots quickly
soaked up the water from
the desert sands.

Elf Owl

The unusual sound of
falling rain woke this
tiny owl from its daytime
sleep. During the day,
the owl hides in this
hole made by a
woodpecker months
ago. At night, it leaves
the nest to hunt

Woodpecker

A loud tap, tap, tap
fills the desert air as
this bird pecks a hole
in the trunk of the
cactus. Today, it will
find plenty of water
inside. Later, another
bird will build a nest in
this hole.

Jack Rabbit

After nibbling tender
young cactus sprouts in
the early morning, this
rabbit has hopped into
the cool shade of the
saguaro. There it can
avoid the scorching sun
until late afternoon.

▲ The desert above is full of different kinds of cactus. Can you find the saguaros?

▼ Sagebrush covers the desert below. Like a cactus, sagebrush grows well in very dry soil.

Life in the Desert

The dry desert climate presents problems for living things. **Climate** is the usual weather of an area over a long time. How do plants and animals live in such a dry climate?

The cactus has a special way of staying alive in the desert. Its long roots spread out around it and are not very deep in the soil. When rain comes, a cactus uses these roots to draw water up into its trunk. The cactus saves the water for use during dry weather.

Animals have their own ways of staying alive in the desert. Many desert animals get much of their water from their food. The little kangaroo rat, for example, gets most of its water from the seeds it eats. Meat also contains water, so predators get water from the animals they eat.

Animals must also find a way to deal with hot desert temperatures. Kangaroo rats dig burrows. The earth is cooler under the desert soil. These animals nest in their burrows during the day. At night when it is cooler, they search for food.

Other animals have different ways of staying comfortable. An iguana crawls into the shade of a rock

when it gets hot. When the iguana becomes cool, it covers its body with sand. The iguana leaves only its head showing. Snakes stay in underground holes or in the shade of rocks and bushes during hot daylight hours. They come out to hunt for food at night.

Desert life is not easy for plants or animals. However, with their special ways of staying alive, the desert is full of life. ■

▲ *This kangaroo rat never needs to drink water. It gets most of its water from seeds like the ones above.*

◄ *A rattlesnake gets its name from the rattle at the end of its tail. Poison shoots out of the snake's two long fangs when it bites.*

■ *Why is life in the desert hard?*

R E V I E W

1. **FOCUS** How do plants and animals adjust to living in the desert?
2. **CONNECT** How is desert soil different from forest and prairie soil?
3. **CRITICAL THINKING** How is desert life during the day different from desert life during the night?

4. **WRITING ACTIVITY** Pretend you have a friend who thinks that nothing grows in deserts. Write a paragraph that explains why the desert is full of life.

The Land Around You

What is the land like where you live? Are there rivers or lakes nearby? Is the land flat or is it hilly? Rivers, lakes, oceans, mountains, and hills are all physical features. You can explore the area where you live to find out more about its physical features.

Get Ready Begin by looking at the land near where you live. Then look at the land near your school and other places you visit close to home. Start a notebook of the physical features you see around you. Write about what you see. Draw pictures of the land you explore. You can also learn more about the land where you live by looking at maps and photographs.

Find Out Make a map of your area to show how the land looks. Use the notes and drawings in your notebook for help. You may also use photographs and maps from books and newspapers for help.

I see a river and a hill.

Move Ahead The map you made is on a flat piece of paper. All the physical features you drew on the map are flat. To show more exactly how the land looks, you can make a model from your map. Build your model with materials that you have at home or in your classroom. Clay and small rocks can be hills or mountains. Aluminum foil or plastic wrap can be rivers or lakes. Can you think of other materials to use?

Explore Some More Share your model with your classmates and other students in your school. Set up a display in your classroom. Label the models and show the maps you drew. Be ready to answer questions about your model and about the land in your area.

Chapter Review

Reviewing Key Terms

climate (p. 54)   physical feature (p. 45)
desert (p. 51)   temperature (p. 45)
mountain (p. 45)   timberline (p. 45)

A. Write the key term for each meaning.
1. how hot or cold something is
2. the place on a mountain above which trees do not grow
3. the usual weather of an area
4. a land feature that has steep sides and a peak
5. a natural part of the earth's surface
6. an area that gets very little rain

B. Write a complete sentence to answer each question.
1. How are bighorn sheep able to live so well on mountains?
2. What are some of the physical features of the area where you live?
3. What kind of plants grow above the timberline?
4. What is the climate where you live?

Exploring Concepts

A. The chart to the right lists one plant and three animals that live in the desert. Copy the chart and fill in the second column. Your chart will show what the plant and the animals do to stay alive in the desert.

B. Write your answer to each question in one or two sentences.
1. How do high mountains affect the land east of them?
2. Why doesn't desert soil hold rain water well?

Plant or Animal	How it lives in the desert
Cactus	
Kangaroo rat	
Iguana	
Elf owl	

Reviewing Skills

1. Copy the map of Wyoming shown below. Add the mountains, lakes, and rivers. Then make a physical features key for your map. Use the map on pages 270–271 for help.

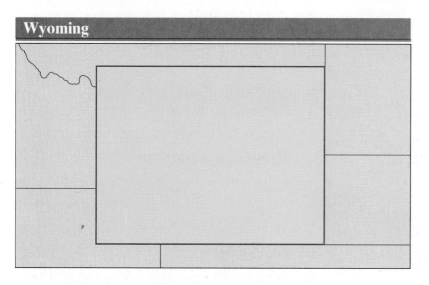

Wyoming

2. Locate your state on the map on pages 270–271. List the physical features that are in your state.

3. Look at the map on pages 268–269. Choose a state. Write three clues that will help a classmate guess the name of the state you choose. Include a cardinal or intermediate direction in each clue. For example, "To get to this state, you must travel northeast from Texas." Take turns trying to name each other's state.

Using Critical Thinking

1. Air conditioning keeps people cool in hot weather. If there were no electricity, how could you stay comfortable in a very hot climate?

2. High mountains are cold and deserts are hot, but in some ways they are alike. Make a list of the ways they are alike.

3. Would you rather live on a mountain top or in a desert? Why?

Preparing for Citizenship

1. **WRITING ACTIVITY** Pretend you and a partner climbed a high mountain. Tape record your reports about what you took with you and what you saw above the timberline.

2. **COLLABORATIVE LEARNING** Prepare a class bulletin board on desert animals. Work in groups and find books about life in the desert. Some group members can draw pictures of desert animals, such as the desert tortoise and the roadrunner. Some group members can write a sentence or two about each animal. Add your pictures and sentences to the bulletin board.

Unit 2

The Land and the First Americans

The first Americans lived all across the land—by the sea, in the forests, on the prairies, and in the deserts. These Native Americans understood the land and lived from it. They chose their clothing, food, and homes from what nature offered them. Items used every day were not only made from natural materials, they were often colored with natural dyes and decorated with artwork that told stories about the land.

Navajo sand painting blanket of the Nightway Chant, 1880.
Werner Forman Archive/Private Collection, New York.

Chapter 4

By the Shining Sea

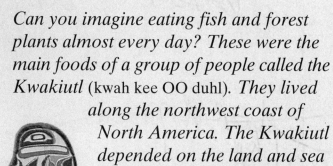

Can you imagine eating fish and forest plants almost every day? These were the main foods of a group of people called the Kwakiutl (kwah kee OO duhl). They lived along the northwest coast of North America. The Kwakiutl depended on the land and sea for all of their needs. In return, these people held celebrations and created beautiful artwork to honor nature.

Tall totem poles stood in front of many Kwakiutl homes, graves, and meeting places. The Kwakiutl carved wood from the forest into works of art.

This piece of clothing was worn as a skirt or a cape. It was made out of tree bark at least 100 years ago by Northwest Coast Indians.

The Kwakiutl made large wooden canoes for fishing and traveling. Sometimes they would dress in special costumes and masks to attend celebrations in nearby villages.

Kwakiutl masks showed the faces of creatures from ancient stories. Dancers sometimes acted out these stories during celebrations.

Between Sea and Forest

Key Terms

- salmon
- cedar
- long house

➤ *This picture of a woman wearing a cedar bark blanket was taken about 1914. Below is a wooden beater that women used to pound the bark before it could be woven into blankets or clothing.*

Kwiskwis is very excited! Today her mother will show her how women make clothes out of tree bark.

"Where do we start?" asks Kwiskwis excitedly.

"With a cedar *(SEE dur)* tree," her mother says.

Kwiskwis and her mother pull long strips of bark off the trees. Then they pull the softer inner bark from these strips. When they collect as much of the softer bark as they can carry, they return to their big wooden house.

"First we pound the bark with this beater until it is not so stiff," says Mother. "Next, we will separate the bark into thin strips. We will weave these strips together on this frame to make a new cape for your grandmother."

Kwiskwis smiles, knowing the gift will keep her grandmother warm and dry.

Sea of Plenty

If you could have visited a Kwakiutl village one hundred or more years ago, you might have seen a girl like Kwiskwis and her mother making clothes from tree bark. The Kwakiutl were one of many Indian groups that lived along the northwest coast of North America. These northwest coast groups lived on a strip of land that stretches from the southern tip of Alaska all the way to northern California. Look at the map. Notice that the Kwakiutl lived in what is now Canada.

Remember what you learned about oceans and forests in Chapters 1 and 2? The Kwakiutl lived in thick forests between the ocean and the high mountains.

Water Provides Food

Water played a large part in the way the Kwakiutl lived. The Pacific Ocean and nearby rivers provided plenty of fish to eat, such as trout, halibut, and **salmon** (*SA muhn*). The Kwakiutl also ate small seafood, such as clams, and large sea animals, such as seals. However, salmon was their favorite food.

The Kwakiutl believed that all things in nature lived in order to help each other. Each year the salmon left the ocean and swam upstream past Kwakiutl villages to lay their eggs. The Kwakiutl caught these fish every spring to feed the villagers.

The Kwakiutl wanted to be sure that the salmon would come back each year. When they ate salmon, they always saved the bones. Then they would return the bones to the

▼ This map's compass rose helps you know that the Pacific Ocean is west of Kwakiutl villages. For help in using a compass rose, see page G4 in the Map and Globe Handbook.

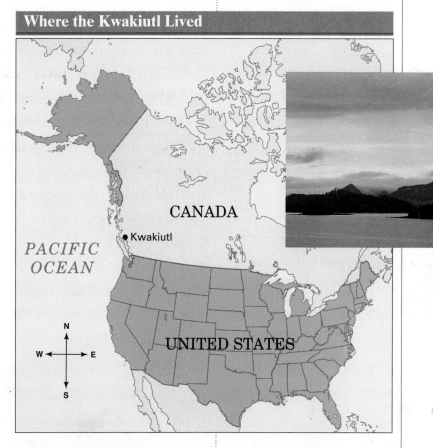

Where the Kwakiutl Lived

CANADA

PACIFIC OCEAN

• Kwakiutl

UNITED STATES

N
W ← → E
S

► The Kwakiutl made fish hooks from wood. First, they heated the wood with steam. Then they bent it to form a hook.

■ How did living near water affect Kwakiutl living?

▼ This wooden box is fitted together and tied with cedar bark rope. Boxes were used for seats and shelves. They were also used to hold food, water, and family treasures.

water where the fish had been caught. They were thankful for the fish that kept them from going hungry.

The Kwakiutl ate fish more than any other food, and they became very good at fishing. The Kwakiutl caught fish with hooks made of wood, bone, or horn. They also used spears and nets. The Kwakiutl caught more than they could eat, so they could dry the extra fish. This gave them food for the winter. ■

Forest Gifts

The forest also helped the Kwakiutl meet their needs. There they could find berries and animals to eat. Wood from the forest was also important to them. They lived in houses made of wood and traveled in wooden canoes. They used wood to make chests, dishes, toys, bows, arrows, and more.

Cedar was the type of wood used most often by the Kwakiutl. A **cedar** is a type of evergreen tree. The Kwakiutl used cedar's soft inner bark to make rope, mats, and clothing. Sometimes they would weave cedar bark and mountain goat wool together to make warm blankets.

The Kwakiutl were careful not to pull too much bark from a cedar tree. They knew that this could kill the

tree. The Kwakiutl believed that cedar trees, like the salmon, were there to help them. Sometimes they sang a song to the cedar, asking it to clothe and shelter them. Then they thanked the tree for giving them so much.

Cedar was the Kwakiutl's favorite wood for building houses. These houses were called **long houses.** They were up to 60 feet long. The Kwakiutl split logs into thin boards to make the walls and roof. Some roof boards could be moved to let out smoke from the cooking fires.

◄ *The artist has drawn this so you can see the inside of a long house. How many different ways do they use wood in this picture?*

Three or four related families usually shared a long house. Each family had its own space and cooking fire in one corner of the house. Kwakiutl long houses were all built close together in a row, facing the sea.

The Kwakiutl cared about what we call nature. They took only what they needed from the land and sea. They gave back what they could. ■

■ *How did forests help the Kwakiutl?*

REVIEW

1. **FOCUS** How did the Kwakiutl meet their basic need for food and shelter?
2. **CONNECT** From what you know about oceans and rivers, where did the Kwakiutl get their freshwater fish?
3. **CRITICAL THINKING** The Kwakiutl believed that all things in the world lived to help each other. How did this affect the way the Kwakiutl lived?
4. **ACTIVITY** Draw a picture that shows how the Kwakiutl used either the sea or the forest in their everyday lives.

Using Timelines

Here's Why It is not easy to keep track of all the events we read about. Timelines can help. A timeline shows events in the order in which they happened. Some timelines show events for a short period of time, such as a week. Many timelines, however, cover more than one year. Years are shown on those timelines. Suppose you wanted to show certain events in the life of a Kwakiutl boy named Weesa.

Here's How You read most timelines from left to right. Events that took place earlier in time are shown on the left side of the timeline. Events that happened later are shown on the right.

Events in Weesa's Life

January
Weesa was born

June
Sister was born

| 1700 | 1701 | 1702 | 1703 | 1704 |

April
Moved to a new village

Look at the left side of the timeline below. What happened to Weesa in the year 1700? Notice that dates are shown by years on the timeline. What happened to Weesa in the year 1701? How old was he then? How old was he when his sister was born?

Try It   You can learn many things about the Kwakiutl boy's life by looking at the timeline. In what year did Weesa help his father carve a mask? Was that before or after he went to the totem-pole raising? How old was Weesa when he helped his father carve a mask? What is the latest date that is shown on the timeline? What happened that year?

Apply It   Make a timeline of your life. Start on the left with the year you were born. Then write the year it is now at the right. Show five or six events on your timeline in the order in which they happened. Draw pictures of some of the events on your timeline.

September
Helped father
carve a mask

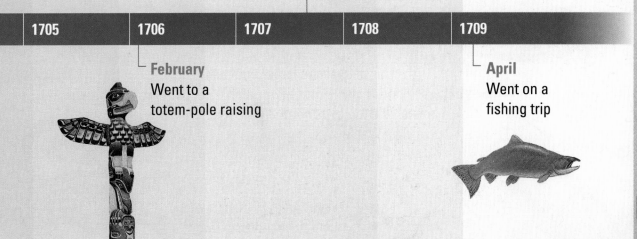

| 1705 | 1706 | 1707 | 1708 | 1709 |

February
Went to a
totem-pole raising

April
Went on a
fishing trip

Of Art and Wood

THINKING
FOCUS

How was wood important to the Kwakiutl?

Key Terms

- totem pole
- ceremony

The Indians of the northwest coast were some of the best woodworkers in North America. They carved animals on many of the things they made. An artist chose certain parts of an animal to carve.

The large front teeth and the wide, flat tail show that this is a beaver.

Big claws help to show that this is a bear.

This animal has large teeth and fins. It also blows air through a hole on the top of its head. It is a killer whale.

What parts of this drawing help to show it is a frog?

Totem Poles and Canoes

Animals like the ones on page 70 were carved into many wooden objects. Carving was an important part of Kwakiutl life.

Remember that Kwakiutl women were weavers. Kwakiutl men were woodcarvers. They taught their sons this skill. If a boy grew up to be a good carver, he became an important person in a Kwakiutl village.

Kwakiutl woodcarvers made beautiful totem poles. A **totem pole** is a wooden pole decorated with figures. Each figure stands for a character in the sacred tales of the Kwakiutl. The character might be an animal or a spirit. The totem explained sacred tales and the family's place in the world.

One of the biggest jobs for a woodcarver was making a canoe like the one shown below. First, he cut down a tall cedar tree and chopped it into the shape of a canoe. Then he used hot stones to burn out the inside of the log. He chipped away the burned parts to form the inside of the canoe.

Across Time & Space

The Kwakiutl still carve totem poles today. A Kwakiutl totem pole can be between 10 and 80 feet tall. In 1980, Kwakiutl carvers in Canada created a totem pole as tall as an eight-story building.

▼ *This colorful Kwakiutl totem pole stands in Canada today. Can you name any of the figures on it?*

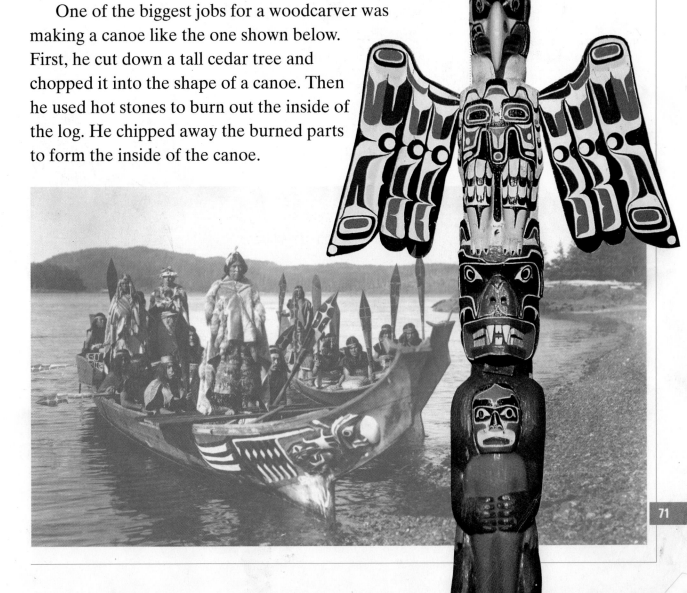

Next, the woodcarver put water into the canoe. He added very hot stones to make steam. The steam softened the wood. Once the sides were soft, they could be stretched. Bigger and bigger sticks were forced between the two sides until the opening was big enough to fit many people in the canoe. A finished canoe could be 50 feet long and hold 40 people.

Finally, like most Kwakiutl items, many canoes were carved and painted. Even Kwakiutl boats became works of art. ■

■ *How did the Kwakiutl use wood in everyday life?*

Special Ceremonies

The Kwakiutl celebrated important events such as weddings or births. There were special words, actions, and songs for each event. The way people act during such important events is called a **ceremony.** Kwakiutl ceremonies were full of dancing, storytelling, and feasting.

The Kwakiutl used finely carved masks, rattles, and puppets during ceremonies. These pieces of art showed animals of the land, water, and air. They were used to tell stories about family histories and sacred tales.

➤ *The Kwakiutl in this picture are wearing costumes that they wore during ceremonies. During these ceremonies, they might have used a rattle like the one pictured below.*

◄ *During Kwakiutl ceremonies, a chief would sit in a wooden seat like this one.*

One Kwakiutl ceremony was a totem-pole raising. A totem-pole raising was held on many special occasions, such as weddings and funerals. Sometimes a family raised a totem pole to call attention to something brave a family member had done.

Not all Kwakiutl families had totem poles. Totem poles showed a family's importance in the community. A family had to be important and rich enough to have one made.

A totem pole was usually set up in front of a house. During the totem-pole raising, a family would gather near the totem pole. In a loud voice, the head of the family would tell sacred tales or stories about his family's past.

The speechmaker used the figures on the totem pole to remind him of these stories. For example, the carving of a sea lion on the pole might remind him of an important event that happened long ago.

A totem-pole raising was an important event. The speechmaker, like the one on the next page, wore special clothes to tell the family's story. People outside of the family were allowed to hear the story, but only a family member was allowed to tell it.

How Do We Know?

Very old Kwakiutl stories tell us that totem poles were carved by Northwest Coast groups as long as 200 years ago. Also, scientists have dug up some old totems that can be seen in museums.

▲ *Even from far away, a Kwakiutl could tell who lived in this house. The totem pole is like a sign that tells which family lives there.*

A Kwakiutl Speechmaker

5:06 P.M., October 20, 1843
In front of a long house on
the northwest coast

Talking Stick
A whale's tail is carved into this stick. The day the speechmaker was born, his mother saw a whale's tail flashing in the sea. Now it is a sign of his family's strength.

Neck Ring
The speechmaker wears this colorful ring made from red cedar bark. He last wore it at his daughter's wedding.

Copper
His thoughts are far from a fight, but the speechmaker is proudly holding a shield called a copper. It is so valuable that he could trade it for 2,500 blankets.

Blanket
The blanket that drapes the speechmaker's shoulders is made from cedar bark and the hair of a mountain goat.

◄ This mask was worn during Kwakiutl ceremonies by a dancer who opened and closed the bird's mouth to make a loud snapping sound. The bird was an evil creature in Kwakiutl myths.

Totem-pole raisings were not the only Kwakiutl ceremonies. The winter days in Kwakiutl villages were filled with the sounds of singing, dancing, speeches, and feasting. Often performers wearing large wooden masks acted out stories of spirits in nature. The masks were carved and painted to look like these spirits. They added to the excitement of Kwakiutl winter ceremonies.

◄ This mask shows the face of a feared giant in Kwakiutl myths. It is made from wood and human hair. At one time it had thick eyebrows and a mustache and beard made from bear fur.

The Kwakiutl had more time for ceremonies in the winter because they didn't spend as much time gathering food. During the warmer days, they caught more fish than they could use. They dried some of these fish to eat during the winter. This gave the Kwakiutl time during the winter for their ceremonies. ■

■ How did the Kwakiutl use wood in their ceremonies?

R E V I E W

1. **FOCUS** How was wood important to the Kwakiutl?

2. **CONNECT** How would Kwakiutl life have been different if these people had lived in a desert?

3. **CRITICAL THINKING** How did the Kwakiutl's ideas about nature affect their art and ceremonies?

4. **WRITING ACTIVITY** Choose an animal from land, sea, or air. Make a drawing of it like the Kwakiutl figures on page 70. Write a short story that a speechmaker might tell about your animal.

Chapter Review

Reviewing Key Terms

cedar (p. 66)　　　salmon (p. 65)
ceremony (p. 72)　　totem pole (p. 71)
long house (p. 67)

A. Write the key term for each meaning.
1. a carved, wooden pole owned by a family
2. a kind of evergreen tree
3. a fish that lives in the Pacific Ocean and swims up rivers to lay eggs
4. a wooden house up to 60 feet long

B. Copy the story below. Change one word in each sentence to make the sentences correct.

Long ago, a Kwakiutl girl lived in a tent with her family. They ate hamburgers for dinner. Her father took her for rides in a boat made of bamboo. Her family had their own flagpole. They celebrated important events with a game.

Exploring Concepts

A. The chart below shows where the Kwakiutl found many useful things. Copy the chart. Fill in the last two columns to show what was used and how it was used.

B. Write two details to support each of the following main ideas.
1. The Kwakiutl took only what they needed from nature.
2. The Kwakiutl made beautiful things.

Where	What was used	How it was used
Forest		
River or ocean		

Reviewing Skills

1. Copy the timeline of a week below. On your timeline, mark the days you go to school, the days you stay home, and the days you have something special planned.

2. Look at the map on page 65 again. What body of water lies west of where the Kwakiutl lived? What state lies north of where the Kwakiutl lived?

Timeline for a Week

School

Monday	Tuesday	Wednesday	Thursday	Friday	Saturday	Sunday

Using Critical Thinking

1. The Kwakiutl used wood from the forest in many ways. How would a forest fire have changed their lives?

2. The Kwakiutl were fine artists and spent long hours making beautiful things. Name some types of art that people today spend a long time making.

3. Compare a Kwakiutl family's totem pole to a family's photo album today. How are they alike?

Preparing for Citizenship

1. **ART ACTIVITY** Work with a partner. Write a story about a Kwakiutl family. Tell something they did or something that happened to them. Then, make a totem pole by rolling and pasting cardboard or heavy paper into a long tube. Decorate your totem pole to match your story.

2. **COLLABORATIVE LEARNING** With your class, have a totem-pole raising. Choose speechmakers to tell the family stories shown on the totem poles you made. Others in the class can make paper neck rings and talking sticks. Gather together to listen to the stories.

Chapter 5

Over Waves of Grass

Finding food was not an easy task for the Cheyenne (shy AN) people. Unlike the Kwakiutl, who had plenty of fish nearby, the Cheyenne had to work hard for their food. Hundreds of years ago, they spent most of their time farming to grow food. Later they had horses and hunted buffalo for meat.

The buffalo lived on the plains in huge herds. The Cheyenne depended on this great beast for food, clothing, and even shelter.

Buffalo hides had many uses. Sometimes the Cheyenne would decorate hides with drawings that told stories of important events, such as hunts or celebrations.

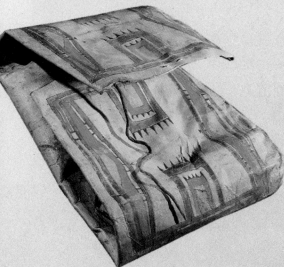

This Cheyenne woman follows the ways of her ancestors.

The Cheyenne used buffalo leather bags to hold many things. This bag is about 200 years old.

Following the Buffalo

THINKING
FOCUS

How did the Cheyenne depend on the buffalo?

Key Terms

- tipi
- natural resource

➤ *This is part of a painting called* Tall Tales on a Full Stomach. *It was painted in 1985 by Paladine Roye, a Native American artist.*

Black Kettle licked buffalo grease from his lips and sighed happily. He looked at the other Cheyenne sitting around the campfire and knew they felt the same way. Their stomachs had not been full for a long time.

Black Kettle knew how it felt to be hungry. The crops had failed to grow this summer. At night, he dreamed about food. Often, he listened to his uncles tell stories about hunger. He wondered how long it would be before they would have another buffalo feast. Hunting buffalo on foot was hard work. His people had followed one herd for almost a week before they got close enough to shoot this buffalo. Even then, the men had been almost too weak from hunger to lift their bows for the kill.

Buffalo Herds in 1600

Key
Buffalo herds, 1600

ATLANTIC OCEAN

N W E S

▲ *The Plains Indians used arrowpoints like these to hunt buffalo as long as two thousand years ago. They were chipped into points with bone or stone tools.*

The Great Provider

If you were a Cheyenne living about 400 years ago, you might have eaten a feast like the one Black Kettle ate. Your family would have farmed and often hunted buffalo in the vast area shown on the map above. The Cheyenne were one of many groups of Plains Indians.

Growing beans, corn, and squash on the plains was difficult. The earth was tough to dig into for planting, and was often dry. If it rained enough, and the Cheyenne had a good harvest, they would eat well. If harvests were small, the Cheyenne hunted whatever animals they could find, such as deer and rabbits. Even so, there often wasn't enough to eat.

Several times during the year, the Cheyenne would leave their homes to hunt buffalo. They camped along the way in tipis *(TEE peez)*. **Tipis** are cone-shaped tents that can be put up and taken down quickly.

To the Cheyenne, the buffalo was a great provider, an important **natural resource**. A natural resource is anything found in nature that helps people live. ■

Across Time & Space

The Cheyenne moved about for a long time. Today, the Cheyenne people are divided into two groups and no longer move. The Northern Cheyenne live in Montana. The Southern Cheyenne live in Oklahoma. Find these states on the United States map on pages 266–267 in the Atlas.

■ *Why was farming on the plains so difficult for the Cheyenne?*

81

The Great Provider

The buffalo was an important source of food for the Cheyenne. A single buffalo could provide enough meat to feed a hundred people. Everything was used. Nothing was wasted. Today we use softened cowhide to make things we use every day, just as the Cheyenne used buffalo hide.

Tipi walls were hides sewn together with a buffalo-bone needle, and thread that was also made from part of the buffalo. The hides were stretched over wooden poles.

Rib bones were tied together with buffalo-hide string to make sleds for moving camp in the snow, or for some winter fun!

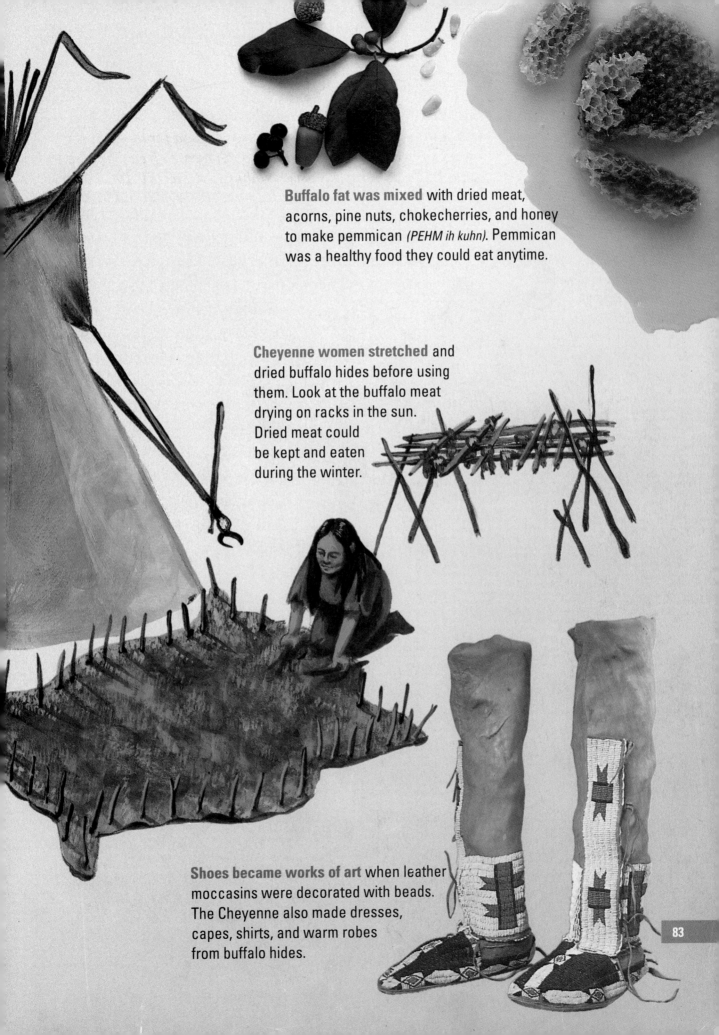

Buffalo fat was mixed with dried meat, acorns, pine nuts, chokecherries, and honey to make pemmican *(PEHM ih kuhn)*. Pemmican was a healthy food they could eat anytime.

Cheyenne women stretched and dried buffalo hides before using them. Look at the buffalo meat drying on racks in the sun. Dried meat could be kept and eaten during the winter.

Shoes became works of art when leather moccasins were decorated with beads. The Cheyenne also made dresses, capes, shirts, and warm robes from buffalo hides.

Help from the Horse

Picture loading all your belongings onto your back! That's what the Cheyenne did when they hunted buffalo. Everyone went on the hunt—grandparents, parents, and children. Women carried the babies and heavy loads. Men carried bows and arrows, in case an animal might run by. Families tied their bundles onto poles pulled by dogs.

Using dogs to travel wasn't easy. They chased rabbits, got into fights, even took naps! Traveling was so slow the Cheyenne moved only five or six miles a day. It was hard to chase buffalo at that speed!

Then the life of the Cheyenne became easier. About 250 years ago, they got horses from their Spanish and Indian neighbors to the south. As the Cheyenne learned to raise their own horses, they became skillful riders. Now hunters could keep up with the herds. Also, horses could pull heavier loads and travel faster than dogs.

Thanks to the horse, the Cheyenne stopped farming. They moved about freely, setting up new camps along the way as they followed the buffalo all year long. The Cheyenne were rarely hungry again. ■

▼ *Cheyenne men pose with their horses that brought them, their tipis, and their families to a summer celebration on the plains.*

■ *Find details to support this statement: The horse made life easier for the Cheyenne.*

R E V I E W

1. **FOCUS** How did the Cheyenne depend on the buffalo?

2. **CONNECT** Remember what you learned about prairies. Do you think the Cheyenne had trouble finding wooden poles to put up the tipi? Why?

3. **CRITICAL THINKING** If you had to move around all the time to search for food, do you think you would keep a lot of things? Why?

4. **ACTIVITY** Imagine that you are a Cheyenne. Tear a piece of brown craft paper so that it looks like a buffalo hide. Draw an important scene from your life.

We Use Natural Resources

The Cheyenne used the buffalo to provide food, clothing, and shelter. The buffalo were a natural resource. A natural resource is anything found in nature that people can use.

Trees, soil, and water were also natural resources for the Cheyenne. The poles that dogs dragged behind them and that held up Cheyenne tipis came from trees. The Cheyenne raised crops in the soil and drank water from streams.

Today, we use many of the same natural resources. We use trees to make everything from houses to paper to clothing. We also use the soil to grow food. We drink water that comes from rivers, lakes, and underground wells.

Natural resources are also found inside the earth. Things like oil, coal, rocks, and metals are natural resources. Today, we use oil to make gasoline for cars. We burn coal in factories, and we use rocks to make cement sidewalks. We build many things, such as cars, with metals. These resources are as important to us as the buffalo were to the Cheyenne.

The Medicine Dance

THINKING
FOCUS

Why was the Medicine Dance important to the Cheyenne?

Key Terms

- myth
- symbol

► *This Indian drum shows the Thunderbird. Many groups of Plains Indians believed that the Thunderbird controlled wind, rain, and snow.*

*L*ong ago, no rain had fallen on the land for many days. Grass died and animals starved. There was nothing to eat.

One day, a Cheyenne man and woman set out on a journey. They traveled for many days until they came to a tree-covered mountain. They pushed aside a rock that hid a cave. Inside, they saw an amazing room! Above and around them were wooden poles covered with buffalo robes. In the center stood a tree trunk with a nest of the magical Thunderbird at its top.

Then they heard the deep voice of the spirit Roaring Thunder. Roaring Thunder told the man and woman how to perform a dance. The dance would bring life back to the grasses of the earth and would bring herds of buffalo back to the people.

Cheyenne myth, retold

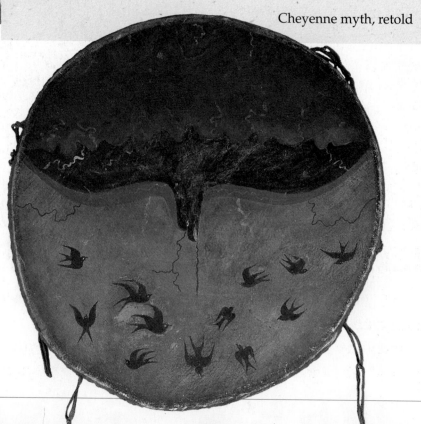

The Cycle of Nature

This myth tells how the Cheyenne ceremony called the Medicine Dance began. A **myth** is a story that explains something about the world. This myth is the Cheyenne's way of explaining changes that repeat over and over. We call this repeating pattern the cycle of life.

To understand this cycle, think about a tree. In the spring, green leaves sprout. The tree grows all summer. In the fall, its leaves turn colors and fall off. During the winter, the tree looks almost dead. When spring comes, new buds appear. Then the cycle begins again.

The Cheyenne saw this cycle all around them. Each year the prairie grass grew and died, the buffalo came and went. The Cheyenne believed there were great powers in the world. They thought of these powers as medicine that could help people. The Cheyenne held a Medicine Dance to get help from these powers.

▼ *Scientists think that Indians from the plains may have held Medicine Dances on this circle called a medicine wheel. It is in Medicine Mountain, Wyoming.*

All the Cheyenne people would arrange their tipis in a huge circle for the eight-day ceremony. A Cheyenne couple took the part of the man and woman in the myth on page 86. The man was a medicine man. The Cheyenne believed that a medicine man could talk with the powers of the natural world, such as Roaring Thunder.

The Cheyenne saw everything around them as part of the cycle of life. All living things begin, grow, and die, but new ones take their place. When the Cheyenne celebrated the Medicine Dance, they were trying to make sure that the cycle of life would continue. They believed that acting out this myth would help bring new life to the grasses, and would bring herds of buffalo back to the people. ■

■ *Why was the cycle of nature important to the Cheyenne?*

➤ *These Cheyenne are ready for a Medicine Dance.*

➤ *This leather rattle was used during Medicine Dance ceremonies. It may have been used by the Cheyenne to make a sound like running buffalo.*

The Medicine Dance Tent

During the Medicine Dance celebration, the Cheyenne made a tent that looked like the mountain room in the myth. In it, they put up a tree like the tree in that room. The tree was the most important symbol in the Medicine Dance. A **symbol** is something that stands for something else. The tree was a symbol of the way life changes and begins again.

The Cheyenne would pick out a special cottonwood tree. Before cutting it down, the chief gave a speech, saying that the tree was a symbol of the cycle of life.

After the Cheyenne cut down the tree and removed its branches, they decorated the top of it with branches and leaves. Women placed bits of brightly colored cloth on the branches. The tree then looked like the nest of the mighty Thunderbird. The nest reminded the Cheyenne of Roaring Thunder because they believed that this spirit flew through the sky in the shape of the Thunderbird.

Next, the Cheyenne put up the decorated tree in the middle of a round tent they had built. The tent was made of a circle of poles tied together. Buffalo robes covered the sides and part of the roof. Standing out from the top of the finished tent was the tree with its nest.

Finally, the dancing began. For the last two days of the ceremony, the Cheyenne would feast and dance around the pole. They celebrated the cycle of life. ■

■ *How did the Cheyenne use symbols in their celebration of the Medicine Dance?*

Building a Medicine Dance Tent

Step One: Poles are put into a circle with an opening facing east.

Step Two: Leaves, branches, and bits of cloth are attached to a tree trunk. This center pole is raised.

Step Three: Buffalo robes are attached to the sides and part of the roof. Now the dance begins.

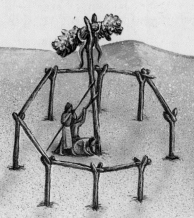

R E V I E W

1. **FOCUS** Why was the Medicine Dance important to the Cheyenne?
2. **CONNECT** How are Cheyenne ideas about the cycle of life like those of the Kwakiutl?
3. **CRITICAL THINKING** Use an acorn to describe the cycle of life.

4. **ACTIVITY** Create your own tree from a cardboard tube. Decorate it and add paper branches and leaves to make a Thunderbird nest. Add bits of colored paper to decorate its branches.

The First American People

Try to imagine what your neighborhood was like a long, long time ago. There were no large houses, or wide streets, or busy highways. There were hundreds of different groups of Indian people who first lived in North America. These groups had different names and their own ways of living. Some of them lived where you live today.

Get Ready In a few places, Native Americans still live where they always did. In other places, you can see what's left of Indian homes. In most places, though, little is left to tell about these early people. How can you learn about the Indians who lived in your area?

Find Out Begin by looking at books and maps to find the names of the Indians who lived in

▲ *Cliff Palace in Mesa Verde National Park, Colorado.*

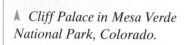

➤ *Wichita Indian lodges made of grass, branches, and earth.*

your area. Then read about how they lived, what they ate, what clothes they wore, and what their homes looked like. Write what you learn in a notebook.

Move Ahead Talk to a Native American living near you. Find out about the history and customs of his or her people. Or read a book about the Native Americans in your area.

Explore Some More Set up a history and geography center about the Indians who lived in your area. Make a map of places in your area that have names from these people. Draw a picture or make a model of their homes. Make something they used, like a basket or a mask. Invite other students in your school to visit your history and geography center.

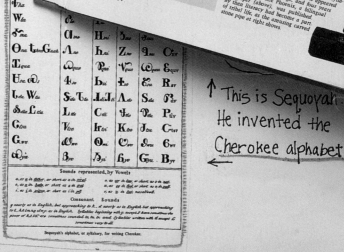

The Cherokee lived near us in Georgia

↑ This is Sequoyah. He invented the Cherokee alphabet

These are masks. They are used in a special dance to help make sick people feel better. This → one is like a buffalo head.

The name Cherokee means "real people."

Chapter Review

Reviewing Key Terms

myth (p. 87) symbol (p. 88)
natural resource (p. 81) tipi (p. 81)

A. Write the key term that best completes each sentence.
1. Something found in nature that people can use is a _____.
2. A _____ is a cone-shaped tent.
3. Something that stands for something else is a _____.
4. A _____ is a story that explains something in nature.

B. Write *true* or *false* for each sentence below. If a sentence is false, rewrite it to make it true.
1. Myths were important in the life of the Cheyenne.
2. To the Cheyenne, a tree was a symbol of the way life changes.
3. Tipis can be put up and taken down quickly.
4. All natural resources are found above ground.

Exploring Concepts

A. The buffalo was very important to the Cheyenne. It supplied food and was used to make clothing and homes. Copy the cluster diagram below. Fill in the empty spaces. Your diagram will show how the Cheyenne used the buffalo.

B. Write a sentence or two to answer the questions below.
1. Why did the Cheyenne hold the Medicine Dances?
2. How did horses change the lives of the Cheyenne?

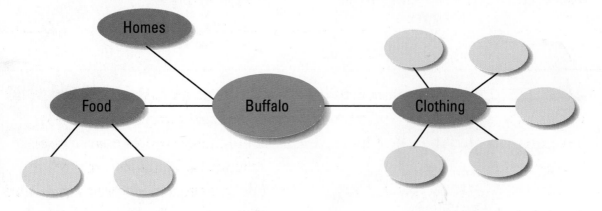

Reviewing Skills

1. The line graph at the right shows how much water was used in a town during a six-month period. In which of the six months was the most water used? In which month was the least used? How many thousand gallons of water were used in July?

2. Look at the map on page 81. Then look at the map on pages 270–271. What physical features are part of the land where the Cheyenne hunted buffalo?

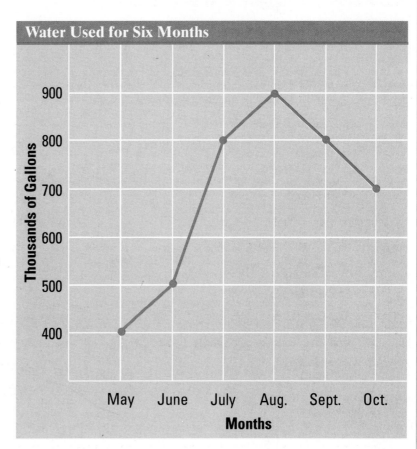

Water Used for Six Months

Thousands of Gallons

900
800
700
600
500
400

May   June   July   Aug.   Sept.   Oct.

Months

Using Critical Thinking

1. When the Cheyenne moved from place to place, they tied their belongings to poles which were pulled by dogs or horses. How do we move our belongings from place to place today?

2. The Cheyenne were not able to grow as many crops as they needed. How might they have improved their farming?

Preparing for Citizenship

1. **ART ACTIVITY** Draw and color pictures to show the cycle of life. You should have one picture for each of the four seasons.

2. **COLLABORATIVE LEARNING** As a class project, make a model of the Cheyenne gathering for a Medicine Dance ceremony. Your model should have tipis in a large circle around the Medicine Dance tent. Use straws, clay, colored paper, and other materials you can find.

Chapter 6

In Red Rock Country

The southwestern deserts do not have oceans alive with fish, or prairies covered with thundering herds of buffalo. The deserts are hot, dry lands where it is difficult to find the resources needed to live. The Navajo (NAV uh hoh) *people, however, discovered many ways to find the food, clothing, and shelter they needed from their red rock country.*

The mud that covers the outside of Navajo homes has always helped protect the people from winter cold and summer heat.

Through sand paintings, the Navajo told stories about the world. The beautiful colors of this painting were made from crushed rock and dried plants.

The Navajo still raise sheep for their wool today.

This painting, called *Navajo Weavers*, shows how women have woven wool rugs and blankets for hundreds of years.

You have read how the desert can be a harsh place to live. How do the people who live there feel about it? Read this excerpt from a book-length poem to find out who calls the desert theirs.

LITERATURE

THE DESERT IS THEIRS

Written by Byrd Baylor

Illustrated by Peter Parnall

This is no place
for anyone
who wants
soft hills
and meadows
and everything
green
green
green . . .

This is for hawks
that like only
the loneliest canyons
and lizards
that run
in the hottest sand
and
coyotes
that choose
the rockiest trails.

It's for them.

And for
birds
that nest
in cactus
and sing out over
a thousand thorns
because
they're where
they want to be.

It's for them.

And for
hard skinny plants
that do without water
for months
at a time.

And it's for
strong brown Desert People
who call the earth
their mother.

They *have* to see
mountains
and *have* to see
deserts
every day . . .
or they don't feel right.

They wouldn't leave
even for rivers
or flowers
or bending grass.
They'd miss
the sand too much.
They'd miss
the sun.

So
it's for them.

Talk to Papago Indians.
They're
Desert People.

They know
desert secrets
that no one else
knows.

Ask
how they live
in a place
so harsh and dry.

They'll say
they *like*
the land they live on
so they treat it well—
the way you'd treat
an old friend.
They sing it songs.
They never hurt it.

And the land knows.

A Desert Homeland

THINKING
FOCUS

How did the Navajo use the natural resources of the land?

Key Terms

- hogan
- livestock
- adaptation

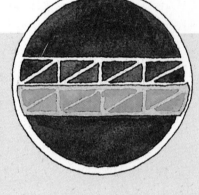

I see the Earth.
I am looking at Her and smile
Because She makes me happy.
The Earth, looking back at me
is smiling too.
May I walk happily
And lightly
on Her.

Ancient Navajo prayer

This prayer is one of many Navajo prayers about the earth. The Navajo called the earth Changing Woman. Changing Woman was one of the most important spirits in Navajo myths. The Navajo believed that she took care of them in many ways.

► *This Navajo is riding through Valley of the Gods in Utah. This area is called red rock country because of the color of the earth.*

Living Close to the Earth

One of the ways the Navajo believed Changing Woman helped them was by giving them the first hogan. A **hogan** is a one-room house. Navajo have lived in hogans for hundreds of years. In Navajo myths, Changing Woman's hogan was made of shells and turquoise (*TUR kwoyz*), a blue-green stone. When the Navajo made hogans, they made them from mud and logs.

The Navajo lived in the deserts of the southwestern United States. Hogans were good houses for desert living. The mud walls and roofs kept hogans cool in summer and warm in winter. A hogan did not have windows, and the doorway faced east toward the rising sun.

One family lived in each hogan. Women sat on the north side of a hogan. Men sat on the south side. The west side, the side that faced the doorway, was saved for guests.

In the center of the hogan was a fire that was used for cooking. There was a hole in the roof above the fire to let out smoke. At night a family slept on sheepskins around the fire. ■

▼ *This Navajo family is standing in front of a hogan in Monument Valley, Utah.*

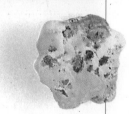

■ *How did hogans help the Navajo stay comfortable in the desert?*

Borrowing from Others

The Navajo had many myths to explain changes in their lives. For example, the Navajo believed that Changing Woman, the spirit who gave them hogans, also taught them how to grow corn. Actually, hundreds of years ago, the Navajo learned how to grow corn from another group of Indians. They probably also learned how to grow beans and squash from these people.

How did the Navajo raise corn and other crops in the dry deserts of the Southwest? They learned to farm near

Across Time & Space

The Navajo are known for their fine weaving. Early Navajo left a hole in each blanket they wove to thank Spider Woman for the gift of weaving. They quit making these holes when they began selling blankets to traders.

▼ *The Navajo still live in the Southwest today. They are the largest group of Native Americans.*

streams so that they would have water for their plants.

Corn became very important to the Navajo as their basic food, and they used it in some ceremonies.

The Gift of Weaving

The Navajo also believed that weaving was a gift from a spirit. Their myths say Spider Woman taught them to weave. She lived in a tall, thin rock called Spider Rock. This rock still stands in what is now Arizona.

The Pueblo people nearby had taught the Navajo to grow crops and also taught them to weave cotton. The Navajo quickly improved on this way of weaving. They discovered that wool was even better than cotton for weaving. Wool was stronger than cotton and easier to dye, or color.

The Navajo were well known for their beautiful weaving. They began making wool cloth by shearing, or shaving, the wool from the sheep they had raised. Then they spun this wool into yarn. They used natural resources of the earth, such as plants and berries, to dye the wool. Then they wove the wool on a wooden loom. Before long, they had a beautiful piece of cloth to make into clothing or blankets.

Raising Animals

Soon after the Navajo learned to weave, they learned how to raise livestock. Animals, such as sheep or horses, that are raised to be used or traded are called **livestock.** The

The Navajo Today

N
W ← → E
S

Utah

Colorado

Navajo

Rio Grande

Arizona

Oklahoma

New Mexico

Texas

MEXICO

Key
☐ Navajo land today

1. Raise sheep   **2.** Shear sheep   **3.** Spin wool into yarn

4. Dye yarn   **5.** Weave yarn on loom   **6.** Finished blanket

Navajo needed sheep so that they would have wool for weaving. They also raised goats and horses.

The way in which the Navajo learned to live in the desert is an example of adaptation. When people change the way they live to fit their surroundings, it is called **adaptation.** The Navajo used natural resources and ideas from others to live well in the desert. ■

■ *What skills did the Navajo learn from their neighbors?*

R E V I E W

1. **FOCUS** How did the Navajo use the natural resources of the land?

2. **CONNECT** How are Navajo hogans different from Kwakiutl long houses and Cheyenne tipis?

3. **CRITICAL THINKING** Why did the Navajo use the name Spider Woman for the spirit who taught them to weave?

4. **WRITING ACTIVITY** Pretend you are sitting inside a Navajo hogan. Write a description of the hogan. Describe its shape and where people are sitting. Draw a picture to go with your description.

We Adapt to Our Surroundings

At one time, the Navajo hunted animals for food. They made clothes from the skins of those animals. When they moved to the hot and dry desert, the Navajo could not find enough wild animals for food and clothing. They had to learn to raise their own animals. They learned how to weave animal hair to make clothing. They also learned how to grow crops, such as corn, beans, and squash. Changing the way we live to fit our surroundings, as the Navajo did, is called adaptation.

Adaptation still takes place today. For example, if you move from Florida to Alaska, you will have to change the way you dress. You will need warmer clothing in Alaska.

Adaptation also happens when people change their surroundings. For example, many people who live in hot climates keep cool by using air conditioning. Farmers in dry climates give their crops water to help them grow, as in the picture below of round corn fields in Kansas.

People often adapt to their surroundings. They change the way they live or they change the area around them.

Sand Painting

A pink sunrise colored the sky as we reached the hogan. My teacher, the medicine man, was quiet. He was thinking about the sick girl he had come to help. The girl's worried family and friends waited outside as we entered. Kneeling beside her, he closed his eyes. Then he began to sing the words of a ceremony used to treat her sickness. The words retold a myth of our people.

Years before, my teacher was a helper like me. He had learned the words from his teacher, a great medicine man who knew hundreds of **chants,** or prayers that are sung. I knew that, in a while, he would finish singing and make pictures of our world. Every chant and picture must be correct so that the girl would get well. I watched him and sighed. How would I ever learn all that I would need to know to become a medicine man myself someday?

Key Terms

* chant
* sand painting

◄ *Today, Navajo medicine men still make sand paintings. This medicine man takes a pinch of color from one of the bowls and sprinkles it in a design to make a beautiful religious work of art.*

Close to Nature

The medicine man's young helper that you just read about believes that the chants and sand paintings had been given to the Navajo by spirits. **Sand paintings** are religious works of art made with bits of crushed rock, plants, and other dry materials. The paintings tell stories about the world and Navajo spirits.

The Navajo believe that, long ago, the spirits told them to paint pictures on the ground with colors of the earth. The spirits warned the Navajo not to save the paintings because people might fight to get them. So the Navajo made sand paintings on the earth floors of their hogans and swept them up after 12 hours. In that time, the power of the painting would have helped those who needed it.

▼ *Here is a finished sand painting. It shows the four Wind People spirits. Each spirit rules the wind from one of the four directions of the earth. In one hand they hold clouds, in the other they hold a feather used to make the winds blow.*

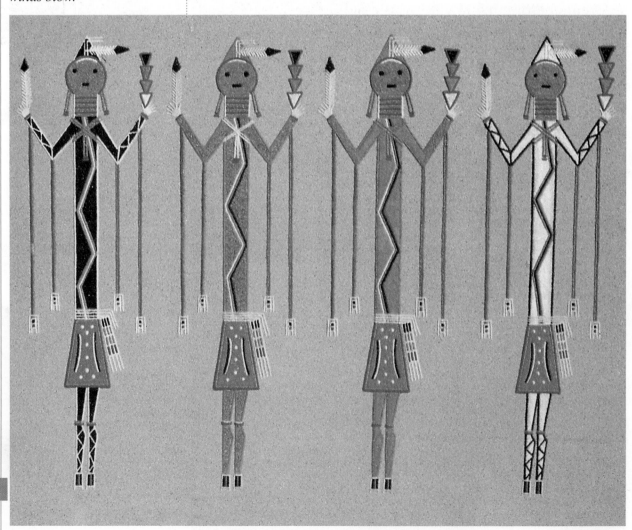

The Navajo first learned sand painting from other Indians who lived nearby. But in Navajo myths, the Wind People taught the Navajo how to make sand paintings. The Wind People are the spirits you just saw in the sand painting on page 104.

The Navajo believe that living happily with the land, the air, and all living things is the only way to stay healthy. If someone gets sick, they believe that using the art of the Wind People in ceremonies will make the person well.

A Navajo ceremony to help someone get well often includes many chants and several sand paintings. A medicine man sings the chants and creates the paintings. Each painting tells a story about the people and spirits found in Navajo myth. The Navajo believe that when a sick person sits inside the painting, its power will help that person get well. ■

◄ *Sand paintings show just about anything in the world of the Navajo. Here, for example, is an otter and a beaver from a sand painting.*

▲ *The Navajo used 500 different sand paintings. A medicine man had to remember each line, since pictures of the paintings were not kept in any book.*

■ *How did the Navajo use sand paintings?*

A Story to Tell

The Navajo have wondered how and why things in the natural world came to be. Why do big rocks exist? Where do mountains come from? What makes the wind blow and the rain fall? The Navajo tell myths to answer these questions.

In myths, things in nature often become spirits who explain why things happen. For example, real rainbows in the sky become the Rainbow People in stories and paintings. Let's look at a sand painting of the Rainbow People and the story it tells about the natural world.

Reading a Sand Painting

This Rainbow People sand painting tells part of a Navajo myth that explains that water is a source of life. The circle in the center of the sand painting is a symbol for the source of all water on earth.

Look at the colors! The Navajo use white to show east, black for north, blue for south, and yellow for west. These colors come from crushed rocks and plants.

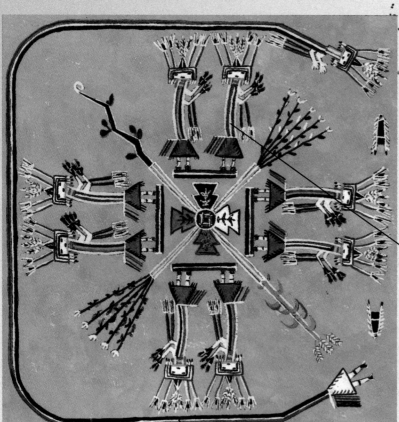

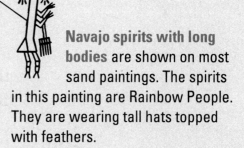

Navajo spirits with long bodies are shown on most sand paintings. The spirits in this painting are Rainbow People. They are wearing tall hats topped with feathers.

To protect the painting's power, another rainbow spirit wraps her extra-long body around three sides of the sand painting. Most sand paintings have protection bands like this.

Why do you think the Navajo tell myths about the Rainbow People? Suppose you lived in a hot, dry desert. What would your most important resource be? If you said "water," you would be right. That's why you would always be happy to see a rainbow. It is a sign that rain has come.

Rainbow People are often used to protect three sides of sand paintings. That is because the Navajo feel safe when they see a rainbow. It is a sign that life-giving rain has brought water to their crops.

Look at the Rainbow People sand painting on page 106. You can see four plants watered by rain. Beans, squash, tobacco, and corn grow between the pairs of Rainbow People. In the center box of the sand painting are symbols for clouds, water, and sunshine. Water and sunshine bring life to the earth because they help plants grow. Water and sunshine also create real rainbows in the sky. That is how this sand painting, and the story it tells, celebrate the beauty of nature. ■

◄ The Navajo use tools like these to grind up rocks and plants to make the colors for their sand paintings. Many of the colors come from the colorful cliffs where they live.

◄ Jet, which is a type of coal found in the Southwest, was often used for the color black in Navajo sand paintings.

■ Describe some of the things the Rainbow People sand painting tells us about nature.

REVIEW

1. **FOCUS** Why is sand painting important to the Navajo?
2. **CONNECT** Compare the ways the Navajo and the Cheyenne see the natural world around them. How are they alike?
3. **CRITICAL THINKING** What skills does a medicine man need to create sand paintings?

4. **ACTIVITY** Draw a picture of a sand painting you would like to make. You might include something from the sky or from the earth, such as the moon, lightning, animals, people, trees, or a river. Make up a story that your sand painting tells.

Using Scale

Here's Why   You can use a map to help you get from one place to another. The scale on a map will help you figure out how far it is from one place to another.

Here's How   Maps are drawn to scale. A scale is a way to show how far apart things are on the real earth. A certain distance on the map is equal to a larger distance on the real earth. Look at the map of the area around Bright Star's village on the next page. Find the scale. It shows that one inch on the map stands for one mile in real distance.

Now take your ruler and measure the distance between Bright Star's village and the place marked *A* on the stream. The two places are about two inches apart on the map. So, they are about two miles apart in real distance.

Measure the distance between Bright Star's village and the place marked *B* on the cliffs. About how far apart are the two places on the map? About how far apart are they in real distance? Bright Star can walk one mile in one-half hour. How long will it take her to walk from her village to place *B* on the cliffs?

Measure the distance between *A* and *B* on the map. About how far apart are the two places on the map? How many miles is that in real distance?

Try It   Measure the distance between other points on the map. About how far away from each other are they in real distance? Use your ruler and the map scale to find out.

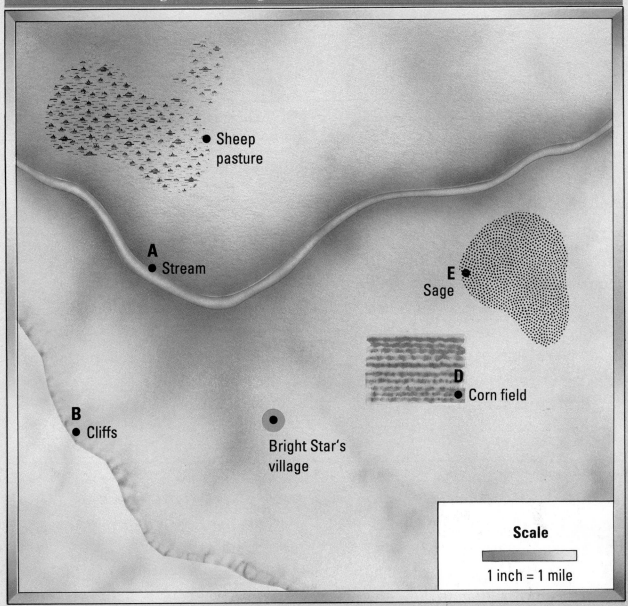

Sheep pasture

A
Stream

E
Sage

D
Corn field

B
Cliffs

Bright Star's village

Scale

1 inch = 1 mile

Apply It Work with a group to make a scale drawing of your classroom. You will need a measuring tape and a large piece of drawing paper. Use the measuring tape to measure the length of each wall. Draw a scale outline of the room on the drawing paper. One inch on your outline should stand for one foot of real distance in your classroom.

Then draw shapes to stand for large objects in your classroom, such as students' desks, teacher's desk, and bookcases. Try to put the objects in your drawing about where they are in your classroom.

109

Chapter Review

Reviewing Key Terms

adaptation (p. 101)　　livestock (p. 100)
chant (p. 103)　　　　 sand painting (p. 104)
hogan (p. 99)

A. Write the key term for each meaning.
1. a song sung on a few notes, often as a prayer
2. a one-room Navajo house
3. a picture made of crushed rock, plants, and other dried materials
4. animals raised to be used or sold

5. a change in the way of life to fit the surroundings

B. Write one or two sentences telling why each of the following sentences is true.
1. A hogan was a very good house for desert living.
2. Raising livestock was important to the Navajo.
3. A Navajo chant was a kind of medicine.

Exploring Concepts

A. Copy the chart below. Fill in the second column to show how the Kwakiutl and the Navajo were alike. Fill in the third column to show how the Kwakiutl and the Navajo were different.

B. Write one or two sentences to answer each question.
1. How did the Navajo adapt to the desert?
2. How did the Navajo use their sand paintings?

Indian people	How they were alike	How they were different
Kwakiutl and Navajo		

Reviewing Skills

A. Use a ruler and the map on the right.

1. About how many miles is it from Sam's house to the school? Use Second Street.

2. About how many miles is it from the school to the library? Use both Maryland Avenue and Third Street.

B. Write a sentence that tells what direction Sam's house is from the library.

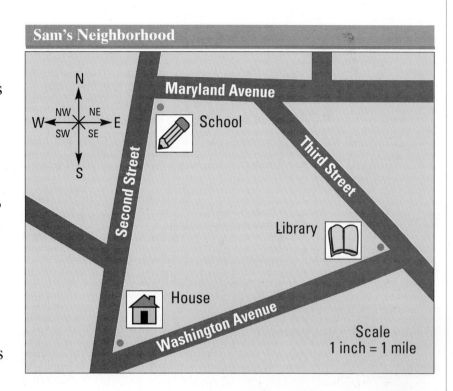

Sam's Neighborhood

Maryland Avenue

School

Third Street

Second Street

Library

House

Washington Avenue

Scale
1 inch = 1 mile

Using Critical Thinking

1. The Navajo learned from their neighbors how to raise livestock and crops. If they had not learned, how would their life have been different?

2. The Navajo made blankets and clothing from wool. Why do you think they used wool?

Preparing for Citizenship

1. **WRITING ACTIVITY** Pretend you live in a Navajo hogan with your family long ago. Write a story about one day in your life. Use your imagination, but include some of the facts about Navajo life that you have learned. Read your story to your class. Listen while other students read their stories. Put all of your stories together into one class book.

2. **COLLABORATIVE LEARNING** Make a mural of a sand painting. First, class members can decide what pictures to include. Some class members can draw the design. Other class members can paint. Choose one person to tell about your sand painting to another class in your school.

Unit 3

Settling the Land

American Indians lived on the land for thousands of years before settlers arrived from Europe. The settlers first built homes along the northeastern coast. As more people arrived, cities sprang up all along the Atlantic coast. Settlers looking for more space moved west. They traveled through thick forests, climbed great mountains, and crossed prairies and deserts on trails leading west. Some people went as far as the Pacific Ocean. Whether they were crossing the ocean or following trails to the Pacific, early settlers hoped that at the end of their journey they would find land to call their own.

Moses Speese Family. Custer County, Nebraska. 1888.
Solomon D. Butcher Collection. Nebraska State Historical Society.

Chapter 7

Settling the Northeast

In 1620, the Pilgrims started out on a long journey from England and landed on the northeast coast of North America. Indians helped the Pilgrims learn how to adapt to the land. As more settlers came and cities grew, people moved away from the coast and cleared land for homes and farms in eastern forests.

Before Pilgrims settled in Plymouth, they landed near Cape Cod. The only other English settlement then was in Virginia.

Thanksgiving with Indians is a painting from the 1940s by N. C. Wyeth. It shows Pilgrims sharing their first harvest with their Indian friends.

This barn was built in 1720 by settlers in eastern Pennsylvania. By that time, many farmers lived in the woods of the Northeast.

By the middle 1700s, many people had settled west of the coastal cities. Farmers used plows like this to turn tree-covered areas into farmland.

Life in Plymouth

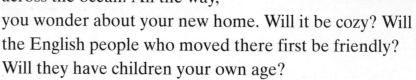

What challenges did the Pilgrims face during their first year in the new homeland?

Key Terms

- colony
- survive

Pretend you are living long ago in England. Your family has decided to make a new home far away, so you leave your home and friends. For 65 days you sail across the ocean. All the way, you wonder about your new home. Will it be cozy? Will the English people who moved there first be friendly? Will they have children your own age?

Tired from the stormy journey, you finally spot land. You search the coast for the neighbors you expected, but there is no sign of them. You can't keep looking. It is getting colder and you must choose a place to stay. As you wade to shore, no one greets you. No one offers you a hot meal or a warm bed. With only a few belongings, you must start a new life in a cold, strange land.

➤ Landing of the Pilgrims *was painted in the early 1800s. Pilgrims did row ashore in small boats, but the painting is incorrect in showing the Indians waiting on shore. The Pilgrims didn't meet the Indians until the following spring.*

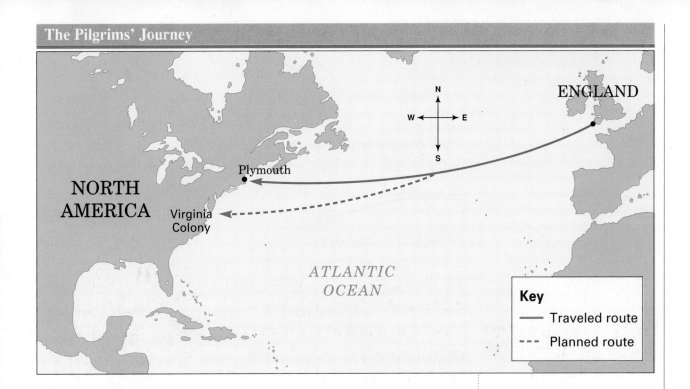

NORTH AMERICA

Plymouth

Virginia Colony

ENGLAND

ATLANTIC OCEAN

Key
—— Traveled route
- - - Planned route

The Pilgrims' First Winter

That's how many Pilgrims felt who sailed from England on a ship called the *Mayflower* in the summer of 1620. The Pilgrims were a religious group who disagreed with the church in England. They decided to raise their children in a whole new place.

The Pilgrims had planned to join a colony already started in Virginia. A **colony** is a settlement ruled by a distant country. However, the *Mayflower* did not follow the route to Virginia. Instead, it landed in late November on what is now the coast of Massachusetts.

Not finding the neighbors they expected, the Pilgrims looked for a place to begin their own colony. Four weeks later, in late December, they chose a spot and named it Plymouth after a town in England. Notice how far Virginia Colony is from Plymouth on the map above.

Plymouth was rich in natural resources. It had good farmland and many streams. Forests were a source for wood and animal meat. From the sea they got lobster, clams, and fish. Still, the Pilgrims barely **survived,** or lived through, that first winter. They had not brought enough extra food with them to last until spring, and there were

Across Time & Space

Historians are not sure what happened to the Mayflower *after the crew returned it to England in the spring of 1621. Some believe that an English farmer bought the* Mayflower *and used part of it as a barn roof. The barn still stands in a village outside London.*

few animals around to be hunted in the wintertime.

During their voyage, the Pilgrims had not eaten any fresh foods. The winter cold destroyed any green vegetables and berries that grew in Plymouth. Without these foods, many Pilgrims got sick. Two or three people died almost every week. To add to their worries, the Pilgrims didn't know if the Indians who lived nearby were going to be friendly.

To make matters even worse, the Pilgrims settled in Plymouth at the beginning of the cold New England winter. They needed to find shelter right away. All winter, the women stayed on board the *Mayflower* to take care of the children. The men rowed ashore to hunt, living in caves or holes dug into the sides of hills. They built rough roofs and doorways out of logs and mud mixed with stones and sticks. These shelters were all that protected the men from the icy weather. ■

■ *Find facts to support this statement: The first winter the Pilgrims spent in America was very difficult.*

Help from the Wampanoag

When spring finally arrived, only half of the 102 people that sailed from England were still alive. Women and children who had survived the winter joined the others on shore. The Pilgrims were determined to build a new English colony at Plymouth. Soon after, the Pilgrims met their Indian neighbors, the Wampanoag *(wahm puh NOH uhg)*.

Without help from the Wampanoag, the Pilgrims may never have been able to survive another winter. They taught the Pilgrims how to grow beans and pumpkins, and corn like that shown here. They also showed the Pilgrims that burying fish makes the soil richer for growing crops. The Wampanoag taught the colonists where and how to hunt and catch fish. The Pilgrims no longer feared that these people might be unfriendly. In fact, the Wampanoag proved to be great friends.

Thanks to the Wampanoag and lots of hard work, the Pilgrims adapted to their new land. That fall, they had a plentiful harvest. The Pilgrims were able to store enough food to last through the winter. They held a feast to give thanks to God. They invited the Wampanoag to share the foods the Wampanoag had made possible. This feast was the first Thanksgiving. ■

■ *How did the Wampanoag help the Pilgrims?*

First Year in Plymouth, From Fall to Fall

Mayflower arrives

Good harvest

1620 Nov.	Dec.	1621 Jan.	Feb.	March	April	May	June	July	Aug.	Sept.	Oct.

Harsh winter

Wampanoag help with crops

First Thanksgiving

R E V I E W

1. **FOCUS** What challenges did the Pilgrims face during their first year in the new homeland?
2. **CONNECT** Compare the materials the Navajo used to build hogans with the materials the Pilgrims used to build shelters that first year at Plymouth.
3. **CRITICAL THINKING** How did the Pilgrims' arrival in winter make their first few months harder than if they had arrived in the spring?
4. **ACTIVITY** Look at the timeline on this page. It shows the Pilgrims' first year at Plymouth. Think about a typical year in your own life. When do you start school? When do you celebrate the New Year? When is your birthday? Make up a timeline for yourself. Draw pictures to show what events you celebrate.

Why Countries Had Colonies

When the Pilgrims began the Plymouth settlement, they were not planning to start a new country with new rulers. Instead, they claimed the land as a part of England. The Pilgrims remained citizens of England, and they were still ruled by English laws. Settlements like theirs, ruled by a country far away, are called colonies.

Having a colony helped a country in several ways. A colony gave the ruling country new land. The ruling country took the natural resources, such as gold, silver, fish, and timber. The ruling country could sell its own products in the colony. It could also sell the colony's products at home or to other countries. Countries with colonies often became rich. A country often paid no attention to the rights of native people who already lived there. Land was taken from the American Indians and given to colonists.

England was just one of many countries that ruled over colonies. France and Spain also had colonies in North America and in other places. Today, most of the colonies are free countries.

Life in the Eastern Forest

A dim lantern glow lit up the log cabin. It was 8:00 P.M., time for Maddie to go to bed. Pulling her nightcap down over her ears, she crawled in beside her sleeping sister. The wooden planks of the bed creaked. Each time Maddie moved, the dry leaves and cornhusks crackled inside the bed padding. During the summer, the deerhide covers felt itchy, and there were often bedbugs in it. But on this cold winter night, the bed felt cozy. Maddie snuggled under the hide, listened for a moment to the trees howling in the wind, then fell fast asleep.

THINKING FOCUS

What was life like for the people who moved from the coastal cities into the wilderness?

Key Terms

- inland
- goods
- wilderness

Moving Inland

Soon after the Pilgrims and other early settlers came to this country, cities began to grow along the Atlantic coast. By the early 1700s, there were several big cities with many people. People began to move **inland,** or away from the coast. Many families like Maddie's moved into the Pennsylvania forests. There they would build a log cabin and rough cornhusk beds and start farming.

CANADA

Lake Ontario

Lake Erie

MOUNTAINS

Boston
Plymouth

New York

Pennsylvania

Philadelphia

APPALACHIAN

Baltimore

ATLANTIC
OCEAN

N
W → E
S

0   250 miles

0   250 kilometers

Key

→ Movement inland

— State borders today

■ *What were some of the reasons settlers moved inland?*

How Do We Know?

Wilderness settlers were very busy, but they still found time to write. They wrote letters to friends and sometimes kept diaries. These writings help us know what life was like for those settlers.

Many of these settlers came from Germany, Ireland, and Scotland. They moved to Pennsylvania for many reasons. Some, like Maddie's family, wanted to own their own land.

These farmers grew food to sell to growing cities like Philadelphia. People in the cities needed more **goods,** or supplies, in order to live. Find Philadelphia on the map.

Trappers and hunters also moved inland. They provided city people with goods from the forest. Forest goods included animal hides and furs, and special plants called herbs. Colonists used hides and furs for clothing and blankets. They used herbs to make medicines. ■

Clearing the Land

Land west of Philadelphia was mostly wilderness. A **wilderness** is land that has not been changed by farms or buildings. Indians living in these forests had built villages and cleared some land for crops. However, most of the land was still covered by thick forests.

The settlers did not move onto land that was not in use. The forested land had been home to American Indians for a long time.

Farmers needed open space to build homes and plant crops. When they found a flat place near fresh water, they cleared the wilderness by cutting down trees. Then they built cabins from logs from the trees. Settlers needed a one-room log cabin and a corn crop to survive the winter.

Settlers could not survive without two important tools—an ax and rifle. They used axes to clear land, chop firewood, and cut logs for the cabin. Settlers used rifles to kill deer, bears, squirrels, and turkey. Without rifles, settlers would not have eaten much meat. ■

■ *Why were axes and rifles so important to settlers in the wilderness?*

Everyday Life

To survive, settlers had to make almost everything they needed themselves. In cities, people could buy goods from stores. There were no stores deep in the wilderness.

Wood was the most important resource in the settlers' everyday lives. Settlers used wood to build their cabins, and nearly everything that went inside. They used wood to make wagons, tools, cradles, benches, and bowls.

Wilderness settlers often lived far apart, but they would gather from miles around to help a new neighbor raise logs for a new cabin. Settlers turned these "log raisings" into a chance to visit. You'll read more about building a log cabin on the next page.

◄ *This settler is cooking supper in her fireplace. How many things can you see in her cabin that are made of wood?*

A Log Raising

Think about your home. Can you imagine building it? What a job! To build their houses, settlers used axes to cut down trees and to make the logs fit together.

U-shaped cuts were chopped into the ends of the logs. The cuts helped the logs fit together.

Helping hands from neighbors made the four main steps in building a log cabin go quickly.

1. Logs were dragged to the spot where the cabin would be built.
2. Bottom logs were put in place.
3. Ropes were used to pull wall logs up poles.
4. Roof and chimney were put up.

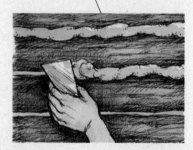

Mud, moss, and stones were mixed to fill the chinks, or holes, between the logs.

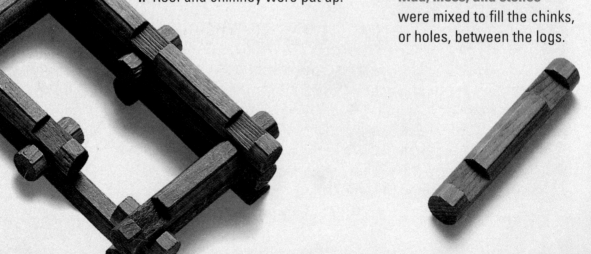

In this 1796 sketch, a settler takes a break from her chores to look at her surroundings.

▼ *Sometimes settlers used axes to plant seeds if they didn't have proper farming tools.*

After all the hard work of putting up a cabin, settlers enjoyed music, feasting, and storytelling. A finished log cabin might have looked like the one above.

Like the Pilgrims, the Pennsylvania settlers learned many of the skills they needed from their Indian neighbors. In the Pennsylvania forests, these were the Delaware Indians.

Like the Wampanoag, the Delaware knew how to use the natural resources of the land. The Delaware taught the settlers how to grow corn, beans, and squash. The Indians even shared recipes for cooking these foods. The Delaware also showed the settlers which wild herbs made the best medicines. ■

■ *How did the settlers adapt to the land?*

R E V I E W

1. **FOCUS** What was life like for the people who moved from the coastal cities into the wilderness?

2. **CONNECT** Compare the way settlers and the Kwakiutl depended on forest goods.

3. **CRITICAL THINKING** Explain how you would feel about moving to the wilderness.

4. **ACTIVITY** Pretend you are a new settler traveling through the wilderness. Write a short description of what you are carrying and how you find food and shelter each day.

"If . . . Then" Statements

Here's Why   You have learned that many settlers moved inland to the wilderness. They must have thought carefully about the move before they made it. They may have thought of many reasons to move and many reasons not to move. They could have used "If . . . then" statements to help them decide.

Here's How   An "If . . . then" statement is a way of thinking about or talking about the results of doing something. Some results may be good. Some may not be so good.

For example, suppose a family were thinking of moving to the wilderness. Here are two possible results:

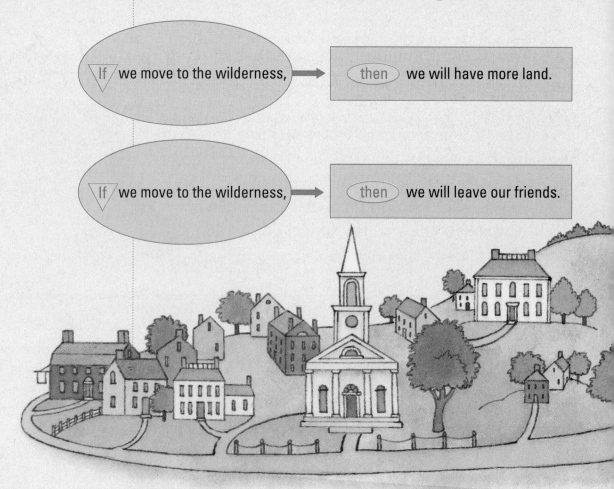

If / we move to the wilderness, → then) we will have more land.

If / we move to the wilderness, → then) we will leave our friends.

Perhaps some families moved because having more land was more important than living near old friends. Why do you think some families decided not to move?

"If . . . then" statements can help us make a decision. They help us see that most things we do have results.

Try It   Think of two other possible results of a family's move to the wilderness. Write each result as an "If . . . then" statement. Share your statements with your class.

Apply It   Suppose your family is thinking of getting a new puppy. Think of some possible results. Then write "If . . . then" statements that tell what might happen.

Early Settlers

*P*retend you are a detective. You have been asked to discover who started your community and what it was like long ago. How would you get this information?

Get Ready Every detective looks for clues to find information. You can find clues about the beginning of your community by looking at the names of streets and buildings. Some of them are named for people who started your community.

Find Out Look through books to find out more about these early settlers. You can also find old pictures or photographs in books. You may even find old maps of your community.

LaClede Landing at Present site of St. Louis

Move Ahead   Write a report on what you discovered about the people who started your community and about its early years. Draw some pictures to go with your report.

Explore Some More   Make a class scrapbook of the early years of your community. Put your written report and pictures in the scrapbook. Include a list of streets and buildings that were named for people who started your community. Add any pictures and maps from the past that you can find. You may want to give your class scrapbook to your school or community library.

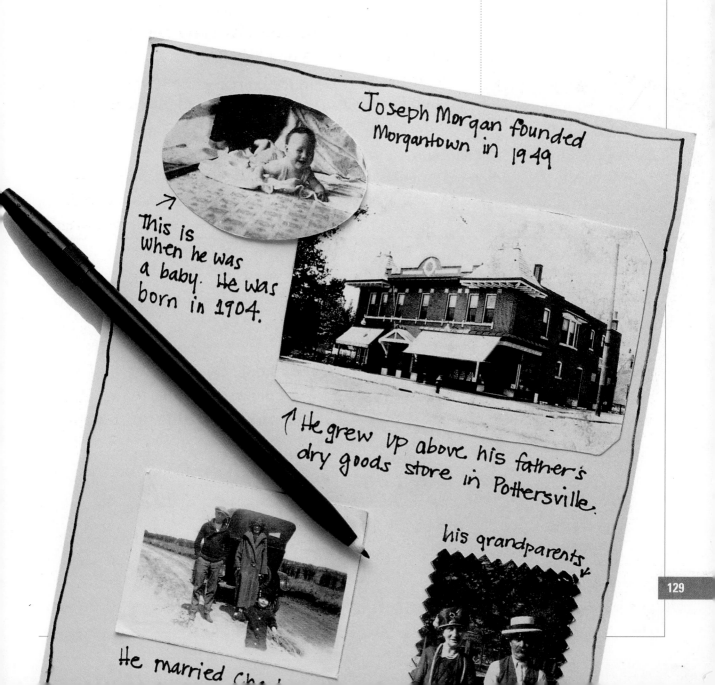

Joseph Morgan founded Morgantown in 1949

This is when he was a baby. He was born in 1904.

He grew up above his father's dry goods store in Pottersville.

his grandparents

He married Cha...

Chapter Review

Reviewing Key Terms

colony (p. 117) survive (p. 117)
goods (p. 122) wilderness (p. 122)
inland (p. 121)

A. Write the key term that best completes each sentence.

1. During their first winter, the Pilgrims were barely able to _____.
2. A _____ is land that has not been changed by people.
3. A settlement ruled by a country far away is called a _____.
4. People buy _____, or supplies.
5. We move _____ when we move away from the coast.

B. Write *true* or *false* for each sentence below. If a sentence is false, rewrite it to make it true.

1. The Wampanoag helped the Pilgrims survive their second winter in Plymouth.
2. Hunters and farmers sold goods to people in cities.
3. In the colonies, the settlers had an easy life.
4. A colony belongs to another country.
5. Wilderness families lived far apart from one another.

Exploring Concepts

A. The Pilgrims and the Navajo learned from other people. Copy the chart below and fill in the last two columns. Your chart will show what the Pilgrims and the Navajo learned and from whom they learned.

B. Answer the questions in one or two sentences.

1. Why were colonies important to their home countries?
2. Why did people move to the wilderness where life was hard?

People	What they learned	From whom
The Navajo		
The Pilgrims		

Reviewing Skills

1. Write two "If . . . then" statements to tell what might happen if you move to a new city.
2. What physical features are shown on the map at the right?
3. Look at the map on the right again. What direction is Philadelphia from New York City? Is the distance between the two cities less than or more than 250 miles?

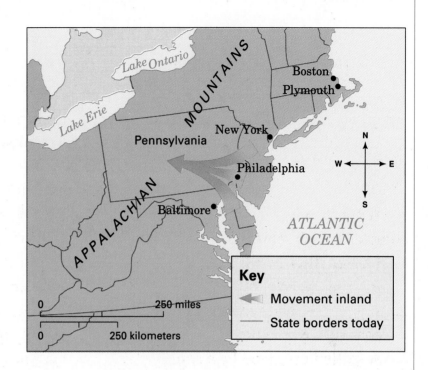

Lake Ontario

Lake Erie

MOUNTAINS

Boston

Plymouth

New York

Pennsylvania

Philadelphia

APPALACHIAN

Baltimore

N
W — E
S

ATLANTIC OCEAN

0   250 miles

0   250 kilometers

Key

Movement inland

State borders today

Using Critical Thinking

1. If the Pilgrims had arrived at a desert in the summer, would more people have survived the first six months? Why?
2. When settlers in the forests built their own homes, other people came to help. What can we do today to help people who have no homes?
3. Rifles and axes were important tools for settlers. What are our most important tools today?

Preparing for Citizenship

1. WRITING ACTIVITY Pretend you are a settler in the wilderness. Write a letter to a friend in England. Tell what you usually do during the day.
2. COLLABORATIVE LEARNING Work with other students in a group. Choose an event in the lives of the Pilgrims or the Pennsylvania settlers. Help your group act out your event for the rest of the class. The landing of the Pilgrims at Plymouth is one event that you could act out. A log raising by the settlers is another. After your group is finished, the rest of the class should try to guess the event you acted out. Try to guess the events acted out by other groups.

Chapter 8

Beyond the Appalachians

As more and more cities grew in the East, many settlers packed all that they owned to journey to new land in the West. First, they had to cross the Appalachian (ap uh LAY chee uhn) Mountains to settle in Kentucky. Later, wagons followed trails that led as far west as Oregon and California. It took about a hundred years, from the end of the 1700s to the end of the 1800s, to settle the West. During this time, the West became a land of growth and change.

This child's cradle was made during the middle 1800s. Babies born along the western trails slept in cradles like this.

Oscar Berninghaus painted *Oregon Trail* in 1951. It shows families making the long trip across the United States.

Some settlers' children attended schools like this one in Kansas. Children of all ages were taught by the same teacher. This one-room schoolhouse was made of big blocks of grass-covered earth.

Here are some of the hunting tools that people took with them on their trip west. The bag held bullets and other hunting materials. In the large horn was powder that would make the rifle fire. The pick and the brush were used to clean the gun, and the tiny horn was used to measure powder.

The Wilderness Road

THINKING FOCUS

Why was the Wilderness Road important for the people who wanted to settle in Kentucky?

Key Terms

- pioneer
- blaze

➤ *The Cumberland Gap is a natural passageway through the Appalachian Mountains. Thousands of settlers traveled through this gap on their way to Kentucky.*

S atrd April 8th—We all pact up and started crost Cumberland gap about one oclock this Day We Met a great many peopel turned Back for fear of the indians but our Company goes on Still with good courage we come to a very ugly Creek with steep Banks and have it to cross several times. . . .

William Calk, from his journal, 1775

William Calk may not have spelled very well, but he had many adventures along the Wilderness Road. Despite the dangers of travel, Calk was determined to reach Kentucky. It was a beautiful land with lots of open space.

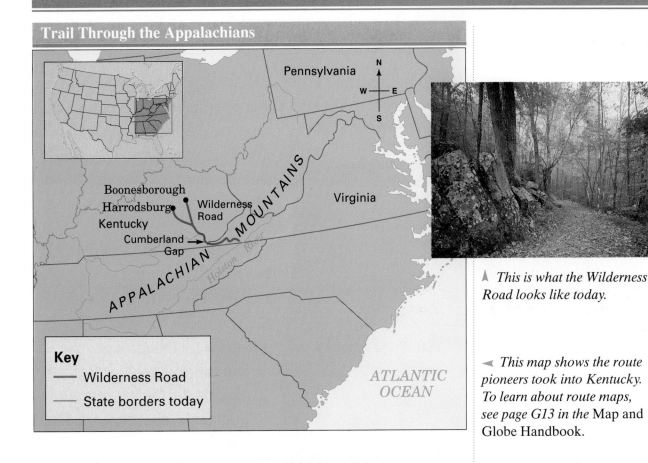

This is what the Wilderness Road looks like today.

◄ This map shows the route pioneers took into Kentucky. To learn about route maps, see page G13 in the Map and Globe Handbook.

A Difficult Crossing

William Calk was a **pioneer,** which is a person who leaves a settled place and moves into the wilderness to make a new home. In the late 1700s and early 1800s, thousands of pioneers like Calk moved to Kentucky. Why did they move to Kentucky? For one thing, land cost less there than along the east coast. For another, Kentucky had rich soil for farming. Herds of buffalo and other wild animals roamed there. People said there were so many birds in Kentucky that they could block out the sun.

Kentucky offered much, but getting there was difficult and dangerous. Notice on the map how the Appalachian Mountains blocked all travel west. If people wanted to reach Kentucky, they first had to haul everything they owned over these rugged mountains.

Narrow Indian or buffalo paths crossed some of these mountains. Pioneers had to follow these paths on foot or by horse. The paths were far too narrow for wagons. ■

■ Why did the Appalachian Mountains present problems to pioneers who wanted to move west?

135

Daniel Boone Leads the Way

Many believe that this piece of tree bark was carved by Daniel Boone in his travels through the Appalachians. It is dated 1775.

■ *How did Daniel Boone help settle the land west of the Appalachian Mountains?*

To help people settle in Kentucky, pioneers needed a better way to get there. Some people bought Kentucky land from the Cherokee *(CHAIR uh kee)* Indians in order to sell it to new settlers. Then these same people hired Daniel Boone to **blaze,** or mark, a trail for the settlers.

To build the Wilderness Road, Daniel Boone gathered a crew of 30 men. Their job was to clear the way from Virginia to Kentucky. The crew had to widen the trails that were already there. Sometimes they made new trails and connected them to the old ones.

Boone led the way, blazing trees to mark the route of the trail. His crew followed, clearing away underbrush and chopping down trees. Look at the map on page 135 again. Trace the Wilderness Road from the Holston River to the Cumberland Gap. At which two Kentucky towns did parts of the road end? ■

Traveling the Wilderness Road

In 1775, Boone's Wilderness Road was finally ready. The road made travel easier, but it was still a difficult trip. Pioneers had to carry everything on horseback or in wagons. Storms caused serious delays. Flooded streams and rivers were hard to cross. Wagon wheels often got stuck in the mud after a heavy rain. Repairing broken wagons was difficult because pioneers had few tools or parts.

Sometimes pioneers were turned back by Cherokee attacks. Kentucky had been Cherokee hunting ground for hundreds of years. The Cherokee had sold part of the land, but people were settling in places that had never been sold. Also, there were more settlers than the Cherokee had expected. The Cherokee were being forced to live in lands farther to the west. Their people were losing the ways that they had lived for hundreds of years.

Until 1818, when other roads opened up for use, thousands of settlers used the Wilderness Road. Many of these first pioneers were the children and grandchildren of the German and other pioneer families who had settled the eastern Pennsylvania forest years before. ■

■ *What made a trip on the Wilderness Road so difficult?*

◄ *This sketch of a pioneer family crossing the Appalachians was drawn by someone who was actually there, Joshua Shaw.*

R E V I E W

1. **FOCUS** Why was the Wilderness Road important to the people who wanted to settle in Kentucky?

2. **CONNECT** Compare problems that Plymouth colonists had with problems that Kentucky pioneers had. What were some of the differences?

3. **CRITICAL THINKING** If you were a Cherokee, how might you feel about settlers moving into your hunting grounds?

4. **WRITING ACTIVITY** Write a journal entry for a day on the Wilderness Road. You have to cross several deep streams with steep banks with your wagon and horses. Describe what you did to get across.

Many years ago, men, women, and children—young and old alike—went west to find a new land to settle. Travel was not easy. Houses and food were hard to find. But, always, other people helped. Read this excerpt from a story about a pioneer family in Kansas.

LITERATURE

WAGON WHEELS

Written by Barbara Brenner

Illustrated by Don Bolognese

Chapter 1—THE DUGOUT

There it is, boys," Daddy said. "Across this river is Nicodemus, Kansas. That is where we are going to build our house. There is free land for everyone here in the West. All we have to do is go and get it."

We had come a long way to get to Kansas. All the way from Kentucky. It had been a hard trip, and a sad one. Mama died on the way. Now there were just the four of us—Daddy, Willie, Little Brother, and me. "Come on, boys," Daddy called. "Let's put our feet on free dirt." We crossed the river, wagon and all.

A man was waiting for us on the other side. "I am Sam Hickman," he said. "Welcome to the town of Nicodemus."

"Why, thank you, Brother," Daddy said. "But where *is* your town?"

"Right here," Mr. Hickman said. We did not see any houses. But we saw smoke coming out of holes in the prairie.

"Shucks!" my Daddy said. "Holes in the ground are for rabbits and snakes, not for free black people. I am a carpenter. I can build fine wood houses for this town."

"No time to build wood houses now," Mr. Hickman told my Daddy. "Winter is coming. And winter in Kansas is *mean*. Better get yourself a dugout before the ground freezes." Daddy knew Sam Hickman was right. We got our shovels and we dug us a dugout.

It wasn't much of a place—dirt floor, dirt walls, no windows. And the roof was just grass and branches. But we were glad to have that dugout when the wind began to whistle across the prairie.

Every night Willie lit the lamp and made a fire. I cooked a rabbit stew or fried a pan of fish fresh from the river. After supper Daddy would always say, "How about a song or two?" He would take out his banjo and *Plink-a-plunk! Plink-a-plunk!* Pretty soon that dugout felt like home.

Chapter II—INDIANS

Winter came. And that Kansas winter *was* mean. It snowed day after day. We could not hunt or fish. We had no more rabbit stew. No more fish fresh from the river. All we had was cornmeal mush to eat.

Then one day there was no more cornmeal. There was not a lick of food in the whole town of Nicodemus. And nothing left to burn for firewood. Little Brother cried all the time—he was so cold and hungry. Daddy wrapped blankets around him. "Hush, baby son," he said to him. "Try to sleep. Supply train will be coming soon." But the supply train did not come. Not that day or the next.

On the third day we heard the sound of horses. Daddy looked out to see who it was. "Oh Lord!" he said. "Indians!" We were *so* scared. We had all heard stories about Indians. I tried to be brave.

"I will get my gun, Daddy," I said.

But Daddy said, "Hold on, Johnny. Wait and see what they do." We watched from the dugout.

Everyone in Nicodemus was watching the Indians. First they made a circle. Then each Indian took something from his saddlebag and dropped it on the ground. The Indians turned and rode straight toward the dugouts. "Now they are coming for us!" Willie cried.

We raised our guns. But the Indians rode right past us and kept on going. We waited a long time to be sure they were gone. Then everyone ran out into the snow to see what the Indians had left. It was FOOD! Everyone talked at once. "Look!" "Fresh deer meat!" "Fish!" "Dried beans and squash!" "And bundles of sticks to keep our fires burning."

There was a feast in Nicodemus that night.
But before we ate, Daddy said to us, "Johnny.
Willie. Little Brother. I want you to remember
this day. When someone says bad things about
Indians, tell them the Osage Indians saved our
lives in Nicodemus."

Passages to the West

Why did people travel on the Oregon Trail and the Santa Fe Trail?

Key Terms

- pass
- wagon train

Reggie walks along the trail in Scotts Bluff National Monument in western Nebraska. He tries to imagine the thousands of wagons that traveled this trail over a hundred years ago. He thinks about how excited the pioneers must have been when they reached Scotts Bluff.

The pioneers spent weeks crossing the Great Plains. The grassy land looked the same mile after mile. The pioneers could not tell how far they had come or how far they had to go. Scotts Bluff was the first sign these tired travelers had that their long prairie crossing was nearing an end. It also meant that their trip through the Rocky Mountains was about to begin.

Heading West

Since the early days of the colonies, Americans had been moving west. First, they moved into places like western Pennsylvania. Then they moved farther west into Kentucky and Missouri. The trail that Reggie saw was made by settlers moving as far west as Oregon. Many of these pioneers were the children, grandchildren, and great-grandchildren of the earlier pioneers.

Many pioneers went west to get away from crowded areas of the East or to start farms on cheap land in the West. Others went west to become miners. Miners are people who dig for gold, silver, and other valuable materials. Still others went west to buy and sell goods.

▼ *Fast-moving water and rocks and holes along river bottoms made river crossings dangerous for pioneers.*

The trip from the East to the far West was difficult. First, pioneers had to cross the Great Plains. This huge grassland lay empty and flat for hundreds of miles. Finding food and drinking water was often a problem. Some of the rivers they had to cross were dangerous.

Pioneers going to the Pacific coast had to cross high mountains. These were steep and sometimes covered with snow. Those going to the Southwest had to travel through a desert where there was little food or water. ■

■ *What were some of the reasons that pioneers traveled west, and why was the trip so difficult?*

147

The Santa Fe Trail

Most travelers used either the Santa Fe *(San tuh Fay)* Trail or the Oregon Trail to go west. The Santa Fe Trail opened in 1821. It was 780 miles long. It began in Independence, Missouri, and crossed the Great Plains. Then it went around the Rocky Mountains. It crossed the Cimarron Valley and ended in Santa Fe, New Mexico. Trace the route of the Santa Fe Trail on the map on page 149.

The area around Santa Fe had first been settled by the Spanish in the 1600s. Later, it was part of Mexico.

Most travelers on the Santa Fe Trail were traders. They went west with cloth, farm tools, and other goods from the East. They sold these goods in the West, where they bought furs, gold, silver, and more. Then they returned to the East for more selling and buying. ■

■ *Why did traders travel the Santa Fe trail?*

▼ *These wagons may have been fuller when they reached the mountains. As pioneers crossed mountains, they often had to dump items to make their wagons easier to pull.*

The Oregon Trail

Unlike the Santa Fe Trail, the Oregon Trail was used by families. Most of them were heading west to find land and to set up farms and build homes.

Look again at the map. Notice that the Oregon Trail also began in Independence, Missouri. From there it wound 2,000 miles toward the Northwest. It crossed the Great Plains and passed over the Rocky Mountains through the South Pass. Going through a **pass,** or a low point in the mountains, made the trip easier for families on the Oregon Trail.

After crossing through South Pass, travelers could continue to what is now the state of Oregon.

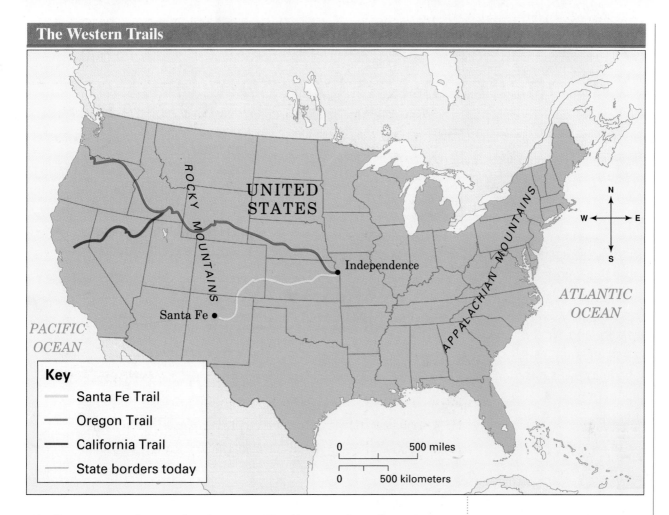

Some people on the Oregon Trail were heading to California. They hoped to find gold there. Those travelers could turn south from the Oregon Trail onto the California Trail.

Pioneer families traveled the Oregon Trail in **wagon trains.** As many as one hundred families would move along the trail in a long line of wagons pulled by oxen and mules. A scout, or guide, traveled with the wagon train. The scout knew where food, water, and good stopping places were.

Travelers on the Oregon Trail had to keep moving. It took four to six months to get to the end of the trail. They had to get through the Rocky Mountains before winter came, or snow and ice might trap them in the mountains. A wagon train usually moved no farther than 15 miles each day and stopped only at noon and at nightfall. Breakdowns or accidents might also force them to stop. The Moment in Time on the next page takes a look at a pioneer during one of these stops.

How Do We Know?

Pioneers on the Oregon Trail sometimes stopped at Independence Rock in Wyoming. Travelers would scratch their names in the rock there. We know this because their names are still there on the rock today.

149

A Pioneer on the Oregon Trail

4:50 P.M. May 7, 1843
On the banks of the Platte River
in central Nebraska

Firewood

Cottonwood branches make a great fire, and this woman plans to keep it going for several hours. After dinner, her new friends will join her family around the fire to talk about their plans to settle in Oregon.

Shawl

This woman's mother wore this colorful shawl when she traveled to America from Ireland. Now it is making another long journey as this pioneer crosses America.

Flint

Striking the rock in her pocket against a metal bar will make sparks to start a cooking fire. Tonight's dinner will be fresh fish from the Platte River.

Dress

Brand new at the start of the journey, this dress is now covered with prairie dust. The woman hopes that soon the wagon train will stop in one place long enough for her to wash it. The other dresses packed in her wagon are too fancy to wear on the trail.

Shoes

Before she left her farm in Ohio, this woman bought these tough leather shoes. The salesman who sold them to her said that they would hold up well on the rough, rocky trails of the mountains.

◄ *This is one of the few photographs taken of people on the Oregon Trail.*

▼ *This box holds medicine made from herbs. Pioneers brought medicine on the trail to help sick or injured travelers.*

The trip west on the Oregon Trail was difficult for travelers. Food, water, and firewood were hard to find along the trail. Sometimes Indians would help pioneers by giving them directions or trading with them. However, not all Indians were friendly. Some Indians were angry that the settlers were forcing them off their land. These Indians would sometimes attack a wagon train. Pioneers were also killed by accidents and sickness during their journey.

The days of pioneer travel were long and hard, but the wagon trains moved on. The pioneers looked forward to starting new lives in the West. ■

■ *What was life like on the Oregon Trail?*

R E V I E W

1. **FOCUS** Why did people travel on the Oregon Trail and the Santa Fe Trail?

2. **CONNECT** How was the journey of the Pilgrims on the *Mayflower* like the journey of the pioneers heading west on the trails? How was it different?

3. **CRITICAL THINKING** What do you think was one of the most difficult parts of a pioneer's life? What was the most exciting part? Explain.

4. **WRITING ACTIVITY** Imagine that you and a group of friends are going west a hundred years ago. You need to find a scout to guide your wagon train. Write a short paragraph that tells what kind of person you are looking for.

Packing Your Wagon for Oregon

Here's Why

Imagine that it is the year 1840. You and your family are going to move west. The trip will take four to six months. Everything you take will have to be packed in a covered wagon. You will have to pack some food and a few necessary items, such as pots and pans. The inside of the wagon is very small, about 16 feet long and 5 feet wide. What will you choose to take?

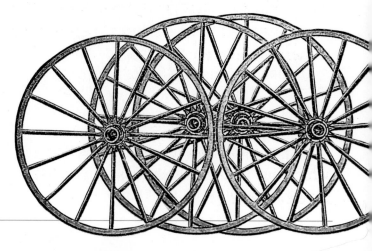

Here's How

Think about the things a pioneer family needed. Look at the items pictured on this page and on page 152 to get some ideas. What other things would you want to take in your wagon? Think about reasons for taking them.

Try It

Work with a partner. Make a list of all the things you would like to pack in your wagon. List those things that you must take. Also, list things that would be nice to take if there is room for them.

Apply It

If you had room in your wagon for only five items, which five would you choose to take? Tell why you would take each one.

An Early Prairie Town

THINKING

FOCUS

Why was Abilene known as a cattle town?

Key Terms

- population
- trade center

➤ *Nat Love was a famous cowboy who drove cattle across the prairies for nearly 20 years.*

Cowboys often sang as they moved cattle across the prairie. This song, "The Old Chisholm (*CHIHZ uhm*) Trail," was one of their favorites:

Oh come along, boys, and listen to my tale,
I'll tell you all my troubles on the ol' Chis'm trail.

Chorus: *Come a-ti yi youpy youpy ya youpy yay,*
Come a-ti yi youpy youpy yay.

On a ten-dollar horse and
a forty-dollar saddle,
I was ridin' and a-punchin'
Texas cattle.

(Chorus)

I'm up in the mornin'
afore daylight,
An' afore I sleep
the moon shines bright.

(Chorus)

It's bacon and beans
most every day,
I'd as soon be eatin'
prairie hay.

(Chorus)

Western Communities

Cowboys sang songs such as "The Old Chisholm Trail" to pass the time and to calm their herds. Cowboys were among the first people from the East to come to the prairies. But as the **population,** or number of people, in the United States grew in the 1860s, more and more people moved west.

The railroad brought many people to the prairies of Illinois, Missouri, and Kansas. Towns sprang up along the railroad line. Many people moved west to set up farms or to start businesses to serve the growing population already living there. The railroad also gave ranchers in the West a way to get cattle to markets in the East. ■

■ *Why did towns start springing up on the prairies?*

▲ *This picture shows Abilene, Kansas, during its peak as a cattle town.*

The Growth of Abilene

One of the fastest-growing prairie towns was Abilene, Kansas. The Chisholm Trail stretched from San Antonio, Texas, to Abilene. This was the main trail for driving cattle out of Texas during the late 1860s. The railroad was also very important to Abilene's growth. For a few years,

Key

||||| Railroad

――― Chisholm Trail

――― State borders today

| 0 | | 250 miles |
| 0 | | 250 kilometers |

Chicago

Illinois

to eastern cities

Abilene

Kansas

Missouri

to eastern cities

Texas

San Antonio

Across Time & Space

Cowboys are now called cowhands. Life for many cowboys has changed. Today some cowhands use helicopters to look for missing cattle. They may move cattle from place to place in trucks.

■ *Why did Abilene grow so quickly?*

the railroad ended in Abilene. Abilene's location at the end of the Chisholm Trail and at the end of the railroad made it an important western town.

People in the East needed beef. Cowboys drove cattle from Texas north along the Chisholm Trail to Abilene. From there, cattle were loaded onto trains and shipped to Chicago where they were prepared to be sold as meat in the East. Use the map to trace the routes used to move cattle from San Antonio to eastern cities.

Visitors to Abilene one hundred years ago could see in a minute that it was a cattle town. Cowboys and cattle were everywhere! Cowboys, happy to be done with a long cattle drive, wandered the streets. Cattle rattled pens and clattered up loading ramps onto trains.

Many businesses moved to Abilene. It quickly grew from a small prairie town into a busy **trade center,** or place to do business. Farmers near the town sold food to the cowboys. Hotels, stores, and other businesses provided cowboys with places to eat, sleep, and buy goods. ■

The Cowboys Move On

By 1872, Abilene's Texas cattle business came to an end. People and businesses started leaving. Abilene was no longer a busy trade center. This graph shows the change in the number of cattle that passed through Abilene.

Abilene's cattle business stopped for many reasons. Some settlers around Abilene were unfriendly to the cowboys. Also, Texas cattle were no longer allowed into areas of Kansas near Abilene. They carried a sickness that made cattle raised on the northern plains very ill. Texas ranchers did not like this new law against their cattle.

The most important reason that Abilene lost cattle business was that new railroads were built. They led to cities that were closer to Texas where cattle were raised than Abilene was. Cowboys no longer had to drive cattle as far as Abilene to reach railroad lines.

Today, visitors come to Abilene to learn about its colorful past. Many people must find it hard to believe that once the streets there were crowded with cowboys. ■

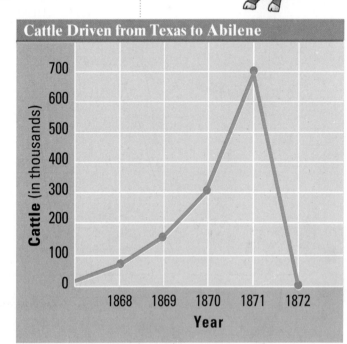

Cattle Driven from Texas to Abilene

■ Why did Abilene's cattle business come to an end?

R E V I E W

1. **FOCUS** Why was Abilene known as a cattle town?

2. **CONNECT** Use the map on page 149 and the map on page 156 to find the Santa Fe Trail, the Oregon Trail, and the Chisholm Trail. Which trail crosses the most states?

3. **CRITICAL THINKING** What kinds of businesses do you think were harmed when cowboys stopped coming to Abilene?

4. **ACTIVITY** Draw a picture that shows some of the things you might have seen in Abilene in 1870. Then draw a picture that shows how the population and businesses had changed by 1872.

Using Grids

Here's Why   You can use a map to locate any place on the earth. Suppose you want to find Wichita, Kansas. You may search on a map of Kansas until you find it. But there is a better, faster way. You can use a grid.

Here's How   A grid is made of columns and rows that cross one another. Here is a grid on a map of Kansas. The columns on this grid have numbers. The rows have letters.

Use the grid to find Wichita. First, find row C. Then find column 5. Move your finger across row C until you come to column 5. Wichita is located in that area.

Can you locate Dodge City on the map of Kansas? It is in the C3 area. What city is located at B6 on the map? In which area of the map is Topeka located?

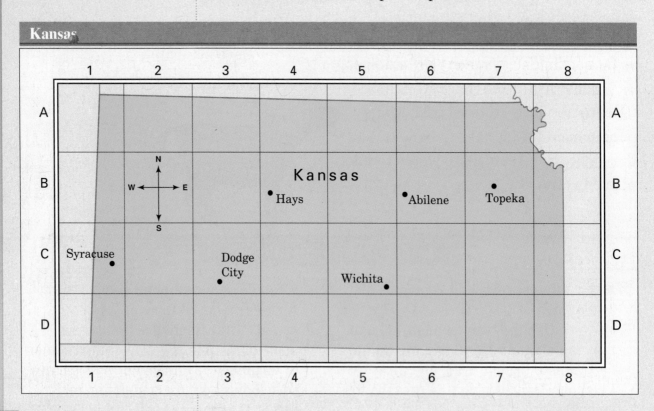

Kansas

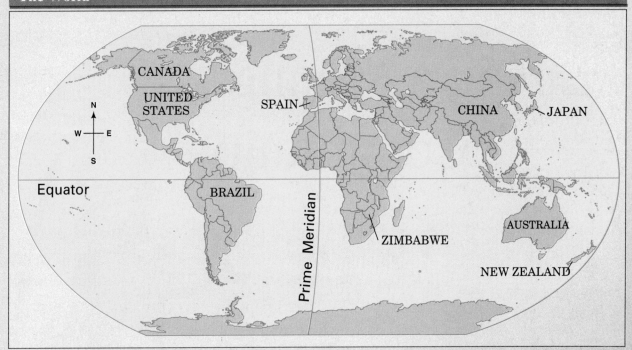

Many lines can be drawn on maps and globes to make grids. One of these lines goes around the globe halfway between the North Pole and the South Pole. It is called the equator. Another line goes from the North Pole to the South Pole. It is called the prime meridian. These are the two most important grid lines on maps and globes.

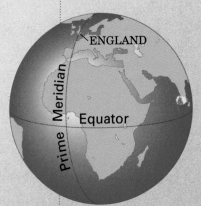

Look at the world map on this page. Find the United States. Is it north or south of the equator? Is the United States east or west of the prime meridian?

Try It   Work with a partner. Use the world map on this page. Take turns naming places. Have the other person say whether your place is north or south of the equator and east or west of the prime meridian.

Apply It   Use the world map on pages 264–265. Make a list of three countries that the equator runs through. List three countries that the prime meridian runs through.

Life in a Mining Community

Why was Leadville known as a boom town?

Key Terms

- vein
- mineral
- boom town

We're rich! We're rich!" shouted the two miners in 1878. They jumped up and down with excitement.

Just a few days before, the two men had walked into a store in Leadville, Colorado. Their clothes were ragged, and they had everything they owned with them. They had come to Leadville hoping to find silver.

The two men asked the owner of the store for supplies. They had no money, so they agreed to give the store owner one-third of any silver they found.

Then the two men went off into the hills. Since it was a warm day, they began digging in a shady spot. A few days later, after digging down 27 feet, the men struck a large **vein,** or strip, of silver. If they had dug a little farther away in any direction, they would have missed the silver completely.

Now the two men—who had started out in rags—were as rich as kings. And there was a very happy store owner in Leadville!

Wealth of the Rockies

Leadville was not the only spot in the Rocky Mountains where gold and silver were found. The map below shows where valuable minerals were found in the West. **Minerals** are materials such as gold and silver that are found in the earth. When news of the discoveries spread, people from all over came to the area, including Chinese, Mexicans, and Chileans.

Towns started where the mines were. The population of these mining towns grew even more rapidly when the railroad came. Trains brought miners, shopkeepers, and heavy mining machines. These mining towns were the first real settlements in the Rockies. ■

▼ *Leadville, Colorado, was one of many mining towns in the Rocky Mountains. This picture was taken in 1901.*

■ *Why did many towns spring up in the Rocky Mountains?*

Gold and Silver in the West

N
W E
S

ROCKY MOUNTAINS

Leadville•

UNITED STATES

PACIFIC OCEAN

Key
- ☐ Gold
- ☐ Silver
- ▨ Gold and silver
- — State borders today

0   500 miles

0   500 kilometers

◄ *The key on this map helps you find where miners got rich in the West. For help in using the key, see page G7 of the* Map and Globe Handbook.

161

A Boom Town

Silver from places like Leadville was used to make many beautiful things. This silver cup was bought for a young child named Richard.

■ *What kind of people came to Leadville when it was known as a boom town?*

➤ *At this Leadville company, silver was melted and made into bars. Later, the silver could be made into coins, platters, cups, or other silver items.*

At the time that the two miners discovered silver, Leadville was a boom town. A **boom town** is a town that grows and becomes wealthy very quickly. News of the silver veins had spread quickly, and people poured into Leadville. Some people came hoping to find silver. Others came to earn money by working in mines owned by others. Business people came to open stores, hotels, and theaters for the new residents. In just one year, the population of Leadville rose from 300 people to 5,000 people!

Several silver veins were found near Leadville. Within one year, there were at least 12 silver mines in the area. People also mined gold, copper, and other valuable minerals. At one time, there were more than 240 mines around Leadville.

The rich residents of Leadville lived well, but not everyone made a lot of money. Many of the people who came to Leadville never found silver or any other valuable mineral. They often worked in mines for little money. ■

The Silver Runs Out

The boom in Leadville did not last. As the chart on this page shows, by 1916 Leadville had lost much of its population. One reason people left Leadville was that silver had become less valuable. Because mine owners were not making as much money selling silver as they had before, they could not pay their workers as much. The workers moved on to better paying jobs in other places.

Population of Leadville	
Year	Population
1877	300
1878	5,000
1879	30,000
1882	16,000
1916	4,500
1990	2,629

People also left Leadville because most of the silver there had been removed from the earth and there were few new discoveries. People went to other places to look for minerals or to work in other mines. Many businesses closed because their customers were gone.

Leadville did not disappear, but its days as a boom town were over. It still attracts many visitors, though. They go to Leadville to enjoy the mountains and to learn about the interesting history of western mining towns. ■

▼ *The home of Horace Tabor still stands in Leadville today. Visitors can learn about this man who made a fortune from silver mines around Leadville during the 1800s.*

■ *What caused Leadville to go from a boom town to a quiet mountain town?*

R E V I E W

1. **FOCUS** Why was Leadville known as a boom town?
2. **CONNECT** Compare the way businesses changed in Abilene, Kansas, and in Leadville, Colorado.
3. **CRITICAL THINKING** Pretend you have just arrived in Leadville and you want to be a miner. What questions would you ask the people in the town about Leadville and about mining?
4. **ACTIVITY** Pretend you are living in the East in 1879. You have heard about Leadville and its silver mines, and you have been given a free railroad ticket to go there. Will you use the ticket? Discuss your answer with your classmates.

Chapter Review

Reviewing Key Terms

blaze (p. 136)
boom town (p. 162)
mineral (p. 161)
pass (p. 148)
pioneer (p. 135)

population (p. 155)
trade center (p. 156)
wagon train (p. 149)
vein (p. 160)

A. Choose the word that best completes the sentence.

1. Pioneers went through a (pass, vein) to get across a steep mountain.
2. A (mineral, population) is usually found in the earth.
3. A (pioneer, vein) is a long strip of a mineral.
4. (Sailors, Pioneers) left settled places and moved to the wilderness.
5. After most of the silver was mined, the (population, pass) of Leadville got smaller.
6. Pioneers traveled along the Oregon Trail in (boats, wagon trains).
7. People buy and sell goods at a (wagon train, trade center).
8. Daniel Boone (closed, blazed) a trail from Virginia to Kentucky.
9. A (mineral, boom town) grows quickly.

Exploring Concepts

1. Pioneers moved to Kentucky and other places for different reasons. Copy and complete the chart to show why they moved.
2. Explain why Daniel Boone's work on the Wilderness Trail was important to the pioneers who moved west.
3. List three problems that pioneers on the Oregon Trail had.
4. How did the railroad help the town of Abilene grow?

Where pioneers moved	Why they moved there
Kentucky	
Leadville	
Oregon	
Santa Fe	

Reviewing Skills

1. Look at the map of New Mexico on the right. Using the grid, tell what area Santa Fe is in. Locate Gallup. Where is Hobbs?

2. Use the political map on pages 264–265 to name two countries south of the equator.

3. Look at the map on page 156. What direction do you travel if you go from Abilene to San Antonio?

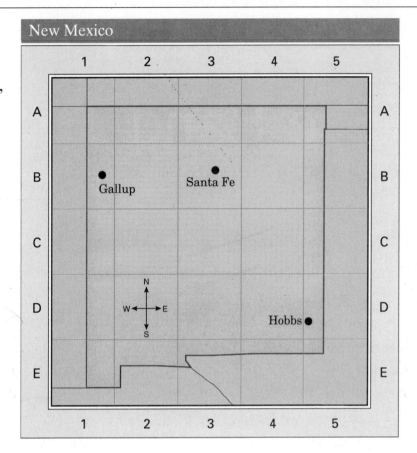

New Mexico

Using Critical Thinking

1. Sometimes a wagon broke down on the rough trails and could not be fixed. What do you think pioneers did when their wagons broke down?

2. When most of the minerals were dug up in Leadville, miners had no jobs and many people had to move away. Where do you think those people moved to? What do you think they did to earn a living?

Preparing for Citizenship

1. **ART ACTIVITY** Pretend you traveled on the Chisholm Trail. Draw a picture of something you saw on the trail. Put your picture with those of your classmates to make a long mural.

2. **COLLABORATIVE LEARNING** As a class project, do a live news report about crossing the mountains in a wagon train. Three students should be the TV reporters. The rest of the students should tell the reporters what happened to them on their trip across the mountains.

The Land Today

The United States is a land of plenty with vast
resources stretching from sea to sea. Today, its
people and cities use many of the same resources
that fed, clothed, and sheltered the American
Indians and pioneers of long ago. New ways of
farming, making products, and moving goods to
market help provide what today's growing
population needs to live. These resources, however,
cannot last forever. If we want to protect the beauty
and the resources of our country, we must care for
our land and all that it stands for.

*Kinuko Y. Craft. Watercolor and oil. Shown at Stars and Stripes
exhibit at the American Institute of Graphic Arts, San Francisco.*

Chapter 9

The Land of Plenty

Can you imagine having to grow your own food and build your own home? The Indians and pioneers had to do this to survive. Today we can depend on other people to farm the land and make building materials. Modern farms and businesses produce goods that are shipped across the country to people who need them. Our land of plenty provides all that we need to live.

Train engines can pull many rail cars at the same time. Trains carry all kinds of goods from livestock to food to automobiles.

Pittsburgh, Pennsylvania, is built near three rivers and large amounts of coal. This location helped it become a major producer of the world's steel.

The San Joaquin
(*SAN waw KEEN*) Valley
produces half of the fruits
and vegetables eaten in the
United States. This valley
also produces crops such as
the cotton shown above.

All farmers in the San Joaquin
Valley depend on water
brought in from other areas to
water their crops.

Farming in the San Joaquin Valley

Key Terms

- agriculture
- irrigation
- fertilizer

► *This machine shakes almond trees so that the nuts fall to the ground. Later, the outer layer of the almonds will be peeled away. When the nuts are sent to stores, they look like the ones above.*

P edro Cruz struggled to hold the heavy bag of almonds.
"Here, let me help you," offered his older sister Rosa.
"No, no," said Pedro. "I'm fine."

Rosa smiled, knowing that Pedro was excited. Both children were on their way to Mexico to see their uncle. Pedro wanted to give him the almonds himself.

The Cruzes had left Mexico to become citizens of the United States. At first Pedro and Rosa's parents moved from state to state picking crops. Now the family lived and worked all year on a farm near Bakersfield, California.

"There it is!" shouted Pedro, pointing to the bus that would take them from Bakersfield to Mexico. He lifted his bag of almonds high, trying to control his excitement!

Rich Soil

Workers like the Cruzes and others from many different countries harvest the crops grown near Bakersfield. One half of the fresh fruits, nuts, and vegetables grown in the United States comes from the San Joaquin Valley. This land is north of Bakersfield in central California.

Find the San Joaquin Valley on the map. Notice that the San Joaquin River runs through this land. Between which two rows of mountains does the San Joaquin Valley lie?

What makes the San Joaquin Valley so good for growing crops? The soil is good for plants. For thousands of years, streams and rivers from nearby mountains have carried rich soil down to the valley. Also, whenever rivers in the area overflowed, they added new soil to the land. Plants grow very well in this rich soil.

More than just rich soil makes the San Joaquin Valley good for **agriculture,** which is the business of farming. The valley also has a good climate in which to grow crops. The spring and fall are warm, and the summer is hot but dry. Winter is cool and wet. Temperatures rarely drop below freezing. With enough water, crops can grow all year in this climate.

Look at the lists on page 172. They show the four kinds of agricultural products that come from the San Joaquin Valley. What are these products? ■

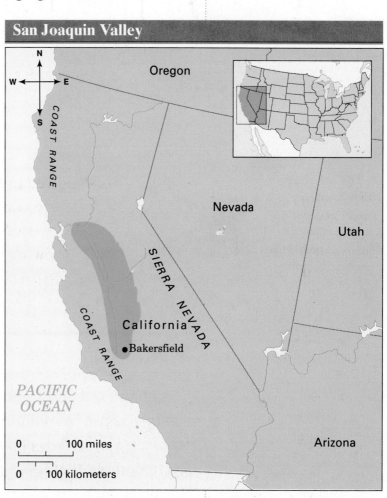

San Joaquin Valley

▲ *How far is it from one end of the San Joaquin Valley to the other? To help you use the map scale to find out, see page G5 in the* Map and Globe Handbook.

■ *What makes the San Joaquin Valley a good place for farming?*

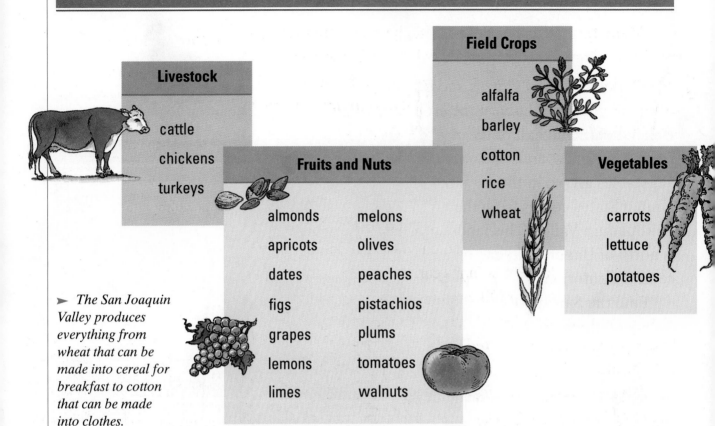

Livestock

cattle

chickens

turkeys

Fruits and Nuts

almonds	melons
apricots	olives
dates	peaches
figs	pistachios
grapes	plums
lemons	tomatoes
limes	walnuts

Field Crops

alfalfa

barley

cotton

rice

wheat

Vegetables

carrots

lettuce

potatoes

➤ *The San Joaquin Valley produces everything from wheat that can be made into cereal for breakfast to cotton that can be made into clothes.*

Across Time & Space

Irrigation is not new. Over 1,000 years ago, Indians used ditches to bring water to huge areas of land in central Arizona.

Working the Land

Are rich soil and a good climate enough to produce such big crops? No. Plants also need lots of water. However, almost half of the San Joaquin Valley is desert. You remember that few plants grow well in deserts because there is not much rain. In the summer, the most important growing season, the San Joaquin Valley gets almost no rain.

How can the farmers in the San Joaquin Valley grow crops in such a dry place? They bring in water from other parts of California. Much of this water comes from the mountains in parts of northern and eastern California. The water is carried from the mountains to the valley through pipes, ditches, or canals. Bringing water to dry land is called **irrigation.**

Rich soil, a good climate, and irrigation help grow strong plants. Farmers also help plants grow by adding fertilizers to the soil. **Fertilizers** are chemicals that feed plants and make them grow stronger and more quickly.

Many farmers spray crops with chemicals that attack weeds and insects. These chemicals help farmers keep crops healthy and free from weeds. Some chemicals that farmers use are dangerous to people and animals, so many farmers try to use those that are safest. ■

■ *How do chemicals and irrigation help farmers?*

▼ *California produces more lemons than any other state in the United States.*

Harvesting the Crops

Once crops are grown, they are harvested. Some crops are harvested by machines, which make the job quick and easy. However, large machines can damage certain crops. Therefore, some crops, like grapes, melons, and lemons, must be carefully harvested by people.

When the crops are ready, families like the Cruzes gather in an area and begin the hard job of harvesting. Thousands of farm workers are hired to pick the crops. The work is long and hard. Often, the living conditions near fields are poor.

After the crops are picked, they are packed and placed on trucks and trains. Products from the San Joaquin Valley are then sent to people throughout the country. ■

■ *How are farmers able to harvest so many crops?*

R E V I E W

1. **FOCUS** What kinds of crops grow in the San Joaquin Valley, and why do they grow so well?
2. **CONNECT** Compare how people use the land of the San Joaquin Valley with the way the Kwakiutl used the land.
3. **CRITICAL THINKING** Why do you think people in many states might worry if insects destroyed crops in the San Joaquin Valley?
4. **ACTIVITY** Look at the lists on page 172. Make your own list of products you have eaten recently that might have come from the San Joaquin Valley.

173

Getting Farm Products to Stores

Y*ou know that many different crops are grown in the San Joaquin Valley of California. You know why they grow so well there. You also know how they are harvested. But do you know how they get from a farm to stores across the country? Let's think about that a little bit.*

Here's Why

Suppose you grow almonds, tomatoes, and carrots on a farm in the San Joaquin Valley. You want to send them to cities in the United States and then to stores within the cities. You have to decide how to get your crops to the stores at the lowest cost before they spoil or rot. How will you send each of them?

Here's How

Your crops can be shipped by truck, airplane, or train. You may have to use more than one method of transportation. Use the chart below to help you decide how to ship your crops.

Comparing Ways of Moving Farm Products

Airplane
Travels faster than trucks or trains.
Costs more than trucks or trains.
Cannot carry products directly to stores.

Truck
Costs less than airplanes or trains.
Can carry products directly to stores.
Travels slower than airplanes and trains.

Train
Can carry more than airplanes or trucks.
Costs more than trucks.
Cannot carry products directly to stores.

Try It

Work with a partner. Discuss how to get your three crops to stores where you now live. Write four or more questions that you must answer before you can decide. One question might be: How much will it cost?

Apply It

Now, make your decision. Write a report that tells how you will get each of your three crops to stores. Tell why you made your decision.

Using Tables

Here's Why   You know that half of our country's fruits and vegetables come from the San Joaquin Valley in California. But what about grain crops, such as the wheat in the picture below? How much grain does California produce? How does its grain production compare with other states? One way you could find this information is to look at a table.

Here's How   A table is one way to organize number information so that it can be understood easily. Look at the table on the next page. It gives grain production from five states for the year 1986. What are the five states? Four grain crops are listed in the table. What are the four crops? Notice that each number shows how many millions of bushels are produced. One million is a large number: 1,000,000.

How can you find out how much of each crop a state produced in 1986? Find the name of the state on the left. Find the name of the crop at the top. Move your finger across the page until you come to the column for the crop you want. For example, to find how much corn was grown in California, go across the California row until you come to the corn column. The number in that space is the number of millions of bushels of corn grown in California in 1986. What is that number?

Grain Production in Millions of Bushels — 1986

States	Barley	Corn	Oats	Wheat
California	24	38	3	52
Colorado	21	99	3	96
Kansas	10	182	11	433
Ohio	1	476	12	48
Texas	2	149	8	120

Try It   Use the table to compare states. For example, if you look at the column of numbers under *wheat,* you can see that Kansas grew the most wheat of these five states. How many millions of bushels of wheat did Kansas grow? Which of these five states grew the smallest amount of wheat? How many millions of bushels of wheat did that state grow?

Apply It   Write three questions that can be answered from the table. Then work with a partner. Ask your partner to find the information in the table that answers your questions. Find the information that answers your partner's three questions.

177

Steel in Pittsburgh

Key Terms

- location
- steel mills
- industry
- services

➤ *In 1930, Thomas Hart Benton painted* Steel. *It shows the inside of a steel mill. What do you think working in a mill would sound like?*

People like to invent tall tales about their heroes. In Pittsburgh, Pennsylvania, a city famous for making steel, people tell stories about Joe Magarac. They say he was the greatest steel worker of all.

Joe Magarac was seven feet of solid steel from head to toe. He worked in a factory, mixing and pouring gallons of bubbling hot steel into big tubs. He stopped only to eat five or six meals a day. Joe stirred the red-hot steel with his bare hands. He would scoop it up and make eight long railroad rails at the same time. He'd squeeze them out from between his fingers, four from each hand.

Joe Magarac wasn't real, of course, but the tale of Joe Magarac shows that steelworkers are American heroes.

Steel City

Steel is a very strong metal. It is so strong that people use it to make cars, airplanes, trains, bridges, buildings, and all kinds of machines we use every day. The city that became best known for making steel is Pittsburgh. It is still called "Steel City."

One reason Pittsburgh became Steel City is that it is in a good location for making steel. The place where something is found is its **location.** Pittsburgh's location is good because it is close to the natural resources that people use to make steel.

The most important natural resources near Pittsburgh for steelmaking are rivers and coal. The rivers allow iron ore from Minnesota to be brought to the city's mills. Miners dig the coal from the earth nearby. Workers in Pittsburgh's **steel mills,** which are factories that make steel, use the coal and iron to make steel. The steel is then shipped out to the world by ships or by trains to make many products. ■

▼ By 1904 there were over 30 steel mills. For help in understanding a land use map like this one, see page G11 in the Map and Globe Handbook.

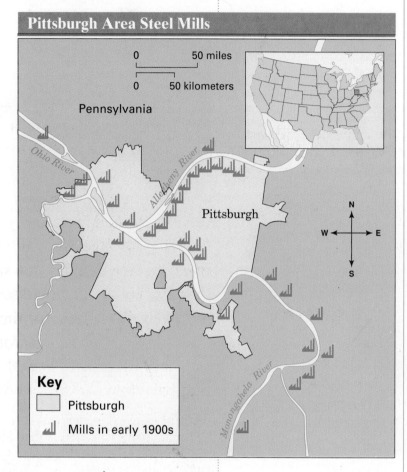

Pittsburgh Area Steel Mills

0   50 miles

0   50 kilometers

Pennsylvania

Ohio River

Allegheny River

Pittsburgh

Monongahela River

Key

Pittsburgh

Mills in early 1900s

■ How does Pittsburgh's location by three rivers help its steel industry?

Pittsburgh Grows

The steel **industry,** or business, helped make Pittsburgh great. Many people moved to Pittsburgh during the early 1900s to get jobs working in the steel industry. Because the steelworkers needed food, clothing, houses, and other goods, more people came to Pittsburgh to provide these things. For years, the city grew and grew.

This view of Pittsburgh in 1911 shows smoky air from the steel mills.

This photograph shows a clear view of Pittsburgh today. What made the difference?

What problems did the steel industry cause?

Over time, the amount of steel produced in Pittsburgh grew. With so many mills, there also came problems.

One problem was dirty air. To make steel, coal is burned. Burning coal sends off smoke. Pittsburgh used to have air filled with smoke. People didn't like living in smoky air. So in 1946, Pittsburgh began a smoke-control program. By 1960, the city had clean air again.

However, Pittsburgh faced another problem in the 1980s. Factories in other parts of the world also made steel. Other countries could make steel cheaper, so most of the steel mills in Steel City closed down. ■

New Beginnings

The people of Pittsburgh went to work to solve this problem, too. They rebuilt the machines in their mills and found new ways to make steel more cheaply. People also started new industries in Pittsburgh, such as computer

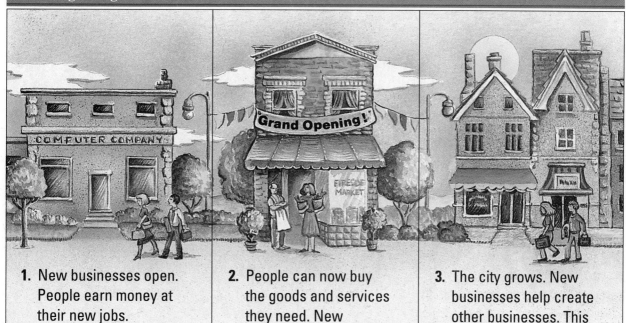

1. New businesses open. People earn money at their new jobs.

2. People can now buy the goods and services they need. New businesses providing goods and services open.

3. The city grows. New businesses help create other businesses. This brings more people to the city.

companies. Soon, more people got jobs in these new businesses.

The chart above shows how new businesses help a city grow. When new businesses open, people move nearby to work. With more people living in an area, more new businesses are needed to serve these people. **Services**— stores, schools, restaurants, gas stations—are businesses that provide people with what they need to live.

In this way, Pittsburgh has been able to keep growing. Some people think that Pittsburgh is one of the best cities in the United States in which to live. Joe Magarac would be proud of this city and how it has grown. ■

■ *In what ways has Pittsburgh kept growing?*

R E V I E W

1. **FOCUS** Why is Pittsburgh in a good location for making steel?

2. **CONNECT** How does the workplace of a steelworker in Pittsburgh differ from the workplace of a farm worker in the San Joaquin Valley?

3. **CRITICAL THINKING** Why is it important for people in a city to try to make the air clean and safe?

4. **WRITING ACTIVITY** Make a list of people you have seen working in services, such as bank tellers and secretaries. Next to it, write the businesses that they would work in, such as banks and offices.

Moving by Rail

How do trains help move goods and people across America?

Key Terms

- freight
- trade
- transportation

Travel

The railroad track is
   miles away,
And the day is loud
   with voices speaking,
Yet there isn't a train
   goes by all day
But I hear its whistle
   shrieking.

All night there isn't a
   train goes by,
Though the night is still
   for sleep and dreaming,
But I see its cinders red
   on the sky,
And hear its engine
   steaming.

My heart is warm with
   the friends I make,
And better friends I'll not
   be knowing;
Yet there isn't a train I
   wouldn't take,
No matter where it's going.

Edna St. Vincent Millay

   This poem captures a good feeling that Americans have about trains. Trains remind us of faraway places that we'd like to visit. However, trains are useful to us in ways that are practical, too.

Trains and Other Ways to Travel

In this chapter you read about farming in the San Joaquin Valley and making steel in Pittsburgh. How do products like farm goods and steel get from where they are grown or made to where people use them?

Many things people need are shipped by train. Trains that carry **freight**—that is, goods like steel and almonds—are called freight trains. Trains that carry people when they travel are called passenger trains. A passenger is a person who rides from place to place.

TWENTY-FIVE TON PASSENGER ENGINE.
LAWRENCE MACHINE SHOP

◄ *This engine got its power from steam. It burned wood or coal to boil water. The steam from the boiling water ran the engine.*

▼ *This advertisement for the St. Louis and San Francisco railroad line shows a brother and sister waiting in the station, ready for a journey by train.*

People have been using freight and passenger trains since the late 1860s, when railroads first crossed the nation from coast to coast. Trains became popular because they made traveling much faster. For example, in the 1880s a trip from Chicago to Denver in a horse-drawn buggy could take 49 days. The same trip by train took only six days, and it was a lot less bumpy!

By the 1920s, however, a new invention became popular, the automobile. Many Americans bought cars so they could travel wherever they wanted. They did not have to take trains, which went only to certain places.

■ *How did cars, trucks, buses, and airplanes affect business on the railroad?*

In the 1950s, many people started to travel by airplane because it was even faster. At that time, a person could fly in a plane from New York to Los Angeles in 18 hours. The same trip by train would take three to four days. ■

Railroads Today

Trains aren't as fast as planes and can't go everywhere that cars and trucks do, but they are still used because they cost less and can carry more. Trains move many of the goods people buy and sell. Buying and selling goods is called **trade.** Trains, ships, trucks, and airplanes help trade. These forms of **transportation,** or ways of moving things, take goods from place to place. Trains help trade between distant states in the United States.

Today, people use what is called "piggybacking" to load freight. Workers can load a box full of goods onto a train car, then stack another box, piggyback, on top of that one. This way, trains are even more useful since twice as many loads can be carried at the same time.

Ships, trains, and trucks work together to move freight. At a seaport, you might see boxes of tuna fish being unloaded from a ship. Those boxes might be put on a freight train and taken to a distant city. Then, they might be loaded on a truck to be delivered to a store near you.

On the next page, you can read more about freight trains—how they move and what they carry.

▼ *This is a freight yard. These cars are waiting to be loaded and hooked up to engines so their goods can be delivered across the country.*

A Freight Train

Modern freight trains have many cars that are used for different purposes. These cars are used to move everything from tanks of liquids to livestock to coal.

Stacked three high, this car carries up to 18 automobiles. Today, freight trains move six out of every ten new automobiles made in the United States.

Piggyback boxcars carry peaches from factories where they were canned to cities where they will be sold. A boxcar is a closed train car that carries almost anything.

An engine leads the way! It has the power to pull all the cars. This modern engine runs on diesel *(DEE zuhl)*, a form of oil. The engineer controls how fast the train goes.

185

➤ *This chart compares travel by steam train and horse before 1929 and between modern trains and airplanes. How many miles per hour can a modern train go compared to a steam-powered train?*

Travel Now and in the Past

550 miles per hour

 79 miles per hour

 21 miles per hour

3 miles per hour

 Jet airplane

 Modern train

 Steam train

 Horse and buggy

▲ *The TGV is a bullet train that travels from Paris to Lyon, France. Its name means "great speed" in French because it can travel 168 miles per hour. How much faster is that than U.S. trains?*

■ *How are railroads helping businesses today?*

Today, most Americans travel long distances by car, bus, or airplane. Compare how much faster airplanes are than trains on the chart above. Even so, people still do ride trains. In 1970, a new passenger railroad called Amtrak began. The name "Amtrak" comes from "**Am**erica," "**tra**vel," and "trac**k**." Thousands ride Amtrak for short trips, often to get to and from work.

People are inventing new kinds of trains, too. One type of new train, called a bullet train, can travel very fast. In the future, bullet trains may carry people to jobs far away from their homes. Because the trains are so fast, people will be able to get to and from work more quickly than ever. ■

R E V I E W

1. **FOCUS** How do trains help move goods and people across the United States?
2. **CONNECT** How might very fast freight trains be helpful to farmers in the San Joaquin Valley?
3. **CRITICAL THINKING** What do you think would happen to the transportation industry if someone invented a faster and cheaper way of moving goods?

4. **ACTIVITY** Work with a group. Make a model freight train out of shoeboxes. Draw on a shoebox to make it look like a certain type of train car. Load your train car with freight. Decide where it is going and then tell the class.

Trade Among Countries

Some food grown in California is sold to other states. Some of it is sold to other countries. The United States buys products from other countries, too. The buying and selling of products among countries is called international trade.

Products that a country sells to another country are called exports. Products that a country buys from another country are called imports. Exports go out. Imports come in.

The United States trades with many countries around the world. Canada is the largest trade partner of the United States. In fact, Canada and the United States sell more products to each other than do any other two countries in the world. Some of these products are shown on the map below.

International trade is important to most countries. When countries export products, they earn money. When they import products, they get things they need.

Trade Between the United States and Canada

cars and car parts

iron

aluminum

natural gas

steel

chemicals

coal

Chapter Review

Reviewing Key Terms

agriculture (p. 171)   location (p. 179)
fertilizer (p. 172)   services (p. 181)
freight (p. 183)   steel mills (p. 179)
industry (p. 179)   trade (p. 184)
irrigation (p. 172)   transportation (p. 184)

A. Write the key term for each meaning.
1. where something is found
2. businesses that perform work or provide people with what they need to live
3. the business of farming
4. materials that are carried by train, ship, truck, or plane
5. factories that make steel
6. chemicals that make plants grow strong and more quickly
7. the buying and selling of goods
8. a business that makes things to sell
9. a way of moving goods or passengers
10. the bringing of water to dry land

Exploring Concepts

A. Copy the timeline below. On your timeline, show when trains, automobiles, and airplanes began to be used a lot for travel. Draw a picture for each of the three dates.

B. Answer each question at the right with one or two sentences.

1. How can crops grow in dry areas like the San Joaquin Valley?
2. Usually a city grows and is a good place to live if there are plenty of jobs for people. Why do you think this is true?
3. Explain how trains and trucks work together to move freight.

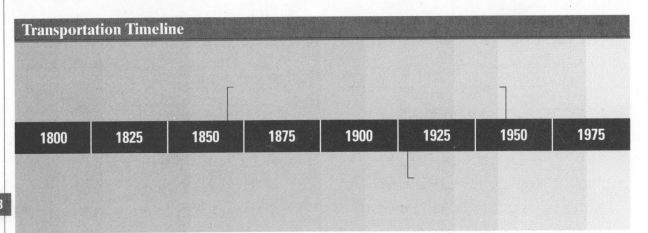

Transportation Timeline

| 1800 | 1825 | 1850 | 1875 | 1900 | 1925 | 1950 | 1975 |

Reviewing Skills

1. The table below shows the amount of land used to grow the main agricultural crops in three states. Write three sentences about what the table shows.

2. Look at the physical map on pages 270–271. What physical features are in Alabama?

State	Thousands of Acres
California	4,922
Alabama	2,267
Arizona	738

Using Critical Thinking

1. Many crops are grown in California and shipped to other states. Why do you think strawberries are not shipped the same way as cotton? How do you think strawberries and cotton are each shipped?

2. In big cities, the air is made dirty by automobile engines. What would you suggest to help solve this problem?

Preparing for Citizenship

1. COLLECTING INFORMATION Work with a partner. Prepare a scrapbook of pictures of goods made of steel. Look through old magazines to find as many pictures as you can.

2. COLLABORATIVE LEARNING Many tall-tale characters are heroes to certain industries. For example, Joe Magarac is a hero to steelmakers, John Henry is a hero to railroaders, and Paul Bunyan is a hero to lumberjacks. Make up your own classroom tall-tale hero. Brainstorm the kinds of things your hero would do. Work in small groups to write stories. Put all the stories together to make a classroom book. Vote on a title for your book. Choose someone to draw a cover.

Chapter 10

Taking Care of Our Land

Our country is a land of great natural beauty. But today we are using resources rapidly and producing large amounts of trash and poisons that harm our land. To protect the beauty of our land, many people are working to clean up our environment and to find ways to use resources wisely.

Every year, more and more people in the United States are saving old newspapers and other kinds of trash that can be used again or made into something new.

These stacks of old boxes will be made into new cardboard items and used again. That means fewer trees will be cut down to make new cardboard.

If we all work together to clean up our resources, more areas can become as clean and beautiful as this protected land in one of our many national parks.

Every day we use clean water in our homes. If we try to use less water each time, we are helping to save our clean water resources.

A tree stump is a home to insects, a scratching post for bears, and a place where people can rest. So who really owns the tree stump? Read a story that answers this question about the land.

ONCE THERE WAS A TREE

Written by Natalia Romanova

Adapted by Anne Schwartz

Illustrated by Gennady Spirin

Once there was a tree. It had grown for many years and now it was growing old.

Dark clouds swept across the sky. Rain fell, thunder roared, and a lightning bolt split the tree in two.

A woodsman came upon the broken tree and sawed it down so that only the stump remained. Soon a bark beetle with long feelers settled in. The beetle loved the stump and laid her eggs under its bark.

The eggs hatched and tiny maggots emerged. All summer long they gnawed tunnels in the bark. Winter came and they slept. When they awoke in the spring with long feelers of their own, it was time to fly away.

But the tree stump was not deserted for long. With all the entrances and exits the maggots had made, here was the perfect place for ants to live. One ant brought a leaf, another a twig, and another a grain of sand. They cleared out the tunnels and made the stump their home. A bear approached the tree stump, sniffed at it, and sharpened her claws on the bark. The stump was hers, like everything else around. Even the ants in the stump were hers, and no other bear would dare disturb them.

A titmouse flew down and landed on the stump.
She spotted an ant dragging a caterpillar and pecked
at it. Now the caterpillar was hers. The ants
were hers, too, and so was the tree stump.
No other birds would come near.

One rainy day a frog found shelter
in a hole in the tree stump. Time and
weather had dug these holes, which
would protect others who also
passed by.

The warm sun dried the tree stump,
and soon a new occupant had moved in—
an earwig. Liking nothing better than the shade,
he crept under the bark to sleep.

A man was walking in the woods and saw the tree stump. He sat down on it to rest, and now the tree stump was his.

The man thought he owned the forest—and the earth—so why not the tree stump?

But who really owns the tree stump? The bark beetle that gnaws tunnels inside it? The ants that travel through the tunnels? The earwig that sleeps under its bark? Or the bear that uses it to sharpen her claws?

Does it belong to the titmouse that flies down upon it? The frog that finds shelter in one of its holes? Or the man who believes he owns the forest?

Maybe the tree stump belongs to all—the beetle and the ants, the bear and the titmouse, the frog, the earwig, and even the man. All must live together.

Meanwhile the tree stump gets older and older. The sun warms it; the rain cools it. Soon it begins to rot. Night comes, and the forest is cast in moonlight. What remains of the tree stump glows in the dark.

Now the tree stump is gone. A new tree has grown in its place. A titmouse is perched in its branches—it is her tree. An ant crawls up high—on her tree. A bear lumbers by and sharpens his claws on the bark. A man lies down to rest in its shade. The tree belongs to all, because it grows from the earth that is home for all.

Saving Our Land

THINKING FOCUS

How can we conserve our natural resources?

Key Terms

- topsoil
- conservation
- environment

➤ *This picture shows a dust storm that took place in southeastern Colorado, in 1937.*

"Mother, what is that?" asks Ellie, pointing to a dark cloud moving toward the house.

"It's a dust storm!" shouts Mother. "Quick! Shut the door!"

Ellie bolts the door and helps her mother close the windows. Just as the last one is latched, the storm hits.

The afternoon becomes dark as dust blocks the sun. Outside, it is almost impossible to see or breathe. Even inside the small farmhouse, dust begins to form layers.

The next morning, all is quiet. Ellie opens the door a crack and looks outside. Dust still falls slowly from the sky. A layer of dust covers the barn, the fence, and even the clothesline. It lies like a thick blanket over the land.

The Need to Protect Land

In the 1930s, strong winds swept across much of the Great Plains. The winds picked up soil from the dry earth, creating huge clouds of dust. The map shows where these storms were. This area was known as the Dust Bowl.

Dust storms wear away the top layer of soil, called **topsoil.** These storms usually happen when land is very dry and when there are not enough plants to hold topsoil in place. Dusty, loose soil can be swept away by strong winds.

Land and water are important natural resources. Events like the storms that took place in the Dust Bowl called attention to the need to conserve these resources.

The Dust Bowl

Key
- Area of the Dust Bowl
- Areas damaged by later dust storms

Conservation Efforts

When the early settlers spread out across the United States, they were amazed by the richness of the land. They saw forests that spread out for miles and miles. The prairies they traveled seemed to be endless.

Today, however, we know that our resources are not endless and that we need to protect them. Protecting our natural resources is called **conservation.**

There are many different ways of protecting our resources. Over a hundred years ago, the leaders of our country began to conserve some wilderness areas. Some of these are called national parks. The land there is protected from changes. On the next pages, you will read about some of these national parks. ■

▲ *The darker orange area on the map shows the Dust Bowl. Why do you think it was called a bowl?*

■ *Why do we need to protect our land?*

199

National Parks

In 1872, the United States government began to set aside certain wilderness areas that would not be changed by people. Since plant and animal life in these areas is protected, visitors can enjoy the land's natural beauty.

Planning a vacation? This map shows national parks across the United States. Use it to find the three national parks pictured on these two pages. Which of these three parks is nearest you?

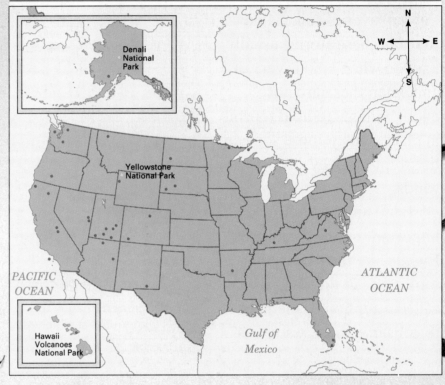

U.S. National Parks

Denali National Park

Yellowstone National Park

PACIFIC OCEAN

Hawaii Volcanoes National Park

ATLANTIC OCEAN

Gulf of Mexico

The first national park in the United States was Yellowstone National Park in Wyoming, Idaho, and Montana. It has thousands of hot springs. Some springs are so hot the water boils. Others shoot water and steam from deep in the ground a hundred feet into the air. These fountains of hot water are called geysers *(GY zuhrz)*.

The highest peak in North America, Mount McKinley, stands in Denali National Park in Alaska. There are also many other mountains in the park. Moose, deer, and other wildlife roam the land there.

Red-hot lava spouts from Kilauea *(kee low AY uh)*. It is a volcano in Hawaii Volcanoes National Park.

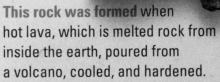

This rock was formed when hot lava, which is melted rock from inside the earth, poured from a volcano, cooled, and hardened.

Conserving Our Resources

We must conserve all of our natural resources. For example, we need rich topsoil to grow food for people and livestock. Plants grow very well in areas with rich topsoil. That is why farmers are so concerned with soil conservation. Look at the chart below to learn ways that farmers conserve topsoil on farmland.

Four Ways That Farmers Conserve Soil

Farmers plant rows of trees, called windbreaks, along the edge of fields. The trees slow the wind so it doesn't cause dust storms.

Farmers plow across hills so that plowed soil forms ridges. The ridges catch the water so it doesn't run downhill and erode the soil.

Farmers cut off a crop and leave the lower part of the plants behind. The roots of these plants hold the soil in place so that rain cannot wash it away.

Farmers plant crops in strips. A crop that holds water well is placed next to a crop that does not. The plants that hold water keep the water from washing soil away.

The conservation of our forests is also important. Forests give us wood for lumber, paper, and much more. They also provide homes for many animals. We can help conserve forests by limiting how many trees are cut. We can also plant new trees where they have been cut down.

You can help conserve forests by using paper wisely. Use paper plates and cups only when you have to. Write on both sides of a piece of notebook paper before throwing it away.

Water is another important resource. People, plants, and animals need water to live. What can you do to conserve water? Try not to waste it. Take shorter showers and turn off the water while you brush your teeth.

Conserving soil, trees, and water helps to create a healthy environment. All the things that surround us — air, water, and land— are a part of our **environment.** We must do more than conserve our natural resources. We must also try to clean those resources that have become too dirty to use. In the next lesson, you will read about what you can do to keep our environment clean. ■

■ *List three natural resources and tell what people can do to conserve them.*

◄ *National forests are areas that are taken care of by the United States government. Trees in national forests can be cut down, but the government makes sure that new trees are planted to replace them.*

R E V I E W

1. **FOCUS** How can we conserve our natural resources?
2. **CONNECT** How does farming in the San Joaquin Valley depend on natural resources?
3. **CRITICAL THINKING** How would your life be different if the place where you live had very little water?

4. **ACTIVITY** Work with a partner. List some of the kinds of plants that need topsoil. Then make a list of the things that can be made from these plants. Finally, tell why topsoil is important.

Protecting Our Resources

THINKING
FOCUS

*Why is it important to
lower the amount of
pollution?*

Key Terms

- pollution
- waste

➤ *This animal rescue worker
is holding a sea otter that was
once covered with oil.*

In the spring of 1989, rescue teams rushed to Alaska. A ship had accidentally spilled millions of gallons of oil into the ocean, harming the plant and animal life there.

Many rescue workers were worried about sea otters. Otters have thick fur that keeps them warm in cold water. When their fur gets oily, however, otters can no longer stay warm. Otters also lick their fur clean. The oil that otters were swallowing was poisoning them.

First, the workers had to catch the otters. Then they washed off the oil with dish detergent. The teams worked hard to save the otters. Many otters died, but thanks to the workers, many healthy otters returned to the sea.

Pollution

In the last lesson, you read about conserving our natural resources. An important part of conservation is keeping our environment clean. Oil spills like the one in Alaska cause pollution. When harmful chemicals make the air, water, or soil unhealthy or poisonous, it is called **pollution.** Besides accidental oil spills, there are other types of pollution that happen every day.

Cars and factories create air pollution. When car engines burn gasoline, they give off poisons that make the air dirty. Some of the smoke that comes from factories also pollutes the air. This type of pollution is harmful to plants and animals, including people.

Air pollution makes the air hard to breathe. It can hurt our lungs and sting our eyes. Sometimes pollution can weaken or kill trees and other plants. It can even wear away the stone in buildings. If this pollution gets into the water of lakes and streams, it can harm animal and plant life there.

How Do We Know?

In large cities, some people's jobs are to test the air each day. If it is very polluted, newspapers and radio and television stations tell people about the unhealthy air. Children, older people, and people with breathing problems must be careful when air is very polluted.

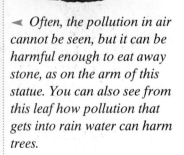

◄ *Often, the pollution in air cannot be seen, but it can be harmful enough to eat away stone, as on the arm of this statue. You can also see from this leaf how pollution that gets into rain water can harm trees.*

Other kinds of water pollution can be caused by communities or factories dumping waste into oceans, rivers, and lakes. **Waste** includes things we don't need anymore and want to throw away, such as garbage and harmful chemicals. Water pollution can kill plant and animal life and can make drinking water unsafe.

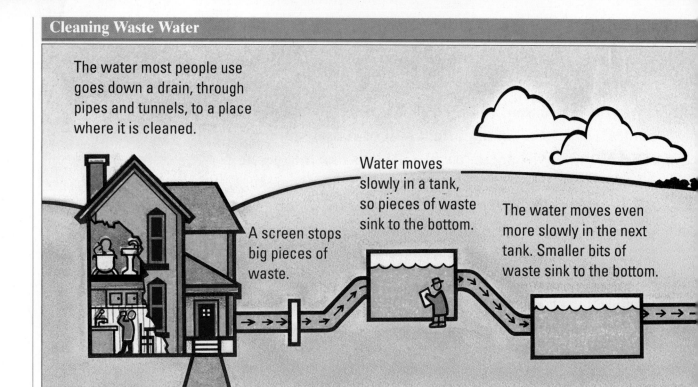

The water most people use goes down a drain, through pipes and tunnels, to a place where it is cleaned.

Water moves slowly in a tank, so pieces of waste sink to the bottom.

A screen stops big pieces of waste.

The water moves even more slowly in the next tank. Smaller bits of waste sink to the bottom.

People use water for many things, for cooking, washing, or drinking. No matter what we use it for, it becomes waste water and has to be cleaned before we can reuse it in our homes. Notice the pipe on the diagram above that carries waste water from a house. Some communities do not clean their waste. They may empty waste water directly into lakes, rivers, or the ocean.

Waste can also pollute the soil. If people don't get rid of home or factory wastes properly, the harmful chemicals can leak into the ground and poison our soil. ■

■ What are some of the causes of pollution?

What We Can Do

The problems of air, water, and soil pollution are not easy to solve. Many people are trying to find answers.

Scientists are working on ways to cut back air pollution. They are inventing new car engines and new types of fuel that produce cleaner air.

There are ways for factories to make less air pollution. Some harmful materials can be replaced with less harmful ones. Factories that must use dangerous materials can use filters. Filters are like nets. They can catch the poisons before they get into the air. ■

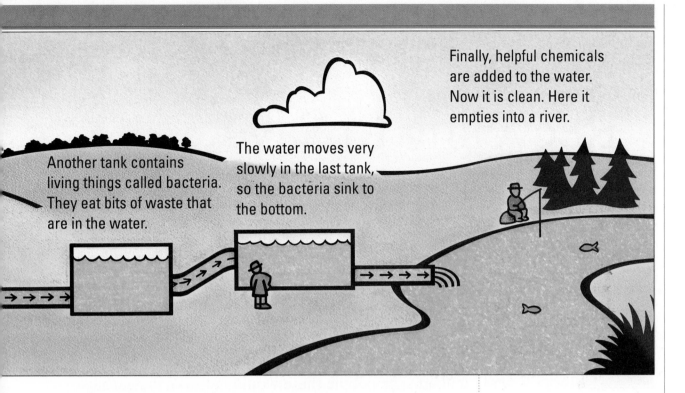

Another tank contains living things called bacteria. They eat bits of waste that are in the water.

The water moves very slowly in the last tank, so the bacteria sink to the bottom.

Finally, helpful chemicals are added to the water. Now it is clean. Here it empties into a river.

Communities and factories can also help stop water pollution. They can stop pouring waste water into lakes, rivers, and oceans. As the diagram shows, waste water needs to be cleaned before it is put back into nature, just as it is cleaned before we can use it again at home.

Dangerous wastes from communities and factories don't have to be dumped on the ground. They can be destroyed, made harmless, or cleaned and used again. If they must be stored underground, they can be sealed in special boxes, so they don't leak into the soil.

You can help solve pollution problems, too. You can encourage your family to walk instead of using the car when it is possible. You may choose to write to people who make laws and tell them to work for clean air and water. What other ways can you think of? ■

■ *What can we do to cut down on soil, water, and air pollution?*

REVIEW

1. **FOCUS** Why is it important to lower the amount of pollution?
2. **CONNECT** Some problems can be caused by chemicals used in farming and by smoke from steel mills. What natural resources can these pollute?
3. **CRITICAL THINKING** Think of three ways that you can get people more interested in pollution.
4. **ACTIVITY** Make posters that show ways people can lower pollution. Display them for others to see.

Recycling to Save Our Resources

Key Terms

- decompose
- recycling

In March of 1987, this boat left New York. It was taking a load of garbage to North Carolina. When the boat arrived in North Carolina, however, it was not allowed to unload. The people there would not take the garbage.

The boat left North Carolina and went to ports in other states and in other countries to try to get rid of its load. The people in these places would not take the garbage either. Finally, after months of traveling from place to place, the boat returned to New York where the garbage was burned.

The Garbage Problem

Some people say that by the year 2000, each person in the United States will throw away about six pounds of garbage a day. Why will we have so much garbage? Half of our garbage is packages that hold items we buy and use.

Think about your garbage. Do you throw away a lot of packages? Americans expect products they buy to be well wrapped. Toothpaste, for example, comes in a plastic tube *and* a cardboard container. Crackers are wrapped in plastic *and* put in a cardboard box. When we use the products, we throw the packages away. We must have a place to put this garbage.

Some of our packages harm the environment because they **decompose,** or rot, very slowly. Plastic, metal, and glass, for example, take many years to decompose. People are trying to find ways of solving the problem. ■

■ *What makes up much of our garbage?*

◄ *These children are doing their part to help the environment. What can you and your friends do?*

Recycling

We throw away so much garbage that we are running out of places to dump it all. How can we throw away less garbage? One way is to turn it into something new that can be used again. This is called **recycling.**

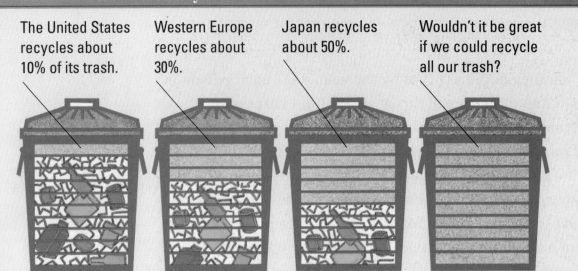

The United States recycles about 10% of its trash.

Western Europe recycles about 30%.

Japan recycles about 50%.

Wouldn't it be great if we could recycle all our trash?

▲ *What are some ways to encourage people in the United States to recycle their garbage?*

■ *Why is recycling important?*

▼ *This chart shows that much of the waste in U.S. homes is made up of materials that can be recycled.*

Some garbage can be recycled into things we need. Old newspapers can be made into new paper or building materials. Plastic bottles can be made into other plastic products. Glass can be made into new glass. Aluminum cans can be made into new cans. These materials and others can be recycled and used again. Recycling helps us make less garbage. ■

You Can Help

Protecting the environment is a big job, but we can all do our part. Planning ahead is a good way to start. We can carefully think about what products to buy before we buy them. This will help us plan what to do with our garbage.

Many communities have recycling centers. Is there a center where you live? If so, can you think of ways to recycle the garbage from your own home? Maybe you could start by sorting your garbage. You could separate cans, plastic, paper, and glass from the rest of your family's garbage. Then take these items to the recycling center. From there, your garbage will be shipped to places where it can be made into new products.

Waste in U.S. Homes

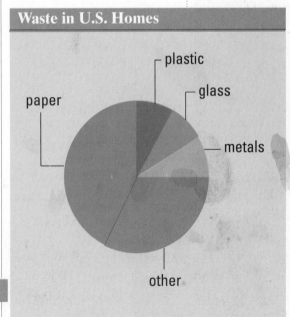

plastic

glass

paper

metals

other

◄ Recycling centers like this one help us to use much of our trash again.

Does your school have a recycling program? If not, can you think of ways to get one started?

Many communities also have programs to make it easy for people to recycle. For example, in some areas people are given containers in which to place newspapers, plastics, and glass. Then on certain days, trucks pick up these items at people's homes.

If you live in an area that does not have a recycling program or recycling centers, there is still something you can do to help protect our natural resources. You may want to write letters to lawmakers and ask them to try to bring recycling centers to your area. You can ask your teacher to give you the names and addresses of the people who make the laws where you live.

Each year, more and more people are becoming interested in recycling. We all must work together to conserve our resources. ■

Across Time & Space

Pioneers recycled things that many of us throw away today. For example, they made old clothing into quilts and used cooking grease to make soap or medicine.

■ How can people help solve our trash problem?

R E V I E W

1. **FOCUS** How does recycling help to make our garbage problem smaller?

2. **CONNECT** How can conservation and recycling help us protect our forest land?

3. **CRITICAL THINKING** Why is it important that people start to recycle their garbage now?

4. **ACTIVITY** Make something useful from an empty package. For example, a juice can can be made into a pencil holder. Share your idea with friends.

211

Recycling Products

Here's Why You have seen how important recycling is to our environment. Recycling helps to save our natural resources. It also helps solve the problem of getting rid of trash.

Suppose you wanted to recycle products. Where would you start?

Here's How You could start by setting up a recycling center in your school or classroom. Your class can work together on the project.

First, decide on the products you are going to recycle. Choose paper, glass, aluminum, plastics, or any combination of products. Then divide your class into small groups. Each group can collect one kind of trash.

Find containers for each type of trash you plan to recycle. If you use plastic bags, be sure they are the kind that can be recycled. The box they come in will tell you if they can be recycled.

You might want to have a theme for your recycling center. Work in groups to draw pictures and make up names for "monsters" that might eat a particular type of waste. For example, children in Toledo, Ohio, feed their glass bottles into the mouth of "Chewbottle." Aluminum cans go into a crusher named "Jaws."

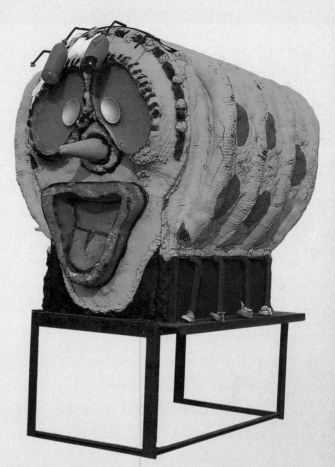

Try It   Each day for a week, pick up trash around your school. Put each kind of trash into its recycling container. Do not mix different kinds of trash in one container. At the end of the week, arrange to have the trash taken to a community recycling center.

Apply It   Set up a recycling center in your home. Work with your family to recycle paper, cans, and other trash. Put each kind of trash in its own container. Help your family take the trash to a community recycling center.

Chapter Review

Reviewing Key Terms

conservation (p. 199) recycling (p.209)
decompose (p. 209) topsoil (p. 199)
environment (p. 203) waste (p. 205)
pollution (p. 205)

A. Write the key term that best completes each sentence.

1. Harmful chemicals and waste in the air, water, or soil cause _____.
2. Some plastic bags may hurt our environment because they do not _____ easily.
3. _____ is blown away in a windstorm when there are no plants to hold it in place.
4. Turning garbage into something that can be used again is called _____.
5. _____ is taking good care of our natural resources.
6. Trash, garbage, and things we often throw away are _____.
7. Our _____ is the air, water, and land around us.

Exploring Concepts

A. The chart below shows some of the many things we throw away. Copy the chart. In the second column, list one or more ways that each thing can be recycled. Try to think of some ideas of your own for ways to recycle.

B. Write one or two sentences to answer each question.

1. What can farmers do to keep from losing topsoil in dust storms?
2. What are some of the things that cause pollution?

Things we throw away	Ways to recycle
Plastic forks	
Metal cans	
Newspapers	
Glass jars	

Reviewing Skills

1. Sometimes you outgrow your clothes and they no longer fit. For a group project, bring some of your outgrown clothes to school. Sort and fold the clothes. Then put them in paper bags. Give your clothes to a group or an organization that gives clothing to people who need it.

2. Write two "If . . . then" statements that tell what might happen if more people learn about the problems of pollution.

Using Critical Thinking

1. What might happen in our cities if we do not try to reduce air pollution?

2. Farmers use chemicals to make crops grow better and to kill insects that eat plants. Do you think the use of such chemicals is good or bad? Why?

3. If we had no national parks, what would our country be like?

Preparing for Citizenship

1. **ART ACTIVITY** Work in small groups. Use waste materials such as plastics, packaging, newspaper, and string to make a model of a national park.

2. **COLLABORATIVE LEARNING** Have a class trial for someone who is accused of throwing trash in the park. Choose a judge, twelve jury members, witnesses, and the person who is accused of the crime. Have the witnesses tell the judge why they think the person is innocent or guilty. Then, the jury should meet and decide if the accused person is innocent or guilty. If the accused person is guilty, the jury should decide what the punishment will be.

Chapter 11

Governing Our Land

Imagine your own community without a government. Who would put up traffic lights? Who would run the schools? Our cities, states, and nation all need a government. You can help your government by being a good citizen. That means obeying the law and helping others where you live.

In big cities and small towns, leaders meet inside city halls and town halls. There, they plan the best ways to take care of their communities.

Citizens of the United States choose their leaders. Some people wear a button to show their choice for President. In 1992, Americans chose Bill Clinton (above) as their President.

Today, we still follow the Constitution's plan for governing our land.

Firefighters and other government workers make their community a better place to live.

If people work together, they can solve problems in their community.

Community Government

Key Terms

- government
- mayor
- council
- taxes

➤ *The playground at Lake Waterford Park needed many repairs.*

Pat Brescia *(BRESH ya)* looked at the playground in Lake Waterford Park. No one ever played there. Pat knew the reason. The swings and slides were broken.

"Why can't someone fix the playground?" Pat asked.

"It will take a lot of money to fix the old playground. The government may not have the money to buy new slides," his father answered.

"There must be a way to get a new playground," Pat said. "Who could we ask?"

His father said, "Getting a new playground is not that easy. We have to tell the government what is wrong. The government is in charge of the playground."

"Who's the government?" Pat asked. "Why is it in charge?"

How Community Government Works

Every community and city has a **government** chosen by the people. The government makes laws that the people must follow. The government decides what to do with the town's land. It decides how much money to spend taking care of the town. It even plans new playgrounds. The government takes care of a community.

The Town Meeting

A town meeting is one kind of government. Anyone in the town can come to a town meeting. At the meeting, the adults plan ways to make their town better. They choose leaders who will run the town for the next year. At such a meeting, someone like Mr. Brescia could tell what's wrong with the playground.

▼ *At this town meeting, people make important decisions about the future of their community.*

Mayor and Council

Most cities are governed by a mayor and a council. A **mayor** is the leader of a town or city. To lead the community, the mayor must work with the council. A **council** is a group of people who make laws and plans for the town. The people of the town or city choose the council. In some places the people choose the mayor. In other towns the council chooses the mayor.

The mayor and the council work together to make the city better. They decide how much money the city government can spend. They decide how many workers the city government can hire. ■

■ *What are two different kinds of community government?*

▲ *The city of Pittsburgh, Pennsylvania, is led by a mayor (above) and a city council.*

➤ *The mayor and council members work together to make plans and pass laws that will improve their town.*

A Mayor–Council Government

The voters elect the mayor and city council.

The mayor leads the city government.

The city council makes laws.

Serving the Community

Government has an important job. Government leaders plan services, or ways of helping people in the community. People in a town need good roads, schools, and parks. These are kinds of services. Building a new playground is a service, too.

Payment for Services

The services a community uses cost money. The people who live in a community and who use the services have to pay for such services. The people pay **taxes,** by paying money to the government.

People pay different kinds of taxes. Workers pay a tax on the money they earn. People also pay a tax each year on the land and buildings they own. When people buy certain items in a store, they may pay a tax. Most of the money used to pay for city services comes from taxes on land and buildings.

▼ *Taxes come from many sources. Taxes pay for the services your government provides.*

Paying Taxes to the Government

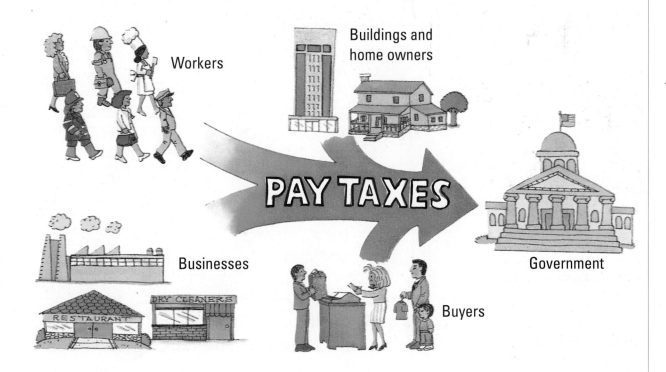

Workers

Buildings and home owners

PAY TAXES

Government

Businesses

Buyers

Services

Leaders set up departments, or offices and groups of workers, to give services to people. One department is in charge of the fire fighters. Another runs the police. Another department takes care of the schools. Some workers make sure city buses run. Often, a city will have one department in charge of parks.

Leaders have to make choices about how to spend tax money. A city may not have money to buy new buses. Instead, the city might fix the old buses. A city may not have money to repair all roads. Then, only busy roads will be fixed. ∎

Paying for Government Services

Government

PAYS FOR

Library

Street lights

Parks

Schools

Safety

Government's services make our towns and cities good places to live. Your lives would be very different without these services.

Solving a Community Problem

Pat's community did not have extra money to build a new playground in the park. Pat and his father had an idea.

They talked to the people at the Department of Parks. The people had been thinking about how to fix the playground. They agreed on a plan with Pat and his father.

The people in the neighborhood would do the work. They would help raise money. Everyone who lived near the park would help build a new playground.

The department workers helped the people find Ms. Wagner, an architect. An architect draws the plans for a building or park. The children told Ms. Wagner the kind of playground they wanted. Ms. Wagner drew all the plans.

Next, the government gave some tax money for swings and slides. Other people gave money, too. Pat's family and neighbors raised the rest of the money. They washed cars. They collected pennies. They sold t-shirts.

Finally the land was cleared. Then the swings were put up. After five days, the playground was finished. Everyone had a party to open the playground. The park was special, because government leaders and people in the community had built it together. ■

■ *How can government leaders and people in the community solve problems?*

▼ *The people who lived near Lake Waterford Park took part in planning, building, and celebrating the new playground.*

NEW PLAYGROUND TO BE CONSTRUCTED ON APRIL 26–30
WE NEED YOUR HELP!
INFO AT OFFICE

THANK YOU WORKERS!!

REVIEW

1. **FOCUS** What is community government?
2. **CONNECT** How can Pat and his friends take care of their new playground?
3. **CRITICAL THINKING** Think about the services in your community. Try to think of a service you would like your community to have. How could you work with adults to get it?
4. **ACTIVITY** Which form of government does your town have, a town meeting or a mayor-council form? See if an adult can help you find out.

A Community's Services

Does a crossing guard help you on your way to school? Do you go to the library? If so, you are using your community's services. You may not know about some services your community offers. How can you find out about them?

Get Ready Make a list of services with your class. Here's how you can get ideas for your list.

Look up the name of your town or city in the phone book. Under the town's name you'll see names of departments like the water plant, library, museum, or park district. Most of these offer services. Put them on your class list.

Ask your teacher and other adults for more names of services. Put these on the list as well.

Then form groups. Each group can learn about one service.

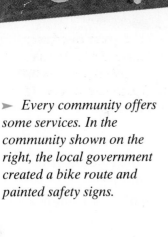

► *Every community offers some services. In the community shown on the right, the local government created a bike route and painted safety signs.*

Find Out   Meet with your group. Decide how you will learn about this service. You can write letters to the department in charge of it. You can call and ask questions. You can visit places like the water plant or library. Collect pictures and pamphlets about the service. Remember the people who help you. When you finish, send them thank-you letters.

Move Ahead   In your group collect all of the information about your service. Then give a report. Explain the service to your class. Tell how the service helps your community. Tell how leaders help. If you can, show pictures and pamphlets about your service.

Explore Some More   Make a poster that tells the class about your service. For example, show how to call the fire department for first aid. Or, you might ask a speaker to come to your class. A worker from the animal shelter could tell how to adopt a pet. Your class might want to put all the information in a community services booklet.

To learn more about your community services, look in pamphlets like these.

You can ask emergency workers to explain to you how to call the police or fire department in your community.

Leaders and Laws

THINKING FOCUS

How do leaders and laws help communities?

Key Terms

- election
- law

➤ *You and your friends could start a club to help protect animals like the hippo (right). Sometimes club members wear club t-shirts (below).*

T he sign in front of the hippo's pool read, "Help Take Care of Me." The third-grade class was visiting the zoo. They had seen many signs like the one in front of the hippo. The zoo asked people for money to help care for an animal. The class decided they wanted to help.

"What a good idea!" the teacher said. "Which animal will you choose? How will you raise the money? Who will write to the zoo?"

The children all had different answers. Everyone talked at once. Then Alma said, "We need to have a person in charge. We should pick a leader."

Choosing Our Leaders

The children picked their leader in the same way people pick government leaders. They had an **election**. They chose the leader by voting. People in towns and cities also vote for their mayor and council members.

In the third-grade class, the children voted by closing their eyes and raising their hands. In government elections, people vote by choosing their leader from a list of names.

Before the election, those who want to be leaders promise voters they will do a good job. Adults use the newspapers, television, and radio to tell people about themselves.

In many towns and cities special meetings are held before an election. Those who want to be elected are the speakers. They explain why they would be good leaders. They tell how they would solve problems. People listen to the speakers. People think about what the speakers say, then decide for whom to vote.

▲ Meetings give candidates a chance to explain their ideas. Voters can listen and decide which candidate they support.

◀ When people vote, no one sees their choices.

227

Finally, election day comes. People go inside a booth to vote. There, no one can see their choices. Then the votes are counted. The person who gets the most votes wins the election. ■

Passing a Law

After an election, the leaders go to work. One of their jobs is to make laws. A **law** is a rule that everyone must follow. A town or city has many laws. Some laws are:

- Do not litter.
- Do not drive faster than the speed limit.
- Do not dump dangerous materials in the river.

Sometimes people ask their leaders to make new laws. Suppose the people in a town want a law about stop signs. Many parents think a street near the school is not safe. They would like the town to make a law. The new law would say that the city must put stop signs on busy streets near the school. The parents ask their council member to try to get the new law passed.

How Do We Know?

You can find out about the laws bicycle riders must follow in your town by calling your city hall or local police station. Many communities have a list of bike laws you can get.

▼ *The council members and the mayor work together to turn a bill into a law.*

How a City Council Passes a Law

A council member suggests a bill to the city council.

The council members debate.

First, the council member suggests the bill to the council. A bill is what a law is called before it is passed. Council members vote to make the bill into a law. This bill says, "If more than ten children cross a street on the way to Baker School, a stop sign will be put up."

Some council members do not want the bill. They think putting up stop signs will cost too much money. They have a debate with the members who want the new law. During a debate, members tell why they are for or against the bill.

After the debate, the council members vote. More council members vote "yes" than "no," and the bill is passed. Now the bill is sent to the mayor. The mayor likes it. The mayor signs the bill and then it becomes a law. The town must put up new stop signs on the busy streets near the school. ■

■ *What is a law? How does a council pass a law?*

The council members vote.

The mayor signs a bill. It is now a law.

Following the Law

▼ *The sign below warns drivers to watch for school children crossing a street.*

Laws protect us. When we obey laws, we help keep our towns and cities safe. For example, traffic laws protect people driving cars and people walking on sidewalks. Here are some traffic laws we obey:

- Stop at a red light.
- Cross a street between the white lines.
- Wear a seat belt.

Bicycle riders also have laws to obey. Your town may have laws like these:

- Use a light at night.
- Wear a helmet if you ride on the street.
- Signal when you turn.

▼ *Police officers help children learn about community laws.*

People who don't obey the laws may get a ticket from the police. If you get a ticket, you have to pay a fine, or money, to the government. Drivers who speed get tickets. In some states, parents of children who do not wear seat belts get a ticket. If you break a bicycle rule, you may get a ticket as well.

Everyone should know the laws where they live and take care to follow the laws every day. When people follow the laws, they help keep their towns safe places to live and work. ■

■ *Why do communities pass laws?*

R E V I E W

1. **FOCUS** How do leaders and laws help communities?

2. **CONNECT** Imagine you are a neighbor of Pat's father from Lesson 1. You want him to become a council member. In a sentence, tell why he would be a good leader.

3. **CRITICAL THINKING** Why do council members debate a bill?

4. **WRITING ACTIVITY** Make a poster that lists some of the rules at your school. Write a reason why students should follow each rule.

Different Points of View

Here's Why   Have you ever had to share your ideas with others? Maybe you helped plan a class project, for example. Your ideas are your point of view. You can learn much more, though, if you listen to what others say, too. That way, the group can put together all the best ideas. Even government leaders, lawmakers, and judges must listen to others.

Here's How   Following these three steps will help you understand what others are saying.

1. *Listen* to everything your classmates say. If you don't listen carefully, you may make a mistake about their ideas.

2. *Ask questions* about any part you don't understand. If your classmate's idea is unclear, ask a question that might help the classmate explain it better.

3. *Think* about what the other person is saying. If you understand their point of view, you may be able to explain your own ideas more clearly.

Try It   Work with a partner. Discuss a school rule. One of you should agree with the rule. The other should disagree. Make sure you both understand each other's ideas.

Apply It   Talk with your family about a subject. Tell your family how to listen to others' points of view before you begin.

231

State and National Government

Key Terms

- capital
- constitution
- President
- Congress

➤ *Visitors can see the state
seal of Mississippi (above)
inside the State Capitol
building in Mississippi (right).*

The third-graders looked in wonder at the golden eagle shining in the sun. The eagle gleamed atop the dome of a tall building.

The children were on a field trip to the city of Jackson, Mississippi. The state's government meets in Jackson. The children came to see their state government at work.

The teacher said that the building was built in 1903. Inside, the class stepped into a large room. Mississippi's lawmakers were voting on a new law.

After the tour, the class got back on the bus. Next, they visited the Jackson Zoological Park. Later they went to the Jackson State Forestry Museum.

The State Capital of Mississippi

Jackson is the capital of Mississippi. A **capital** is the city where government leaders meet to plan and carry out government business.

Like other state capitals, Jackson has many government buildings. Visitors can see courthouses and tour a library that holds important papers from Mississippi's past.

Many visitors enjoy touring Jackson's Old Capitol building. There they can see the state historical museum. Visitors enjoy going to the art museum, the science museum, and Jackson's many parks. ■

Across Time & Space

In 1792, a fur trader set up a trading post in what is now Jackson. In 1821, state lawmakers chose the town as their capital. They named it after Andrew Jackson, who became the seventh President of the United States.

■ Why does a state need a capital?

◄ The map shows some of the places you can visit on a trip to Jackson, Mississippi.

Downtown Jackson, Mississippi

N
W E
S

High
To I-55
Hamilton
■5
College
Madison
Monroe
Griffith
Mississippi
West
Yazoo
Greymont
Lamar
Congress
President
Jefferson
Amite
■6
E. Capitol
State
Farish
■7 ■4
Pearl
■1
Pascagoula
To I-55
■2 ■3
Tombigbee

1 City Hall
2 Planetarium
3 Museum of Art
4 Natural Science Museum
5 State Capitol Building
6 State Fairgrounds
7 Old Capitol Museum

Mississippi
★Jackson

CITY HALL

ANDREW JACKSON

▲ In Jackson, Mississippi, you can see a statue of Andrew Jackson in front of the old city hall of the 1800s (above). You can also visit a model space station (left).

MISSISSIPPI
Student
Space Station

Governing a State

The people of a state elect their leaders. Many of these leaders are lawmakers, who come to the capital from different parts of the state.

State lawmakers meet in a legislature. They pass many different laws. For example, they might pass a law that says all third graders must take a test about government. Lawmakers also decide how much tax money people pay to the state and vote on when to fix the state highways.

State lawmakers meet the same way city council members do. They listen to ideas from all the people. They debate. Then they pass or vote down laws.

The rules lawmakers follow to pass laws are found in the state's constitution. A **constitution** tells how a government should be run and what rights the people have.

The Mississippi lawmakers discuss a proposed state law (photograph). Lawmakers are one part of a state's government. The other two parts are made up of the governor and state workers as well as the state courts (chart).

The Three Parts of a State Government

Lawmakers
- write and pass new laws for the state

Governor
- signs new laws
- makes sure laws are carried out
- chooses some state workers

Courts
- decide if people have broken state laws

Instead of a mayor, a state has a governor. A governor is the head of the government of the state. People in the state elect the governor. The governor suggests ideas for bills to the lawmakers. The governor also signs bills so they can become laws. Then the governor makes sure these laws are carried out.

The governor has the job of choosing some government workers and certain judges for the courts. The governor also picks some of the workers for departments that serve the state. Some of these departments repair roads and bridges, issue driver's licenses, run state parks, and help people get health care.

The courts of a state decide if people have broken the law. The State Supreme Court decides if the other courts in the state have made the right decisions. ■

◄ *As in other states, Mississippi's government provides important services. This photograph shows people visiting a state health clinic.*

▼ *State governments also provide parks, like the one in which these children are playing.*

■ *Who are some of the elected leaders of a state and what do they do?*

Governing the Nation

The people of a state elect leaders for the nation as well as for their state. The national government is like a state government in some ways. The national government has a leader and lawmakers. The President heads the national government. National lawmakers debate and vote on bills. Like states, the nation has a capital. The Closer Look on page 236 is a tour of Washington, D.C., the national capital.

Washington, D.C.

Follow along on a quick tour of the nation's capital city, Washington, D.C. The city was named for George Washington, the first President. D.C. stands for the District of Columbia.

The President of the United States lives and works in the White House. Over the years, millions of tourists have visited this 132-room house.

Many tearful visitors stand by the Vietnam Veterans Memorial. Some leave flowers for friends or relatives who died in the Vietnam War.

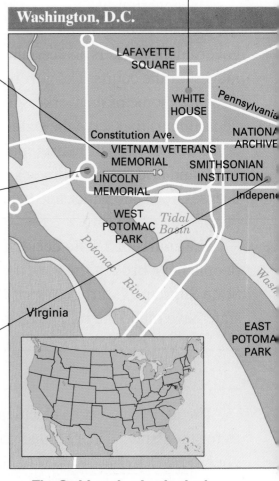

Washington, D.C.

LAFAYETTE SQUARE

WHITE HOUSE

Pennsylvania

Constitution Ave.

VIETNAM VETERANS MEMORIAL

NATIONAL ARCHIVE

LINCOLN MEMORIAL

SMITHSONIAN INSTITUTION

Independe

WEST POTOMAC PARK

Tidal Basin

Potomac River

Wash

Virginia

EAST POTOMA PARK

The Lincoln Memorial reminds visitors of Abraham Lincoln, the sixteenth President. In the memorial is a marble statue of President Lincoln.

236

The Smithsonian Institution's National Museum of American History shows objects from America's past. A Southeast Indian carver made this figure.

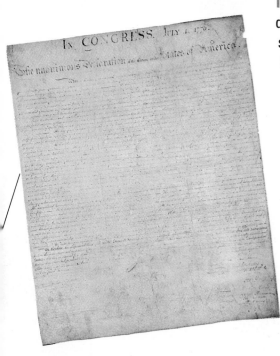

The National Archives displays important papers, such as the Declaration of Independence shown here. The Founders of the United States wrote this paper to declare that they were free from British rule. Visitors can also see the Constitution of the United States.

In the Supreme Court Building, the judges of the U.S. Supreme Court make important decisions about our country's laws. Visitors can attend meetings of the Supreme Court.

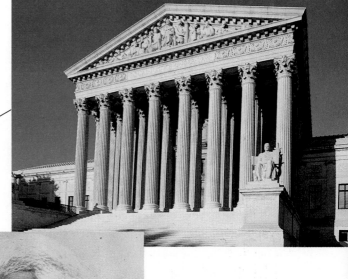

Frederick Douglass escaped from slavery and became an important writer and speaker. The house where he lived is now a popular tourist sight.

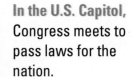

In the U.S. Capitol, Congress meets to pass laws for the nation.

237

The Constitution of the United States describes how our country should be governed. The Constitution divides the national government into three parts. The President, the Congress, and the courts make up the three parts. The diagram below shows the main job of each part.

The Three Parts of Our Nation's Government

Congress
- writes and passes new laws for the country

President
- signs new laws
- makes sure laws are carried out
- chooses some national workers

Courts
- decide if people have broken national laws

▲ *Compare this diagram to the one of state government on page 234. On this diagram, find the President, the law-makers, and the courts.*

▼ *Below is the seal of the President, who heads one of the three branches.*

The President

The leader of the United States is the **President**. The President plans how the government should spend the money from taxes. He sends this plan to Congress. The President also signs bills that the national lawmakers pass to make them laws. Then the President makes sure these laws are carried out.

The President picks the heads of different departments. These departments help run the country and provide services to the people.

The President picks the head of the Army, the Navy, and other armed forces. The President talks with leaders from other nations. They meet to make decisions about events in the world.

The Congress

National lawmakers form a group called the **Congress**. There are members of Congress from each state.

Congress has other jobs besides passing laws. It has the power to declare war on another country. Congress must approve any agreements between the United States and other countries. Congress can suggest its own plan for spending tax money.

The Courts

The courts make up another part of the nation's government. The courts decide if people have broken the law. Lawbreakers are punished by the courts. The President picks judges for all of the national courts. The President also picks the nine judges who sit on the United States Supreme Court.

The picture shows the Supreme Court of the early 1990s. Sandra Day O'Connor (bottom row, right) is the first woman to serve on the court.

The United States Supreme Court is the most important court in the nation. The Supreme Court judges listen to cases about local, state, and national laws. They decide if these laws are fair. They also decide if the decisions of state courts are fair. The judges of the Supreme Court vote on their decisions. More than half must agree before a law or decision is changed. To help them decide, the judges review the United States Constitution. ■

■ *Name the three parts of our national government. Name the main job of each part.*

REVIEW

1. **FOCUS** How are state and national governments organized?

2. **CONNECT** How are state government and city government alike? How are they different?

3. **CRITICAL THINKING** Why might the Supreme Court change a law that Congress passed?

4. **WRITING ACTIVITY** Write a letter to your mayor, your governor, or a city or state lawmaker. In the letter tell why your city or state is a good place to live. Then suggest some changes that might make it an even better place. For example, your suggestions might be about schools or parks.

Choosing Our President

The United States became a nation over two hundred years ago. Then, the leaders of most countries were kings or queens. These people were born into families that had always governed. Most kings and queens ruled their countries for as long as they lived.

The founders of our country changed the way Americans got their leaders. They wrote in the Constitution that Americans would elect a President.

In an election, people vote for their leaders. Every four years, citizens of the United States elect their President. People must decide which candidate will get their vote. Candidates are the people who want to be elected. Usually there are at least two candidates for President. A party, or a large political group, called the Democrats chooses one candidate. A party called the Republicans chooses another candidate. In 1992, the Democrats chose Bill Clinton. That year the Republicans chose George Bush.

On Election Day in November, United States citizens who are eighteen or older vote. The candidate who wins will be President for the next four years. In 1992, Bill Clinton was elected President.

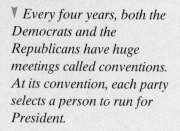

▼ *Every four years, both the Democrats and the Republicans have huge meetings called conventions. At its convention, each party selects a person to run for President.*

Good Citizenship

The special day had arrived. Ina, her sisters, and her parents woke up early. They dressed in their best clothes. Then they went to the courthouse.

People crowded into the courtroom. Every person there had been born in another country. Today, all would become citizens of the United States.

The judge spoke. She told what being a citizen means. Then everyone said the words of an oath, or promise. Ina had practiced the words at home. In the oath, Ina's family promised to follow the rules set forth in the Constitution.

Later, the judge passed out papers. Ina's paper said that she became a citizen on September 17, 1994. That day is a holiday called Citizenship Day. Ina was glad the judge picked September 17 to make her a citizen. Ina smiled as the judge handed her an American flag.

THINKING FOCUS

What is good citizenship?

Key Terms

- citizen
- volunteer

◄ *Many people become citizens on September 17, Citizenship Day.*

241

What Is a Citizen?

A **citizen** is a member of a nation. Anyone born in the United States is a citizen of this country. The people in the courtroom were born in other countries. Then they came to the United States. They learned to speak English. They learned about their new country. They passed a test. Finally they took the oath and became United States citizens.

Not everyone living in the country is a citizen of the United States. But anyone living in the United States is expected to show good citizenship. Good citizenship means following the rules of the United States and paying taxes. It means helping people who are in need and taking care of the land. All people can help make their community a better place to live.

Children can practice good citizenship, too. They can put the papers from their lunch in the trash. They can help younger children cross a street or find a book at the library. How do you practice good citizenship? ■

■ *What is a citizen?*

➤ *Like the oath that new citizens take, the Pledge of Allegiance is a promise we all make to be good citizens. Above is another sign of citizenship—a U.S. passport. U.S. citizens carry passports when they travel to most other countries.*

The Rights of Citizenship

All the people who live in the United States have certain rights. The early leaders of our country believed that everyone should have these rights. Our Constitution protects these rights. Here are some of the rights people in the United States have:

- You can worship where you choose.
- You can say what you think.
- You can go to meetings and express your ideas.
- If you are arrested, you must be put on trial quickly. The trial cannot be secret.
- If you are tried for a crime and found not guilty, you cannot be tried for that crime again.
- If you publish a newspaper, the government can't tell you what to print.

No one may take away a person's rights. Lawmakers pass laws to protect people's rights. Judges hold trials to protect people's rights. ■

▲ *United States citizens have the right to speak their minds, as in this Earth Day rally (above). They also have the right to print what they think in newspapers (left).*

243

The Duties of Citizenship

Duties are actions that people should carry out. Some duties are laws that must be obeyed. Drivers must obey traffic laws. Adults must sit on a jury at a trial if asked. People on a jury decide if the person on trial is guilty.

Other duties are not laws but are good and helpful actions. Adult citizens should vote in elections. All people should keep the streets and parks clean.

Some girls from El Segundo, California, found a way to practice good citizenship. The girls started a club called the Tree Musketeers. The club planted trees. They gave speeches to groups about taking care of the earth. The girls wrote stories for the newspaper. They also got the government to start a recycling center.

One year, the Tree Musketeers wanted to celebrate Arbor Day. Usually, people plant trees on Arbor Day. The girls wanted to plant more trees than ever before. Also, they wanted to plant the trees along a highway. The event would take lots of work and help from the people in El Segundo.

▼ Citizens have the duty to vote and elect the best leaders. Some voters wear buttons such as those below to remind others to vote in elections.

➤ Adult citizens can learn about our laws and courts when they serve on juries.

244

The girls went to the city council. They explained where they wanted to plant the trees. The council agreed to let the girls organize the tree planting.

The Tree Musketeers asked people in the town for help. Some people helped buy the trees. Others helped plant the trees. When the work was done, the girls were very proud. They had made their city more beautiful.

The girls in the Tree Musketeers were **volunteers**, people who work without being paid. Many towns and cities depend on volunteers. Parents who coach soccer teams or who help at school are practicing good citizenship. Young people who help in libraries or in hospitals help their communities as well. People can do many jobs to make their community a good place to live. ■

▲ *Volunteers like the Tree Musketeers (left) and others find many ways to practice good citizenship.*

■ *Name one way a person can practice good citizenship.*

R E V I E W

1. **FOCUS** What is good citizenship?
2. **CONNECT** In Lesson 1 you read about some people who built a playground for their community. In what way were these people practicing good citizenship?
3. **CRITICAL THINKING** Why do you think people want to work as volunteers in their community?
4. **ACTIVITY** The Tree Musketeers practiced good citizenship. With your class, list ways you can practice good citizenship.

245

Chapter Review

Reviewing Key Terms

capital (p. 233)   government (p. 219)
citizen (p. 242)   law (p. 228)
Congress (p. 239)   mayor (p. 220)
constitution (p. 234) President (p. 238)
council (p. 220)   taxes (p. 221)
election (p. 227)   volunteer (p. 245)

A. Write the key term that best completes each sentence.

1. The leader of the United States is the _____.
2. The plan for governing a state or nation is described in its _____.
3. National lawmakers form a group called _____.
4. A _____ is a member of a nation.
5. People must obey every _____ in their community.
6. People choose their leaders by voting in an _____.
7. Washington, D.C., is the _____ of the United States.
8. People pay _____ to pay for roads and schools and police.
9. People who pass laws and provide services work in the _____.
10. A _____ does not get paid for working.
11. A city's leader is the _____.
12. The _____ makes laws and plans for a town or city.

Exploring Concepts

A. Copy the chart below. Fill in the columns by writing the name of the leader and lawmakers of each level of government. For example, the leader of a city is the mayor. Your chart will compare community, state, and national government.

B. Answer the following questions in one or two sentences.

1. Why does a community need government leaders?
2. Give an example of an important law. Tell why you think it is important.

	Leader	Lawmakers
City		
State		
United States		

Reviewing Skills

1. Your point of view is your idea on a subject. Different people have different points of view. With a partner, talk about this topic: Gym class should be held once a week. Then, write a paragraph telling your point of view and your partner's.

2. Look at the map of Jackson, Mississippi, on page 233. Use the compass rose and tell in which direction the state fairground is from the Old Capitol Museum. In which direction must you walk to get from the art museum to the Planetarium?

3. Where would you find the answers to these questions about services?
   - What day of the year do the city swimming pools open?
   - When is the first day of school?
   - Does your library have a summer reading club?

Using Critical Thinking

1. Imagine living in a community that has no laws. What would living in this community be like?

2. What kind of club would you like to start to do volunteer work? How would this work help your community?

Preparing for Citizenship

1. **INTERVIEWING** If you could interview your mayor or council member, what questions would you ask? Write a list of possible questions to ask your community leader. You might want to find out why he or she decided to become a community leader or what the person does in the government.

2. **COLLABORATIVE LEARNING** In this chapter you learned about how people choose their leaders—from mayor to President. Your class can research and perform a skit about the nation's first President, George Washington. Your classmates can form three groups. The first group will find out about President Washington. The second group will use the information to make up a short skit. The third group will draw posters advertising the skit. Your teacher will help you decide who will play each part. After you practice the skit, perform it for another class.

Chapter 12

Our Holidays and Symbols

We the people of the United States of America are proud of our country. We set aside holidays that celebrate important events from our history and honor special people. We choose symbols that remind us that we are a nation of people who are free and proud of our land.

These children are celebrating Arbor Day by wearing evergreen tree hats. On this day we plant trees to show our pride in the beauty of the land.

The flag is a national symbol that shows some of the history of our nation. Each stripe stands for one of the first 13 colonies. The 50 stars stand for the 50 states that today make up the United States.

The bald eagle is also a
symbol of the United
States. This strong, proud
bird shows our courage,
our respect for the land,
and our love of freedom.

The Washington Monument
is a national symbol that
honors George Washington,
our first president. It stands
in our country's capital,
Washington, D.C.

Celebrating Our Land

Johnny Appleseed

Of Jonathan Chapman
Two things are known,
That he loved apples,
That he walked alone.

For fifty years over
Of harvest and dew,
He planted his apples
Where no apples grew.

Why did he do it?
We do not know.
He wished that apples
might root and grow.

Rosemary Carr and Stephen Vincent Benet

Arbor Day

Many poems and tales have been written about Johnny Appleseed. Most of these are a mix of truth and imagination. The stories are based on a real man named John Chapman. He lived during the late 1700s and early 1800s. For forty years, he traveled from Pennsylvania to Illinois planting apple trees.

Few apple trees grew where John Chapman traveled so he planted apple trees from the East as he went. He would also give apple trees and apple seeds to settlers he met. People began to call him Johnny Appleseed.

Settlers said that Johnny Appleseed traveled barefooted through the wilderness giving apple seeds or small apple trees to every person he met along the way.

J. Sterling Morton's Arbor Day was not the first time trees were planted on a special day. Hundreds of years ago, a group of people that lived in Mexico planted a tree whenever a child was born.

Some people remember Johnny Appleseed and his trees on Arbor Day. This is a holiday that is set aside for planting trees. It is called Arbor Day because an arbor is a place that is shaded by trees.

Arbor Day was started by J. Sterling Morton, who worked with lawmakers in Nebraska. Because Nebraska is part of the dry plains of the United States, few trees grow there naturally. Morton saw that trees were needed to provide wood for the people who were moving to Nebraska. Trees would also protect the land. The plains received very little rain. Tree roots would help keep the soil in place and hold water. They would also slow the wind during dust storms and snow storms.

Today some people in the United States celebrate Arbor Day by planting trees.

251

▲ *This 1932 painting by Grant Wood is called* Arbor Day. *It shows a teacher and students planting a tree in front of their school on Arbor Day.*

■ *On Arbor Day, how do people show that they care for the land?*

J. Sterling Morton planned a tree-planting day. That day, April 10, 1872, was the first Arbor Day. The whole state of Nebraska celebrated by planting trees. As news of Arbor Day spread, more and more states began to celebrate this special day.

Arbor Day is still a holiday in Nebraska, though it is now celebrated on April 22. This day was Morton's birthday. Different states celebrate this holiday on different days of the year, but it is celebrated throughout most of the United States and in some parts of Canada. Other countries also set aside days and even weeks as a time to plant trees.

Celebrating Arbor Day gives people the chance to give back to the land some of the things that are taken from it. It also reminds us that it is important to protect our natural resources, especially the land. ■

National Holidays

Arbor Day became a Nebraska holiday when lawmakers there decided the state would celebrate it each year. Other states celebrate Arbor Day, too. In the United States, each state can choose different holidays that its citizens will celebrate.

Some holidays are celebrated by every state in our country. Holidays that are called by the national government and that honor our country and its people are called **national holidays.** The chart on this page shows some of the national holidays that we celebrate.

National Holidays		
Holiday	**Date**	**What We Honor**
Martin L. King, Jr., Day	Third Monday in January	Martin L. King, Jr.'s, birthday
Presidents' Day	Third Monday in February	George Washington's and Abraham Lincoln's birthdays
Memorial Day	Last Monday in May	U.S. soldiers killed in war
Independence Day	July 4	Independence from England
Labor Day	First Monday in September	Working people
Columbus Day	Second Monday in October	European arrival in America
Veterans' Day	November 11	U.S. soldiers who fought in wars
Thanksgiving Day	Fourth Thursday in November	Pilgrims' first harvest

Some national holidays celebrate famous events in history. On Thanksgiving Day, for example, we remember how the Pilgrims thanked God for their harvest and celebrated with the Wampanoag, who had helped them. On Independence Day, we remember July 4, 1776, the day early leaders of America stated that the United States was free from England. Today on July 4, we also celebrate the freedoms that American citizens have. Each year, new citizens, like the one on the next page, join the United States to enjoy the rights and freedoms of our country.

An Immigrant on July 4

1:15 P.M., July 4, 1991
At an Independence Day parade
in Corpus Christi, Texas

Flag
This young immigrant happily tells everyone she meets that she is now a citizen of the United States. Waving the flag is another way for her to say that she is proud of her new country.

Lone Star Button
For her, living in the United States also means living in Texas. This button shows a star, the symbol of Texas. She plans to pin it on her uncle when he moves to the United States next year.

Camera
The pictures she takes of today's celebration will be a wonderful surprise for her friend Tina in Guatemala. The two girls write to each other each week. Tina hopes to visit the United States someday.

Purse
She was given this purse for her ninth birthday. The colorful Guatemalan fabric was woven by hand by her grandmother.

Two of our national holidays honor well-known citizens of our country. We honor George Washington and Abraham Lincoln on Presidents' Day. On Martin Luther King, Jr., Day, we remember this man who fought for freedom for all people.

Some national holidays honor many of our citizens. On Labor Day, we honor all people who work, or labor, to provide things we need. On Veterans' Day, we remember Americans who have fought to keep our country free. Memorial Day is a holiday when we remember soldiers who have died during wars. All of these holidays remind us of the ideas and the beliefs that make our land great. ■

■ *What kinds of people and events do our national holidays celebrate?*

◄ *For many people national holidays are a time to remember our country and all that it gives us.*

R E V I E W

1. **FOCUS** Why do Americans celebrate state and national holidays?

2. **CONNECT** How do stories about men like Johnny Appleseed and Joe Magarac help us remember good things about our country?

3. **CRITICAL THINKING** Think of a person or an event that is important enough to be honored as a national holiday. Write a paragraph telling why.

4. **ACTIVITY** Choose two holidays that you know. Draw a picture that shows what we honor on these days. Make a holiday book that contains your picture and your classmates' pictures.

Using Main Ideas

Look at what you've read

Main Idea

detail

detail

detail

Main Idea

detail

detail

Remember main ideas

detail

detail

detail

detail

detail

Main Idea

Main Idea

Retell main ideas in your own words

Summary

Here's Why Have you ever had to remember something you read? Maybe it was for a test. Or maybe you wanted to tell a friend. How do you go about remembering what you read? A good way to remember what you read is to make a summary of it.

Here's How A summary is a few sentences that tell the main ideas of what you read. You should use as few words as possible in a summary. They should be your own words.

In the last lesson, you read about Arbor Day. What would you include in a summary about Arbor Day? Think about the main ideas. The meaning of Arbor Day is one important idea to remember. When we celebrate Arbor Day is another. The number of years that Johnny Appleseed planted trees is a detail. Details are not as important as main ideas. They are not part of a summary.

Try It Work with a partner. Write a summary of the information about Arbor Day on pages 251 and 252.

Apply It Write a summary of something you have read in a book or magazine. Read your summary to the class.

National Symbols

What would you think if a wild turkey were our national symbol? Over 200 years ago, Benjamin Franklin suggested that the turkey be chosen to stand for the United States. Franklin didn't much like the eagle. He thought that the turkey was a wise and clever bird. He also knew that it had played a role in the history of our nation. The wild turkey was an important food for early settlers.

Other people thought the eagle was a better symbol for the freedom and power of our nation. The bald eagle has great strength. With its huge wings, it flies high and free above the land. An eagle's eye can see movement below from hundreds of feet in the air. For all these reasons, the bald eagle became our national symbol.

THINKING

FOCUS

Why do we have national symbols?

Key Terms

- liberty
- monument

Today the eagle is on some of our coins. Look at the coins above. One of them is what a quarter might look like if Benjamin Franklin had gotten his way. Which bird do you think is the best symbol of the United States?

The Liberty Bell has been cracked twice. It hasn't been rung since 1835, the second time it broke.

Different nations use different symbols to show their feelings about themselves and their land. We Americans pick national symbols that stand for what is special about our country. Our symbols stand for our pride and good feelings about the United States.

For example, the Liberty Bell is a symbol of the **liberty,** or freedom, that Americans believe in. The Liberty Bell was rung in 1776 when the United States declared its independence from England. Today it hangs in Philadelphia, Pennsylvania.

Other cities have monuments that are national symbols. A **monument** is a building that honors a person or an event. If you were to visit our nation's capital, Washington, D.C., you could see the tall Washington Monument. It was built to honor George Washington. The Gateway Arch stands west of the Mississippi River in St. Louis, Missouri. This stainless steel monument honors the pioneers who moved West to settle the land.

Preserving Our Symbols

These symbols are special because they remind us of important ideas and beliefs about our country and our land. That is why we should try to preserve them.

Today the bald eagle is so rare that it is in danger of dying out. Pollution and hunting have put the bald eagle in danger. Changes to the land have made it hard for the eagle to find food to eat and places to build nests.

How Do We Know?

How do we know that eagles are in danger? The U.S. Fish and Wildlife Service sends out teams of people to study bald eagles and keep track of how many new ones are born each year. The teams usually watch the birds with binoculars from a distance. That way, the eagles aren't frightened.

◄ *An important reason the bald eagle was chosen as a national symbol was that it lived only in North America. The bald eagle has been seen in each of the United States, except Hawaii.*

If we work together to care for bald eagles, however, we can help them become plentiful again. As long as they are not hunted and have trees, clean food, and clean land to live on, they will be safe. ■

■ *Why is the eagle a good symbol of the United States?*

Old Glory

The best-known symbol of the United States is our flag. Sometimes it is called "Old Glory." The flag is a symbol of the idea that we are one nation made up of separate states.

Look at the flag on this stamp. It has 50 stars. Each star stands for one state in our country. The 50 stars mean our nation has 50 states. Our flag also has 13 stripes. Each stripe stands for one of the 13 English colonies that were settled in America.

Our flag is a symbol both of our history and of our nation today, but it has not always looked as it does now. The postage stamps we use to mail letters all over the country have shown a history of our flag. On the next page you can see some of the forms our flag has taken.

◄ *This 1988 stamp shows "Old Glory" as it looks today. The U.S. Postal Service makes sure that it has an up-to-date flag stamp at all times.*

▼ *What is wrong with this can of asparagus? It's against the law to use the flag to advertise or sell products.*

This 1775 flag shows a snake warning enemies not to tread, or step, on it. It was flown on Continental Navy ships.

In 1777 the Congress decided on a flag of 13 red and white stripes and 13 white stars against a blue background. The stars and stripes stood for the original 13 colonies.

This flag is the "Star Spangled Banner." Our national anthem was written about this flag with 15 stars and stripes. It was our country's flag from 1795 to 1818.

In 1959 the flag had 48 stars, as this one does. Two more stars were added later that year when Alaska and Hawaii became our 49th and 50th states.

■ *How does the flag symbolize our history, as well as our nation today?*

As you can see, the flag has changed from the time before we won our independence from England to today. As states joined the union, stars were added to the flag. Whatever form the flag took, it has always stood for a single nation that believes in "liberty and justice for all." ■

R E V I E W

1. **FOCUS** Why do we have national symbols?
2. **CONNECT** How was the flag changed as our nation moved West?
3. **CRITICAL THINKING** Name other things that might be used as a national symbol.

4. **ACTIVITY** Create your own flag. Choose designs that remind you of the land and people that you learned about in this book. Let these be the symbols on your flag. Display and discuss your design with your classmates.

Chapter Review

Reviewing Key Terms

liberty (p. 258)
national holiday (p. 253)
monument (p. 258)

A. Write *true* or *false* for each sentence. If a sentence is false, rewrite it to make it true.

1. A national holiday celebrates a famous event in our history or honors people of our country.
2. A place to hold indoor games is called a monument.

3. Liberty is freedom from control by others.

B. Write the correct key term for each numbered blank.

Presidents' Day is a __1__ when people throughout the country honor the past presidents of the United States. In Washington, D.C., people may visit a __2__ that honors Abraham Lincoln. Our presidents must work for __3__ and justice for all.

Exploring Concepts

A. The bald eagle is our national symbol. Copy the chart. Fill in the second column to show what the early Indians might have chosen for their symbols.

B. Long ago the bald eagle was chosen to be our national symbol. Write two reasons why you think that was a good choice.

Indian people	Symbol
Kwakiutl	
Cheyenne	
Navajo	

Reviewing Skills

1. Read the second paragraph on page 251 again. In one or two sentences, write a summary of the paragraph in your own words.

2. Draw a map to show that Johnny Appleseed walked ten miles in one day from one town to another. Use a scale of one inch for one mile.

Using Critical Thinking

1. The Wampanoag and the Delaware helped the Pilgrims and the early settlers survive in the wilderness. Do you think monuments should be built in their honor? If so, where?

2. The picture shows children planting trees on Arbor Day many years ago. Today, some towns celebrate Arbor Day and hold tree-planting ceremonies. Do you think Arbor Day should be a national holiday? Why?

Preparing for Citizenship

1. **ART ACTIVITY** The Liberty Bell is a symbol of our liberty and freedom. Draw a picture of something else that you think would be a good symbol of our liberty. Show your picture to the class. Tell them why it is a good symbol of liberty.

2. **COLLABORATIVE LEARNING** Divide the class into four groups. Each group should prepare a short skit, song, or poem about someone who did something special for our country. Perform your skits, songs, or poems for other classes in your school.

Time/Space Databank

WORLD: *Political*

ABBREVIATIONS

BOS. AND HERZ.
    Bosnia and Herzegovina
CEN. AFR. REP.
    Central African Republic
DEN.   Denmark
FR.   France
GR.   Greece
IT.   Italy
N.   North, Northern
NETH. Netherlands
N.Z. New Zealand
PORT. Portugal
S.   South
SP.   Spain
U.A.E. United Arab
    Emirates
U.K. United Kingdom
U.S. United States
W.   Western

—— National boundary

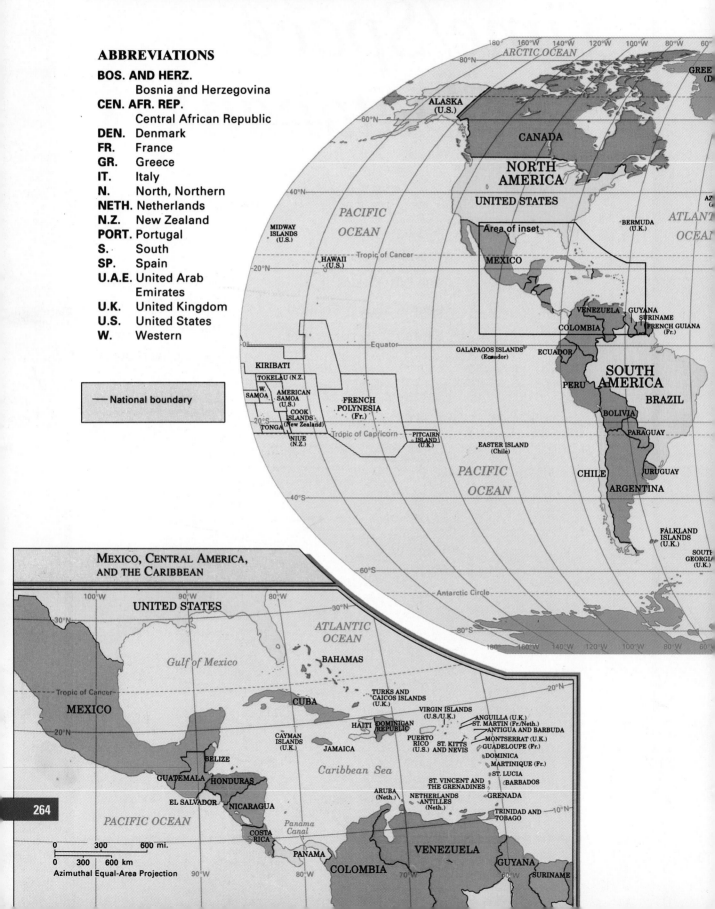

MEXICO, CENTRAL AMERICA, AND THE CARIBBEAN

Azimuthal Equal-Area Projection

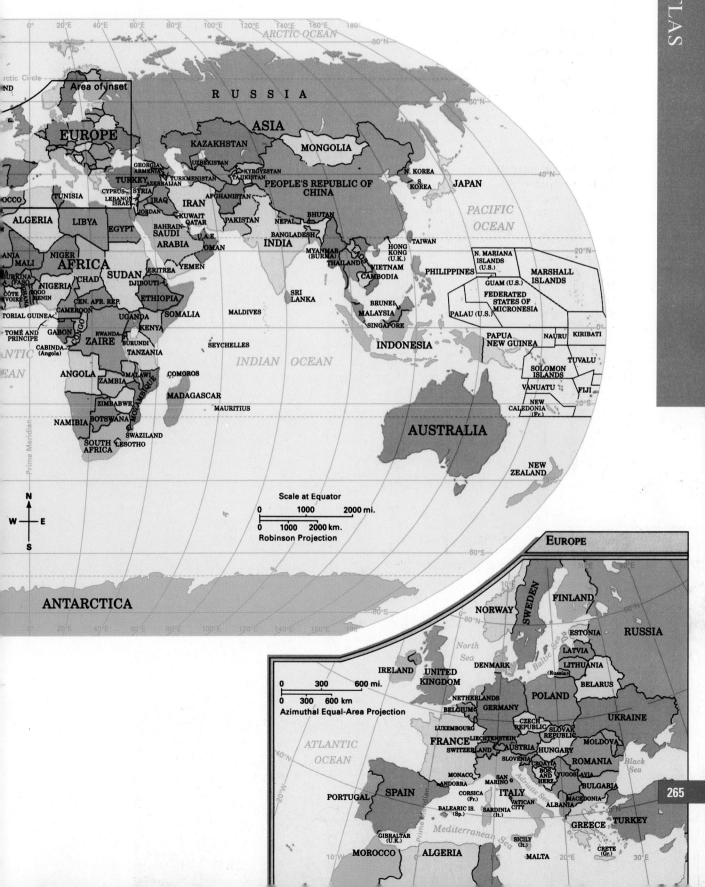

Area of inset

ARCTIC OCEAN

80°N

rctic Circle

ND

EUROPE

RUSSIA

60°N

ASIA

KAZAKHSTAN

MONGOLIA

OCCO

GEORGIA
ARMENIA
AZERBAIJAN

UZBEKISTAN

KYRGYZSTAN

N. KOREA

40°N

JAPAN

TURKEY

TUNISIA

CYPRUS
LEBANON
ISRAEL

SYRIA

IRAQ

JORDAN

TURKMENISTAN

TAJIKISTAN

PEOPLE'S REPUBLIC OF
CHINA

S.
KOREA

PACIFIC
OCEAN

ALGERIA

LIBYA

EGYPT

IRAN

AFGHANISTAN

BHUTAN

KUWAIT
QATAR

PAKISTAN

NEPAL

ANIA

NIGER

AFRICA

SUDAN

BAHRAIN
SAUDI
ARABIA

U.A.E.
OMAN

BANGLADESH

INDIA

20°N

MALI

BURKINA
FASO

NIGERIA

CHAD

ERITREA

DJIBOUTI

YEMEN

MYANMAR
(BURMA)
THAILAND

LAOS

HONG
KONG
(U.K.)

TAIWAN

N. MARIANA
ISLANDS
(U.S.)

MARSHALL
ISLANDS

CÔTE D'IVOIRE
TOGO
BENIN

CEN. AFR. REP.

ETHIOPIA

VIETNAM
CAMBODIA

PHILIPPINES

GUAM (U.S.)

TORIAL GUINEA

CAMEROON

UGANDA

SOMALIA

MALDIVES

SRI
LANKA

FEDERATED
STATES OF
MICRONESIA

TOMÉ AND
PRINCIPE

GABON

KENYA

BRUNEI
MALAYSIA
SINGAPORE

PALAU (U.S.)

NTIC

CABINDA
(Angola)

ZAIRE

RWANDA
BURUNDI

TANZANIA

SEYCHELLES

INDIAN OCEAN

PAPUA
NEW GUINEA

NAURU

KIRIBATI

EAN

ANGOLA

ZAMBIA

MALAWI

MOZAMBIQUE

COMOROS

INDONESIA

TUVALU

MADAGASCAR

SOLOMON
ISLANDS

ZIMBABWE

MAURITIUS

VANUATU

FIJI

NAMIBIA

BOTSWANA

SWAZILAND

AUSTRALIA

NEW
CALEDONIA
(Fr.)

20°S

SOUTH
AFRICA

LESOTHO

NEW
ZEALAND

N
W — **E**
S

Scale at Equator

0   1000   2000 mi.

0   1000   2000 km.

Robinson Projection

60°S

ANTARCTICA

80°S

0° 20°E 40°E 60°E 80°E 100°E 120°E 140°E 160°E 180°

Prime Meridian

EUROPE

NORWAY

SWEDEN

FINLAND

60°N

ESTONIA

RUSSIA

North
Sea

DENMARK

Baltic Sea

LATVIA

LITHUANIA

IRELAND

UNITED
KINGDOM

(Russia)

0   300   600 mi.

0   300   600 km.

Azimuthal Equal-Area Projection

NETHERLANDS

BELGIUM

GERMANY

POLAND

BELARUS

UKRAINE

LUXEMBOURG

CZECH
REPUBLIC

SLOVAK
REPUBLIC

MOLDOVA

FRANCE

LIECHTENSTEIN

AUSTRIA

HUNGARY

ROMANIA

SWITZERLAND

SLOVENIA

CROATIA

BOS.
AND
HERZ.

YUGOSLAVIA

Black
Sea

ATLANTIC
OCEAN

MONACO

SAN
MARINO

BULGARIA

ANDORRA

CORSICA
(Fr.)

ITALY

MACEDONIA

PORTUGAL

SPAIN

VATICAN
CITY

ALBANIA

BALEARIC IS.
(Sp.)

SARDINIA
(It.)

GREECE

TURKEY

GIBRALTAR
(U.K.)

SICILY
(It.)

CRETE
(Gr.)

30°E

MOROCCO

ALGERIA

Mediterranean Sea

MALTA

20°E

THE FIFTY STATES

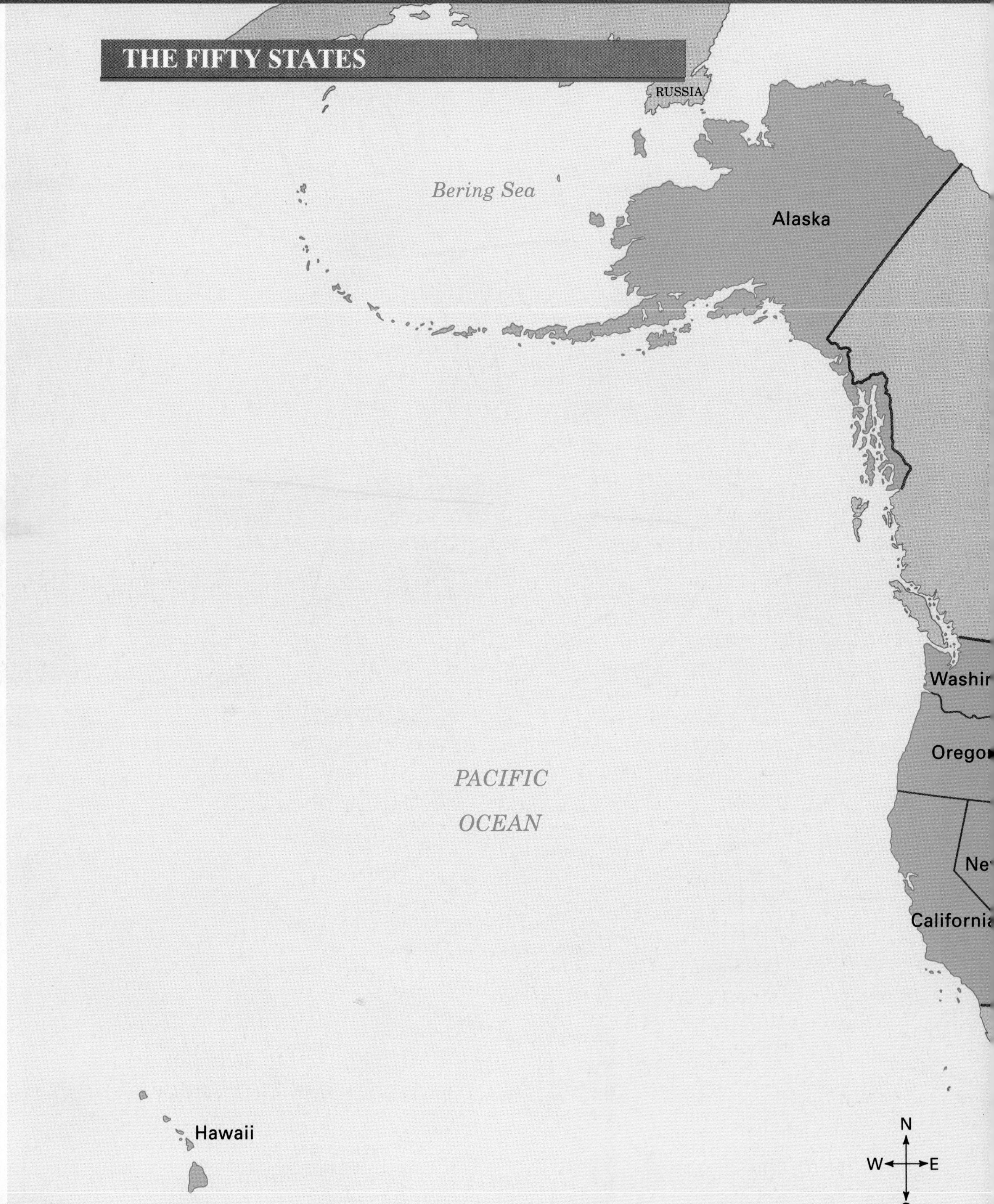
RUSSIA
Bering Sea
Alaska
Washir
Orego
Ne
California
PACIFIC
OCEAN
Hawaii
N
W
E
S

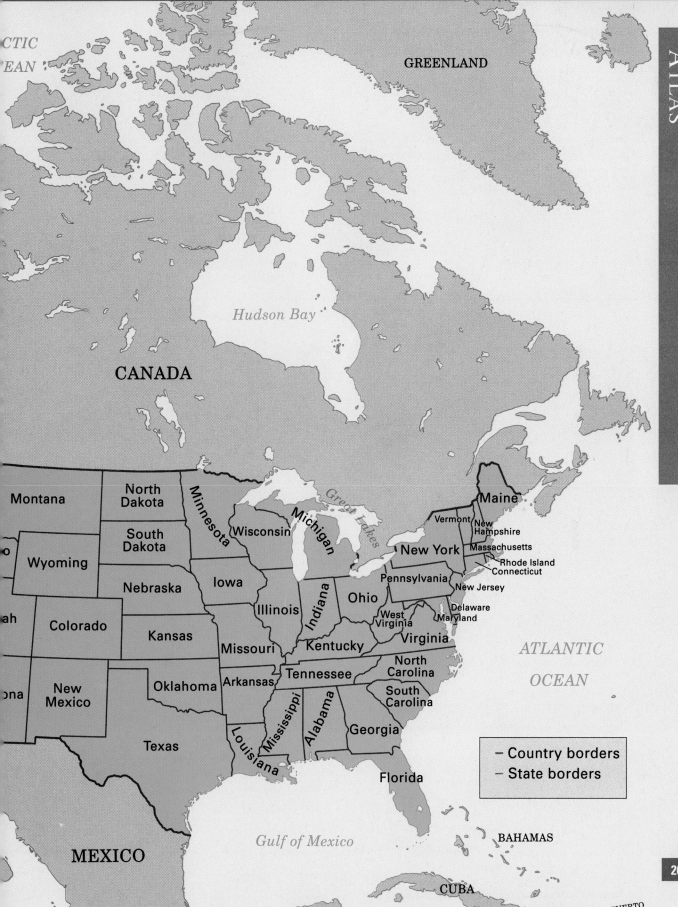

CTIC
EAN

GREENLAND

Hudson Bay

CANADA

Great Lakes

Montana | North Dakota | Minnesota | Wisconsin | Michigan | Maine

Vermont | New Hampshire

South Dakota | New York | Massachusetts

Wyoming | Rhode Island | Connecticut

Nebraska | Iowa | Pennsylvania | New Jersey

Illinois | Indiana | Ohio | Delaware | Maryland

Colorado | West Virginia

Kansas | Missouri | Kentucky | Virginia

ATLANTIC

OCEAN

North Carolina

Oklahoma | Arkansas | Tennessee | South Carolina

New Mexico | Mississippi | Alabama | Georgia

Louisiana

Texas | Florida

— Country borders
— State borders

Gulf of Mexico

BAHAMAS

MEXICO

267

CUBA

PUERTO RICO (U.S.)

UNITED STATES: *Political*

ALASKA

ARCTIC OCEAN

RUSSIA

Arctic Circle

Yukon River

Alaska

Fairbanks

CANADA

Anchorage

Juneau

ALEUTIAN

ISLANDS

0   300   600 mi.
0   300   600 km

PACIFIC

OCEAN

Seattle
Washington
Olympia

Columbia River

Portland
Salem

Oregon

Helena

Montan

Billin

Idaho

Boise

Snake River

Pocatello

Wyomi

Caspe

Nevada

Carson City

Salt Lake City
Provo

San
Francisco

Sacramento

Utah

De

Colorad

California

Las Vegas

Colorado River

Los Angeles

Arizona

Santa Fe
Albuquerque

San Diego

Phoenix

New Mexi

Tucson

MEXI

HAWAII

KAUAI

NIIHAU

OAHU

Honolulu

MOLOKAI

LANAI

MAUI

PACIFIC

KAHOOLAWE

OCEAN

Hawaii

HAWAII

Hilo

0   100   200 mi.
0   100   200 km

⊕ National capital

★ State capital

● Major city

— National boundary

— State boundary

100°W 95°W 90°W 85°W 80°W 75°W 70°W 55°N 65°W 60°W

50°N

C A N A D A

Lake Superior

North Dakota

marck Fargo

Minnesota

Lake Huron

Michigan

Lake Ontario

45°N

Maine

Augusta

Vermont

Burlington

Montpelier New Portland

Hampshire Concord

St. Paul

Minneapolis

Wisconsin

Lake Michigan

Lansing

Albany Boston

New York Massachusetts Providence

Rhode Island

Hartford Connecticut

Pierre

South Dakota

Sioux Falls

Milwaukee

Madison

Detroit

Lake Erie

New Haven New York

Sioux City

Iowa

Des Moines

Chicago

Cleveland

Ohio

Columbus

Pennsylvania

Harrisburg

Pittsburgh

New Trenton

Jersey Philadelphia

Wilmington Dover

Delaware

40°N

Nebraska

Platte River

Omaha

Lincoln

Missouri River

Illinois

Indiana

Springfield Indianapolis

Ohio River

West

Charleston

Virginia

Baltimore

Washington Annapolis

Maryland

Virginia

Richmond Norfolk

Kansas City

Topeka

Kansas

sas River

Wichita

St. Louis

Jefferson City

Missouri

Louisville Frankfort

Evansville

Kentucky

Nashville

35°N

70°W

Raleigh

North Carolina

Charlotte

ATLANTIC

Tulsa

Oklahoma City

Oklahoma

Red River

Arkansas

Fort Smith

Little Rock

Mississippi River

Memphis

Tennessee

South

Columbia

Carolina

Charleston

OCEAN

Greenville

Birmingham

Atlanta

Georgia

Savannah

30°N

Dallas

Texas

Austin

Houston

Rio Grande

Louisiana

Baton Rouge New Orleans

Jackson

Mississippi

Alabama

Montgomery

Tallahassee

N

W E

S

Gulf of Mexico

Florida

Tampa

BAHAMAS

25°N

Miami

CUBA

20°N

0 200 400 mi.

0 200 400 km

Albers Equal-Area Projection

100°W 95°W 90°W 85°W 80°W 75°W

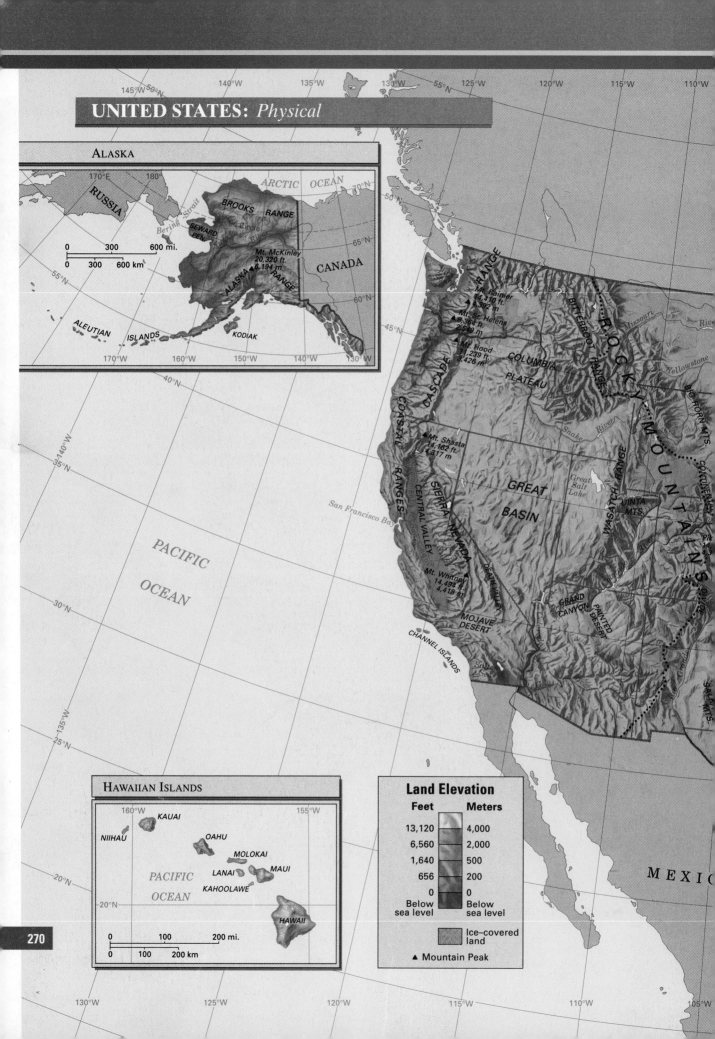

ALASKA

ARCTIC OCEAN

RUSSIA

BROOKS RANGE

SEWARD PEN.

Bering Strait

Arctic Circle

Mt. McKinley
20,320 ft.
6,194 m

ALASKA RANGE

CANADA

70°N
65°N
60°N
55°N

170°E
180°
170°W
160°W
150°W
140°W
130°W

0   300   600 mi.
0   300   600 km

ALEUTIAN ISLANDS

KODIAK

PACIFIC OCEAN

COASTAL RANGES

San Francisco Bay

CASCADE RANGE

Mt. Rainier
14,410 ft.
4,392 m

Mt. St. Helens
8,364 ft.
2,549 m

Mt. Hood
11,239 ft.
3,426 m

COLUMBIA PLATEAU

BITTERROOT RANGE

ROCKY MOUNTAINS

Missouri River

Yellowstone

BIG HORN MTS.

Snake River

Mt. Shasta
14,162 ft.
4,317 m

SIERRA NEVADA

CENTRAL VALLEY

GREAT BASIN

Great Salt Lake

WASATCH RANGE

UINTA MTS.

CONTINENTAL DIVIDE

Pike

Mt. Whitney
14,494 ft.
4,418 m

DEATH VALLEY

GRAND CANYON

PAINTED DESERT

MOJAVE DESERT

CHANNEL ISLANDS

SAN MTS.

Rio Grande

MEXICO

HAWAIIAN ISLANDS

KAUAI

NIIHAU

OAHU

MOLOKAI

LANAI   MAUI

KAHOOLAWE

PACIFIC OCEAN

HAWAII

160°W   155°W

20°N

0   100   200 mi.
0   100   200 km

Land Elevation

Feet		Meters
13,120		4,000
6,560		2,000
1,640		500
656		200
0		0
Below sea level		Below sea level

Ice-covered land

▲ Mountain Peak

CANADA

Lake of the Woods

MESABI RANGE

Lake Superior

Lake Huron

Lake Michigan

St. Lawrence River

WHITE MTS.
Mt. Washington
6,288 ft.
1,917 m

ADIRONDACK MTS.

Lake Ontario

CATSKILL MTS.

NANTUCKET

MARTHA'S VINEYARD

LONG ISLAND

Red River

Lake Erie

Susquehanna River

ALLEGHENY PLATEAU

Delaware Bay

Mississippi River

Des Moines River

CENTRAL PLAINS

Chesapeake Bay

AND HILLS

Platte River

OZARK PLATEAU

River

CUMBERLAND PLATEAU

APPALACHIAN MOUNTAINS

FALL LINE

ATLANTIC COASTAL PLAIN

ATLANTIC OCEAN

as River

Arkansas River

OUACHITA MOUNTAINS

Red River

BLUE RIDGE MTS.
Mt. Mitchell
6,684 ft.
2,037 m

JO ADO

Brazos River

Sabine River

EDWARDS PLATEAU

Colorado River

Pensacola Bay

Mobile Bay

GULF COASTAL PLAIN

Galveston Bay

Tampa Bay

Lake Okeechobee

BAHAMAS

Gulf of Mexico

EVERGLADES

N
W E
S

FLORIDA KEYS

CUBA

0   200   400 mi.
0   200   400 km
Albers Equal-Area Projection

This gazetteer will help you locate many of the places discussed in this book. The page number tells you where to find each place on a map.

A

Abilene Prairie town in Kansas. It became a booming cattle town in the 1860s. (p. 156)

Africa The earth's second largest continent. It lies between the Atlantic and Indian oceans. (pp. 264–265)

Alabama Southeastern state on the Gulf of Mexico. Its capital is Montgomery. (pp. 268–269)

Alaska State farthest north of all states. Its capital is Juneau. (pp. 268–269)

Allegheny River River in eastern United States. It joins the Monongahela River at Pittsburgh to form the Ohio River. (p. 179)

Appalachian Mountains Mountain range in eastern North America. It extends about 1,600 miles from southern Canada to Alabama. (p. 122)

Arizona Southwestern state on the Mexican border. Its capital is Phoenix. (pp. 268–269)

Arkansas South central state. Its capital is Little Rock. (pp. 268–269)

Asia The earth's largest continent. It is separated from Europe by the Ural Mountains. (pp. 264–265)

Atlantic Ocean The earth's second largest body of water. It borders the eastern coast of the United States. (p. 5)

B

Bakersfield City in south central California at the southern end of the San Joaquin Valley. (p. 171)

Boonesborough Pioneer settlement in central Kentucky. Named after Daniel Boone. (p. 135)

C

California Western state on the Pacific coast. Its capital is Sacramento. (pp. 268–269)

California Trail Southern branch of the Oregon Trail. It was used by pioneers traveling to California. (p. 149)

Canada Country to the north of the United States. Its capital is Ottawa. (pp. 264–265)

Chicago City in northeastern Illinois on the shore of Lake Michigan. (p. 156)

Chisholm Trail Main trail for cattle drives out of Texas in the 1860s. It extended from San Antonio, Texas, to Abilene, Kansas. (p. 156)

Colorado Western state. Its capital is Denver. (pp. 268–269)

Colorado River River in southwestern United States. It begins in the mountains of Colorado and flows into the Gulf of California. (p. 21)

Connecticut Northeastern state. Its capital is Hartford. (pp. 268–269)

Cumberland Gap A pass through the Appalachian Mountains where Kentucky, Virginia, and Tennessee join. (p. 135)

D

Delaware Eastern state on the Atlantic coast. Its capital is Dover. (pp. 268–269)

Denver City in north central Colorado. (pp. 268–269)

Detroit City of southeastern Michigan. (p. G14)

Dodge City City in southwestern Kansas. (p. 158)

E

England The southern part of the island of Great Britain. People from England started many colonies in North America. (p. 117)

Europe The earth's second smallest continent. It extends west from the Ural Mountains. (pp. 264–265)

F

Florida Southeastern state on the Atlantic coast. Its capital is Tallahassee. (pp. 268–269)

France Country in western Europe. People from France settled in North America beginning in the 1600s. (p. 265)

G

Georgia Southeastern state on the Atlantic coast. Its capital is Atlanta. (pp. 268–269)

Germany Country in Europe. Its capital is Berlin. German people came to settle eastern North America in the early 1700s. (p. 265)

Grand Canyon Canyon of the Colorado River in northwestern Arizona. It is 217 miles long and 4 to 18 miles wide. (p. 21)

Great Lakes Group of five lakes between Canada and the United States, including Lakes Superior, Huron, Erie, Ontario, and Michigan. (p. 49)

Guatemala Country in Central America. (p. 264)

Gulf of Mexico Part of the Atlantic Ocean that borders the southern part of the United States and the eastern part of Mexico. (p. 49)

H

Harrodsburg One of two pioneer towns in central Kentucky (with Boonesboro) at which branches of the Wilderness Trail ended. (p. 135)

Hawaii State and island group in the central Pacific Ocean. Its capital is Honolulu. (pp. 268–269)

Holston River River in northeastern Tennessee and southwestern Virginia. The Wilderness Road began there. (p. 135)

Hudson River River in New York. It begins in the mountains of northern New York and flows into the Atlantic Ocean at New York City. (p. 19)

I

Idaho Northwestern state. Its capital is Boise. (pp. 268–269)

Illinois North central state. Its capital is Springfield. (pp. 268–269)

Independence City in western Missouri. In pioneer days, it was the starting point for travelers using the Oregon and Santa Fe Trails. (p. 149)

Indiana North central state. Its capital is Indianapolis. (pp. 268–269)

Iowa North central state. Its capital is Des Moines. (pp. 268–269)

Ireland Small country in the British Isles. People from Ireland settled in eastern North America in the early 1700s. (p. 265)

J

Jackson The capital of Mississippi. (p. G6)

K

Kansas Central state. Its capital is Topeka. (p. G7)

Kentucky Southeastern state. Its capital is Frankfort. (pp. 268–269)

Kilauea One of two volcanoes in Hawaii Volcanoes National Park. (p. 201)

L

Lake Ontario One of the five Great Lakes, which lie between the United States and Canada. (p. 49)

Lansing The capital of Michigan. (p. G14)

Leadville Town in central Colorado. It became a silver mining boom town during the 1870s. (p. 161)

Los Angeles City in southern California on the Pacific coast. In pioneer days, it became the end of the Santa Fe Trail. (pp. 268–269)

Louisiana Southeastern state on the Gulf of Mexico. Its capital is Baton Rouge. (pp. 268–269)

M

Maine Northeastern state on the Atlantic coast. Its capital is Augusta. (pp. 268–269)

Maryland Eastern state on the Atlantic coast. Its capital is Annapolis. (pp. 268–269)

Massachusetts Northeastern state on the Atlantic coast. Its capital is Boston. (pp. 268–269)

Mauna Loa One of two volcanoes in Hawaii Volcanoes National Park. (p. 201)

Mexico Country to the south of and bordering the United States. Its capital is Mexico City. (p. 21)

Michigan North central state. Its capital is Lansing. (p. G14)

Milwaukee City in southeastern Wisconsin on Lake Michigan. (p. G13)

Minnesota North central state. Its capital is St. Paul. (pp. 268–269)

Mississippi Southern state on the Gulf of Mexico. Its capital is Jackson. (p. G8)

Mississippi River The longest river in the United States. It begins in northern Minnesota and flows into the Gulf of Mexico at New Orleans. (p. 49)

Missouri Central state. Its capital is Jefferson City. (pp. 268–269)

Missouri River One of the longest rivers in the United States. It begins in western Montana and flows into the Mississippi River near St. Louis. (pp. 268–269)

Monongahela River River in the eastern United States. It joins the Allegheny River at Pittsburgh to form the Ohio River. (p. 179)

Montana Northwestern state. Its capital is Helena. (pp. 268–269)

Mount McKinley Mountain peak in south central Alaska. It is the highest peak in North America at 20,320 feet. (pp. 270–271)

N

Nebraska North central state in the Great Plains. Its capital is Lincoln. (pp. 268–269)

Nevada Western state. Its capital is Carson City. (pp. 268–269)

New Hampshire Northeastern state on the Atlantic coast. Its capital is Concord. (pp. 268–269)

New Jersey Northeastern state on the Atlantic coast. Its capital is Trenton. (pp. 268–269)

New Mexico Southwestern state on the Mexican border. Its capital is Santa Fe. (pp. 268–269)

New York Northeastern state. Its capital is Albany. (pp. 268–269)

New York City City in New York at the mouth of the Hudson River. It is the largest city in the United States. (p. 122)

North America The third largest continent. It includes the countries of the United States, Canada, Mexico, and those of Central America. (pp. 264–265)

North Carolina Southeastern state on the Atlantic coast. Its capital is Raleigh. (pp. 268–269)

North Dakota North central state. Its capital is Bismarck. (pp. 268–269)

North Pole The most northern point of the earth. (p. 159)

O

Ohio North central state. Its capital is Columbus. (pp. 268–269)

Ohio River River formed in Pennsylvania where the Allegheny and the Monongahela rivers join. It flows into the Mississippi River at the southern tip of Illinois. (p. 179)

Oklahoma Southwestern state. Its capital is Oklahoma City. (pp. 268–269)

Oregon Northwestern state on the Pacific coast. Its capital is Salem. (pp. 268–269)

Oregon Trail Pioneer route from Independence, Missouri, to the West. (p. 149)

P

Pacific Ocean The earth's largest body of water. It borders the western coast of the United States. (p. 5)

Pennsylvania Northeastern state. Its capital is Harrisburg. (pp. 268–269)

Philadelphia City in southeastern Pennsylvania on the Delaware River. (p. 122)

Pittsburgh City in southwestern Pennsylvania at the place where the Allegheny and Monongahela rivers meet to form the Ohio River. (p. 179)

Platte River Most important river in Nebraska. Its two branches begin in the mountains of Colorado. (pp. 268–269)

Plymouth Harbor town in southeastern Massachusetts. (p. 117)

Plymouth Colony Second English settlement in America. It was founded by Pilgrims in 1620. (p. 117)

R

Rhode Island Northeastern state on the Atlantic coast. Its capital is Providence. (pp. 268–269)

Rocky Mountains Longest mountain range in North America. It extends more than 3,000 miles from northern Alaska to northern New Mexico. (pp. 270–271)

S

St. Louis City in eastern Missouri on the Mississippi River. (pp. 268–269)

San Antonio City in southern Texas. It was the beginning of the Chisholm Trail during the 1860s. (p. 156)

San Joaquin Valley Rich farming area in central California. The San Joaquin River runs through this land. (p. 171)

Santa Fe City in north central New Mexico. It is the capital of New Mexico. In pioneer days, it was an important stop on the Santa Fe Trail. (p. 149)

Santa Fe Trail Pioneer route from Independence, Missouri, to Santa Fe, New Mexico. It was later extended to Los Angeles, California. (p. 149)

Scotland Northern part of the island of Great Britain. People from Scotland settled in the eastern part of North America in the early 1700s. (p. 265)

Sonoran Desert Desert in southwestern United States and northwestern Mexico. (p. 52)

South America The earth's fourth largest continent. It lies between the Atlantic Ocean and the Pacific Ocean. (pp. 264–265)

South Carolina Southeastern state on the Atlantic coast. Its capital is Columbia. (pp. 268–269)

South Dakota North central state. Its capital is Pierre. (pp. 268–269)

South Pole The most southern point of the earth. (p. 159)

Spain Country in southwestern Europe. People from Spain came to North America to start colonies. (p. 265)

T

Tennessee Southeastern state. Its capital is Nashville. (pp. 268–269)

Teton Mountains Range of the Rocky Mountains in northwestern Wyoming and southeastern Idaho. Grand Teton is the highest peak in the range. (pp. 270–271)

Texas South central state on the Gulf of Mexico coast. Its capital is Austin. (pp. 268–269)

U

United States Country of central and northwestern North America. It is made up of 50 states. Its capital is Washington, D.C. Its abbreviation is U.S. (pp. 264–265)

Utah Western state. Its capital is Salt Lake City. (pp. 268–269)

V

Vermont Northeastern state. Its capital is Montpelier. (pp. 268–269)

Virginia Southeastern state on the Atlantic coast. Its capital is Richmond. (pp. 268–269)

Virginia Colony First English colony in North America, made up of several settlements. (p. 117)

W

Washington Northwestern state on the Pacific coast. Its capital is Olympia. (pp. 268–269)

Washington, D.C. Eastern city on the Potomac River. It is the capital of the United States. (pp. 268–269)

West Virginia East central state. Its capital is Charleston. (pp. 268–269)

Wichita City in south central Kansas. (p. G7)

Wilderness Road Pioneer road from Virginia to Kentucky through the Cumberland Mountains. Daniel Boone led the men who cut the trail for the road. (p. 135)

Wisconsin North central state. Its capital is Madison. (p. G13)

Wyoming Western state. Its capital is Cheyenne. (pp. 268–269)

Y

Yellowstone National Park Oldest and largest United States national park. Most of it is in northwestern Wyoming. It is famous for its hot springs. (p. 200)

GLOSSARY OF GEOGRAPHIC TERMS

ocean
a salty body of water covering a large area of the earth (also, **sea**)

mountain
a steeply raised mass of land, much higher than the surrounding country

mountain range
a row of mountains

tree line
on a mountain, the area above which no trees grow

valley
low land between hills or mountains

highland
land that is higher than most of the surrounding land

forest
a large area of land where many trees grow

hill
a raised mass of land, smaller than a mountain

prairie
a large, level area of grassland without trees

desert
a dry area where few plants grow

plain
a broad, flat area of land

sea level
the level of the surface
of the ocean

harbor
a protected body of water
where ships can safely stop

coast
the land next to
the ocean

river
a large stream of water that
runs into a lake, ocean, or
another river

bay
part of a lake or ocean extend-
ing into the land

island
a body of land with
water all around it

shore
the land along the edge of a
lake, sea, or ocean

lowland
land that is lower than most
of the surrounding land

lake
a body of water with
land all around it

277

Glossary

Pronunciation Key

Spellings	Symbol	Spellings	Symbol	Spellings	Symbol
pat	ă	kick, cat, pique	k	thin	th
pay	ā	lid, needle	l	this	*th*
care	âr	mum	m	cut	ŭ
father	ä	no, sudden	n	urge, term, firm,	ûr
bib	b	thing	ng	word, heard	
church	ch	pot, horrid	ŏ	valve	v
deed, milled	d	toe	ō	with	w
pet	ĕ	caught, paw, for	ô	yes	y
bee	ē	noise	oi	zebra, xylem	z
life, phase, rough	f	took	o͝o	vision, pleasure,	zh
gag	g	boot	o͞o	garage	
hat	h	out	ou	about, item, edible,	ə
which	hw	pop	p	gallop, circus	
pit	ĭ	roar	r	butter	ər
pie, by	ī	sauce	s		
pier	îr	ship, dish	sh	Primary stress ´	
judge	j	tight, stopped	t	Secondary stress ´	

A

adaptation (ăd´ăp-tā´shən) A change in the way of life of people, animals, or plants in order to fit the surroundings in which they live. (p. 101)

agriculture (ăg´rĭ-kŭl´chər) The business of working the soil, growing crops, and raising livestock. (p. 171)

B

blaze (blāz) To mark a trail by cutting bark from a tree. (p. 136)

boom town (bo͞om´ toun´) A town that grows and becomes wealthy very quickly. (p. 162)

C

capital (kăp´ ĭ-tl) The city where government leaders meet. (p. 233)

cedar (sē´dər) A type of evergreen tree whose wood is often reddish in color. (p. 66)

ceremony (sĕr´ə-mō´nē) An act that is performed in honor of an important event. (p. 72)

chant (chănt) A song that is sung on the same note or on a few notes, often as a form of prayer. (p. 103)

citizen (sĭt´ĭ-zən) A person who is a member of a nation. (p. 242)

climate (klī´mĭt) The weather of an area over a long time. (p. 54)

coast (kōst) The land beside a sea. (p. 5)

colony (kŏl´ə-nē) An area that is settled by people from a faraway country and ruled by that home country. (p. 117)

Congress (kŏng´grĭs) National lawmakers from every state who meet in Washington, D.C. (p. 239)

conservation (kŏn´sûr-vā´shən) The protection or wise use of things found in nature. (p. 199)

constitution (kŏn´stĭ-tōō´shən) A list of the rights of the people and of how their government will be run. (p. 234)

council (kōun´səl) A group of people who pass laws. Part of the government of a town or city. (p. 220)

D

decompose (dē´kəm-pōz´) To rot, or fall apart, slowly. (p. 209)

desert (dĕz´ərt) A dry, sandy area that gets very little rain. (p. 51)

E

election (ĭ-lĕk´shən) The time when people vote. (p. 227)

environment (ĕn-vī´rən-mənt) The surroundings in which animals, people, and plants live. (p. 203)

erosion (ĭ-rō´zhən) The slow wearing away of land. (p. 5)

F

fertilizer (fûr´tl-ī´zər) Chemicals that are added to soil to make plants grow healthier and more quickly. (p. 172)

flood (flŭd) Water that overflows to cover land that is normally dry. (p. 23)

forest (fôr´ĭst) A large area of land that is covered with trees. (p. 28)

freight (frāt) Materials carried by train, ship, truck, or airplane. (p. 183)

G

goods (gŏŏdz) Things that people buy and sell. (p. 122)

government (gŭv´ərn-mənt) The group of people who pass laws and take care of a community, a state, or a country. (p. 219)

H

hogan (hō´gän´) A one-room Navajo house made of logs and mud. (p. 99)

humus (hyōō´məs) The brown or black matter that is found in soil. (p. 30)

I

industry (ĭn´də-strē) Businesses that make things or provide services. (p. 179)

inland (ĭn´lənd) Away from the coast. (p. 121)

irrigation (ĭr´ĭ-gā´shən) To bring water to dry land through the use of ditches, canals, or pipes. (p. 172)

L

lake (lāk) A large body of water with land all around it. (p. 19)

law (lô) A rule that everyone must keep. (p. 228)

liberty (lĭb´ər-tē) Freedom from control by others. (p. 258)

livestock (līv´stŏk´) Animals, such as sheep or horses, that are raised for home use or to be sold. (p. 100)

location (lō-kā´shən) The place where something could be or is found. (p. 179)

long house (lông´ hous´) A house, up to 60 feet long, used by eastern and western North American Indians. (p. 67)

M

mayor (mā´ər) The leader of a town or city. (p. 220)

mineral (mĭn´ər-əl) A naturally occurring material, such as gold or iron, found in the earth. (p. 161)

monument (mŏn´yə-mənt) A statue or building that honors a person or an event. (p. 258)

mountain (moun´tən) A steep-sided mass of land much higher than the surrounding country. (p. 45)

myth (mĭth) A sacred story, often about gods, that helps to explain something about the nature of the world. (p. 87)

N

national holiday (năsh´ə-nəl hŏl´ĭ-dā´) A holiday that is set aside by the national government to honor a country and its people. (p. 253)

natural resource (năch´ər-əl rē´sôrs´) Anything that is found in nature that people can use. (p. 81)

O

ocean (ō´shən) A large body of salt water. Oceans cover much of the earth's surface. (p. 5)

P

pass (păs) A narrow passage at a low point between mountains. (p. 148)

physical feature (fĭz´ĭ-kəl fē´chər) A natural part of the earth's surface. (p. 45)

pioneer (pī´ə-nîr´) A person who is the first to settle in a wilderness area, leading the way for others to follow. (p. 135)

pollution (pə-lōō´shən) Harmful material that makes the air, water, or soil dirty. (p. 205)

population (pŏp´yə-lā´shən) The number of people that live in an area. (p. 155)

prairie (prâr´ē) A large area of flat or hilly land covered by grasses. (p. 34)

predator (prĕd´ə-tər) An animal that lives by hunting other animals for food. (p. 35)

President (prĕz´ĭ-dənt) The elected leader of the United States. (p. 238)

R

recycling (rē-sī´klĭng) The process of treating trash so that it can be used again. (p. 209)

river (rĭv´ər) A large moving stream of water that flows into an ocean, lake, or other body of water. (p. 18)

S

salmon (săm´ən) A type of fish. (p. 65)

sand painting (sănd´ pān´tĭng) A special picture made on the ground by a Navajo medicine man. (p. 104)

services (sûr´vĭs-əz) Businesses that perform work or provide help instead of making goods. (p. 181)

steel mills (stēl´ mĭlz´) Factories that make steel. (p. 179)

survive (sər-vīv´) To stay alive. (p. 117)

symbol (sĭm´bəl) Something that stands for something else. (p. 88)

T

taxes (tăks´ĕs) Money paid to the government to provide services. (p. 221)

temperature (tĕm´pər-ə-chŏŏr´) A measurement of heat and cold. (p. 45)

timberline (tĭm´bər-līn´) The height on a mountain above which trees do not grow. (p. 45)

tipi (tē´pē) A cone-shaped tent made of animal skins or bark used by some North American Indians. (p. 81)

topsoil (tŏp´soil´) The top layer of soil, usually darker and richer than the soil beneath it. (p. 199)

totem pole (tō´təm pōl´) A wooden pole with carved figures made by Northwest Coast Indians. (p. 71)

trade (trād) The business of buying and selling goods. (p. 184)

trade center (trād´ sĕn´tər) A town or city where people buy and sell goods and services. (p. 156)

transportation (trăns´pər-tā´shən) A way to move passengers or goods. (p. 184)

V

vein (vān) A long strip of mineral found in rock. (p. 160)

volunteer (vŏl´ən-tîr´) A person who works without pay. (p. 245)

W

wagon train (wăg´ən trān´) A line of wagons pulled by oxen, mules, or horses that was used to transport people and goods across the country. (p. 149)

waste (wāst) Materials that are no longer useful and are thrown away. (p. 205)

wilderness (wĭl´dər-nĭs) Land that has not been changed by people or their actions. (p. 122)

Italic numbers refer to pages on which illustrations appear.

Text *(continued from page iv)*

96–97 Reprinted with permission of Charles Scribner's Sons, an imprint of Macmillan Publishing Company from *The Desert Is Theirs* by Byrd Baylor, illustrated by Peter Parnall. Text copyright © 1975 Byrd Baylor. Illustrations copyright © 1975 Peter Parnall. **98** untitled Navajo poem, Copyright © 1978 by Richard Erdoes. Reprinted by permission of Sterling Publishing Co., Inc., 387 Park Ave. S., New York, NY 10016. **138–45 (xvi–xvii)** Chapters 1 and 2 from *Wagon Wheels* by Barbara Brenner, illustrated by Don Bolognese. Text Copyright © 1978 by Barbara Brenner. Illustrations Copyright © 1978 by Don Bolognese. Reprinted by permission of Harper & Row, Publishers, Inc. **154** "The Old Chisolm Trail", Copyright © 1939 by Kansas State Historical Society. Reprinted by permission of Kansas State Historical Society. **182** "Travel" by Edna St. Vincent Millay. From *Collected Poems*, Harper & Row. Copyright 1921, 1948 by Edna St. Vincent Millay. Reprinted by permission. **192–97 (text)** *Once There Was a Tree* by Natalia Romanova, adapted by Anne Schwarz. Copyright © 1985 by K. Thienemanns Verlag, Stuttgart. English translation © 1985 by Dial Books for Young Readers. Reprinted by permission of the publisher, Dial Books for Young Readers. (illustrations) *Once There Was a Tree* by Natalia Romanova, adapted by Anne Schwarz, pictures by Gennady Spirin. Copyright © 1985 by K. Thienemanns Verlag, Stuttgart. Reproduced by permission of the publisher, Dial Books for Young Readers, and VAAP on behalf of the artist. **250** From "Johnny Appleseed" from *A Book of Americans,* Rosemary and Stephen Vincent Benet. Copyright 1933 by Rosemary & Stephen Vincent Benet. Copyright renewed © 1961 by Rosemary Carr Benet. Reprinted by permission of Brandt & Brandt Literary Agents, Inc. **278** Pronunciation key copyright © 1985 by Houghton Mifflin Company. Adapted and reprinted by permission from *The American Heritage Dictionary,* Second College Edition.

Illustrations

Literature border design by Peggy Skycraft. **Ligature** 35, 37. **B. Battles** 68, 69, 107. **H. Berelson** 53, 74, 150, 254. **J. Brunnick** 82, 83. **R. Chewning** 45, 47, 119. **S. David** 6, 22. **R. Dondis** 105, 106(r). **E. Dudley** 48. **M. Evans** 234, 238. **R. Fleck** 70, 98, 106(l). **M. Langeneckert** 32, 56, 85. **J. LeMonnier** 5, 109. **R. Lipking** 220, 228. **A. Lorenz** 67, 124. **L. Lydecker** 36. **K. Mitchell** 89, 101, 181. **J. Needham** 29, 202. **E. Parker** 9, 120, 126–127, 172, 257. **J. Reed** 157. **R. Schanzer** 221, 222. **G. Toressi** 276–277. **N. L. Walter** G4, G5, G9. **C. Wrobel** 186, 187, 191, 206–7, 210. **O. Yourke** 185. **Other:** 104 Source of painting: *Navajo Sandpainting Art* by E. Baatsoslanii, J. and M. Bahti, Copyright © 1978, Treasure Chest Publications.

Maps

Ligature 59, 111, 165. **R. R. Donnelley & Sons Company Cartographic Services** Back Cover, 264–65, 266–67, 268–69, 270–71. **JAK Graphics** 19, 21, 35, 49, 52, 81, 100, 117, 122, 131, 135, 149, 156, 158, 159, 161, 171, 179, 199, 200. **Mapping Specialists** G2–G14, 233, 236-37.

Photographs

AL—Alan Landau; **BD**—Bob Daemmrich; **GH**—Grant Heilman Photography; **LC**—Library of Congress; **MA**—Museum of the American Indian; **NYPL**—New York Public Library; **PH**—Photographic Resources; **PI**—PHOTRI; **PR**—Photo Researchers, Inc.; **RBC**—Royal British Columbia Museum, Victoria, BC, Canada; **RR**—Root Resources; **SB**—Stock Boston; **SK**—Stephen Kennedy; **SY**—SYGMA; **TBM**—The Thomas Burke Memorial Washington State Museum; **TIB**— The Image Bank; **TS**—Tom Stack & Associates; **TSW**—TSW—Click/Chicago Ltd.

Front cover P. Bosey. **G1** D. Maenza, TIB. **G4** © SuperStock, Inc. **G6** R. Brunke. **G7** J. Avery, PI. **G8** PI. **G10** NASA (t); R. Brunke (b). **G12** R. Brunke; AL. **G13** The Mitchell Indian Museum, Evanston, IL, AL. **G15** AL (l, r, b). **xviii–1** © D. Muench. **2** © J. Apoian, Nawrocki Stock Photo (tl,br); © G. Corsi, TS (c). **2-3** C. Bjornberg, PR. **3** © G. Heilman, GH. **4** SK (t,bl,br); © L. Migdale, PR (b). **5** © B. Parker, TS. **7** SK (t); © Superstock (l); © E. Simmons, SB (cr). **8–9** SK. **18** © L. L. T. Rhodes, TSW (tr); © F. Oberle, PH (c). **19** © J. Appleyard. **20** © F. McConnaughey, PR (tl); © A. Thomas, PR (b). **20–21** SK. **21** Smithsonian (tl); D. Hamm, National Park Service (br). **22** © T. G. Rampton, GH. **23** © S. Proehl, TIB. **25** T. G. Rampton, GH (t); S. Proehl, TIB. **26** © R. Dixon (tl); © D. L. Stratton, TS (c), C. Bjornberg, PR (r). **26–27** © G. Heilman, GH. **27** © H. Spencer, PR (tr); © B. McKeever, TS (br). **28** © S. Maslowski, PR (t); © T. Mareschal, TIB (b). **30** SK (tl,tr,bl,br); © J. Kaprielian, PR (tc). **31** SK (tl,cr); © S. Maslowski, PR (tc); © J. Lapore, PR (c). **33** Thomas Gilcrease Institute of American History and Art (l); SK (r). **34** G. Heilman, GH. **35** © D. L. Stratton, TS. **36** SK; © R. Planck, PR (l); © L. L. Rue III, PR (r). **37** © B. Parker, TS (l); © L. P. Brock, TS (r). **38** SK. **39** SK. **42** C. Bjornberg, PR (t), © J. H. Robinson, PR (r); © J. McDonald, TS (b). **42–43** © B. Firth. **43** © K.

W. Fink, RR. **44** © D. Stoecklein, Stock Market (tr); SK (r); © D. Murie, Meyers Photo-Art (b). **46** © G. Brettnacher, TSW (t); © L. L. Rue III, TSW (b). **50** © F. Oberle, PH (t); © F. Siteman, PH (b). **51** © G. C. Kelley, PR. **52** © G. Heilman, GH. **54** © M. Rand, TS (t); © S. Krasemann, PR (b). **55** SK (tl); © J. Cancalosi, TS (tr); © B. McKeever, TS(b). **56–57** SK. **60–61** © Werner Forman Archive/Private Collection. **62** © C. Speedie, Image Finders (l); RBC (r). **62–63** E. Curtis, LC. **63** E. Calderon, TBM. **64** RBC (l); E. Curtis, University of Washington Libraries (detail) (r). **65** © Werner Forman Archive. **66** E. Calderon, TBM (t); TBM (b). **71** LC (bl); © D. Fivehouse, Image Finders (br). **72** TBM (bl); LC (br). **73** © Werner Forman Archive/Provincial Museum, Victoria, BC (t); H. I. Smith, American Museum of Natural History (b). **75** TBM. **78** © B. Parker, TS (l); Philbrook Museum of Art, University of Tulsa Collection (r). **79** © P. Conklin (t); Smithsonian (b). **80** © Native American Images. **81** Museum of the Great Plains. **82** © B. Parker, TS. **82–83** SK. **83** MA (c). **84** Smithsonian. **86** Field Museum of Natural History. **87** USDA-NFS. **88** MA (l); Field Museum of Natural History (c). **90** Mesa Verde National Park (l); PR (b). **91** SK (r): NYPL; The Denver Art Museum; Peter Kaplan; Philadelphia Museum of Art; Georgia Historical Society; MA; Reader's Digest; SK (b): Holmes & Meier Publishers; MA. **94** © M. Bahti (l); © L. Moulton, TSW (c). **94–95** © M. Keegan. **95** Philbrook Art Center, Tulsa, OK (b). **98** © C. Aurness, West Light. **99** SK (t,b); © R. Wolken, TSW (cr). **102** Grant Heilman, GH. **103** © T. Eiler, SB. **104** © M. Bahti. **105** © T. Eiler, SB. **107** SK. **112–13** Nebraska State Historical Society. **114** © UPI/ Bettman Newsphoto. **114–15** M. Varon, Metropolitan Life. **115** © J. Apoian, PR (t); New York State Historical Assn. (b). **116** NYPL (t); Plymouth Pilgrim Society (b). **118** © UPI/Bettman Newsphoto. **121** SK. **123** © North Wind Picture Archives. **125** NYPL (t); The Farmer's Museum, NY (r). **126** SK. **128** SK, St. Louis Public Library (l); Missouri Historical Society (b). **129** SK, J. Knirr Archive. **132** © Esto Photographics (l); Private Collection (c). **132–33** The Kansas State Historical Society, Topeka; © Time-Life, H. Beville, Anne and Madison Grant. **134** © D. Muench. **135** © D. Muench. **136** © W. Strode. **137** J. Shaw, Museum of Science and Industry, Chicago. **146** © L. E. Schaefer, RR. **147** The Granger Collection, NY. **148** Elmer Fryer, K. Spangler Archive. **151** Denver Public Library (t); from The Old West: The Pioneers, H. Sund © 1974 Time-Life Books, Inc. (b). **152** USDA (t); © M. Root, RR. **153** National Archives. **154** © William Loren Katz Collection. **155** NYPL. **160** © North Wind Picture Archives. **161** LC. **162** Yale University Art Gallery (t); W. H. Jackson, Culver Pictures, Inc. (b). **163** © J. Parsons, The Stock Broker. **166–67** © 1987 Kinuko Y. Craft. **168** © T. Schanuel, PH (l); Greater Pittsburgh Office of Promotion (r); **168–69** © G. Heilman, GH. **169** © J. Livezey. **170** SK(t,l); © GH (b). **173** SK (t); © G. Heilman, GH (b). **174** © L. Balterman, Gartman Agency. **174–75** SK. **175** © W. J. Kennedy, TIB (t); © H. Wendler, TIB (c); © M. Melford, TIB (b). **176** © S. Wilkinson, TIB. **178** © Collection of the Equitable Life Assurance Society of the United States. **180** © Detroit Publishing Co., LC. (r); © R. Colton, Black Star (l). **182** © B. Taylor, FPG International. **183** Coverdale & Colpitts (l); LC (r). **184** © D. Gleiter, FPG International. **185** SK(t); © T. Tracy, FPG International (b). **186** © C. O'Rear, West Light. **190** © D. Stock, Magnum Photos (l); © A. Upitis, TIB (c); **190–91** USDA-NPS. **198** D. L. Kernodle for FSA, LC. **200** © S. Swanger, TS. **201** © J. Buitenkant, PR (t); © G. Vaughn, TS (b). **203** USDA-FS Bauermeister (l); USDA-FS, F. Erickson (r). **204** © M. Mathers, Black Star. **205** © M. Andrews, Animals, Animals/Earth Scenes (l); © R. J. Cheng (tr). **208** © D. Capolongo, Black Star. **209** R. Benkof. **211** SK. **212** SK. **213** © J. Fong. **215** SK. **216** AL (t); © W. Johnson, SB (l); A. Tannenbaum, SY (r). **217** H. Talman, National Archives; © BD,TSW; © J. Nettis, SB. **218** L. Shore, Anne Arundel County, Maryland. **219** C. Blouin, TSW. **220** Courtesy The City of Pittsburgh, Office of the Mayor. **223** J. Cuccia (tr); L. Shore, Anne Arundel County, Maryland (tl, bl, br). **224** © L. L. T. Rhodes, TSW (l); © G. Bumgarner, TSW (r). **225** AL (t, b) **226** AL (l); H. Hartman, TIB (r). **227** BD (t); © BD, SB (b). **230** © L. Migdale. **231** AL. **232** © J. D. Schwalm, Stock South (l); Mississippi Dept. of Economic and Community Development (r). **233** J. D. Schwalm, Stock South (c, b). **234** Mississippi Dept. of Economic and Community Development. **235** Mississippi State Dept. of Health (t); Mississippi Dept. of Economic and Community Development (b). **236** © B. Kulik, PI (tl); J. Feingersh, SB (tr); S. Weber, SB (cl); National Museum of American History (b). **237** National Archives (tl); P. Salutos, PH (tr) ; National Park Service (c); H. Armstrong Roberts (b). **238** The Bettmann Archive. **239** UPI/Bettmann. **240** L. Stone, SY (l); A. Tannenbaum, SY (r). **241** F. Lee Corkran. **242** R. Brunke (t); L. Migdale (b). **243** AL (l); M. Reinstein, FPG International. **244** AL (tl); H. A. Roberts (b). **245** Tree Musketeers (tl); ©BD (tr); C. Gupton, TSW (br). **248** © B. Jones. **248–49** © R. Macia, PR (b); © J. G. Herron, SB (t); **249** © G. Spencer, PR. **250** SK. **251** Granger Collection, NY (tl); SK (tr); © J. Lei, SB (b). **252** Grant Wood, © Associated American Artists, NY. **255** © COMSTOCK. **258** © Minardi, Uniphoto Picture Agency. **259** © T. Kitchin, TS (t); SK, U. S. Postal Service (c); © Pentagram (b); **259–60** SK, U. S. Postal Service. **262** Grant Wood, © Associated American Artists, NY.